NOTES
ON A
CALIFORNIA
CELLARBOOK

BY BOB THOMPSON

Notes on a California Cellarbook: Reflections on Memorable Wines

Webster's Wine Tours: California, Oregon and Washington

Cheese

The University of California/Sotheby Book of California Wine (CO-EDITOR)

The American Express Pocket Guide to California

The Pocket Encyclopedia of California Wine

Sunset Travel Guide to Washington

The California Wine Book (with Hugh Johnson)

American Wine and Wine Cooking (with Shirley Sarvis)

California Wine Country

Beachcomber's Guide to the Pacific Coast

OMPSON

NOTES ON A CALIFORNIA CELLARBOOK

Reflections on Memorable Wines

BⲒB
BEECH TREE BOOKS
WILLIAM MORROW
New York

Library of Congress Cataloging-in-Publication Data

Thompson, Bob, 1934–
    Notes on a California cellarbook.

    Includes index.
    1. Wine and wine making—California.   I. Title.
TP557.T487   1988   641.2'22'09794   87-33496
ISBN 0-688-07007-8

Printed in the United States of America

2 3 4 5 6 7 8 9 10

BOOK DESIGN BY KATHLEEN CAREY

The word "book" is said to derive from *boka,* or beech.
The beech tree has been the patron tree of writers since ancient times and
represents the flowering of literature and knowledge.

FOR HAROLYN

my not-quite-silent partner

ACKNOWLEDGMENTS

In the course of thirty years of wine, I have come to owe a debt of some sort to nearly every winemaker and winery owner in the business, to merchants by the scores, and to at least a dozen teachers (formal and informal). In particular I would like to thank the following for their special help along the way.

Among winemakers and vineyardists, Tucker Catlin, Jack Davies, Dawnine Dyer, Greg Fowler, Joe Heitz, Louis P. Martini, Michael Martini, Edmund Maudière, Robert Mondavi, Tim Mondavi, and Zelma Long all have taken extra pains to sit me down and make me look until I see something of why wines are what they are.

Dan Berger (San Diego National Wine Competition, Riverside Farmers Fair), Nathan Chroman (Los Angeles County Fair), Bob Foster (San Diego National Wine Competition), Nancy Johnston (Riverside Farmers Fair), Rebecca Murphy (*Dallas*

Morning News National Wine Competition), Harvey Steiman (San Francisco Fair & Exposition), Rich Thomas (Sonoma Harvest Fair, El Dorado West Coast Wine Competition), and Wilfred Wong (San Francisco Fair & Exposition) all have allowed me to sit as a judge, and so learn many of the hard lessons major wine competitions teach about noticing the fine points.

Dr. Bernard Rhodes, Belle Rhodes, Dr. Robert Adamson, Dorothy Adamson, Shirley Sarvis, Tor Kenward, Susan Costner Kenward, Earl Thollander, and Janet Thollander have helped keep me from getting too immersed in the technical side of wine at the expense of the pleasurable one.

To Narcisse Chamberlain I owe a particular debt for getting this project off the ground.

To Jim Landis I owe an equally sizable debt for seeing it through as my editor.

Last, to Deborah Weiss I offer thanks for the copyediting.

CONTENTS

The more you study the less surprised you are, but no matter how hard you study you are still surprised agreeably often, and the prizes that come to the studious are especially delicious.

—GEORGE WILL

NOTES
ON A
CALIFORNIA
CELLARBOOK

THE VIEW FROM MY CELLAR

THESE RECOLLECTIONS OF CALIFORNIA WINES from the past forty vintages are what they are because of all the trouble I have buying record players and because I am a wine nut.

Every few years I go into a record-player store to buy a new record player so I can play my old, beat-up twelve-inch LPs of Schubert, Ellington, the MJQ—pops, hisses, and all. The problem is, there is no longer any such thing as a record-player store, or a record player. The available item is the sound system, sold by sound-system nuts who have wanted me to buy ever-more-complicated stereos. Last time around they wanted me to throw out my LPs and buy a CD. They drown me in ohms and impedance and tracking error and will not listen to my explanation that records are, for me, the auditory equivalent of home movies, a way to jog memories of the real thing. So I go home, weighed down by insults, sore as hell at sound-system nuts, and buy something through the mail.

Meanwhile, things have reached the pass where I will stand around on concrete in a cold cellar for hours of a bleak winter afternoon talking about the Pommard clone and TA and pH and PSU-I and heavy-toast Allier oak, which are the ohms and impedance of wine nuts.

Can anyone so immersed in a subject say anything sensible to someone else who wants only the simple pleasure of it? I try not to talk like a wine nut. But will a normal human being like the same wine a nut likes? I cling to the hope.

My wife and I do eat funny stuff like sweetbreads and snails and baked garlic, and we drink what would have to be called interesting wines—all on purpose, but not often. What we like to eat fifteen nights out of sixteen is pasta, salmon fillets, baked chicken, shrimp Louis, steak and potatoes, things like that. The wines we drink when we are eating normal?

Aha. At last, the nub of it. After thirty years, I keep a little list of soul warmers, the ones that have earned me a reputation for incurable optimism, that make me hurry to dinner and then linger over it. On the list are the couple of hundred names that start going through my head when I go out to get a bottle for honored guests, because they are the ones that more than once have made friends at our table happy. This book is that list.

It is not, however, a list of California's best wines. Although we Americans have bogged ourselves down in the Super Bowl syndrome, there cannot be any such thing as a best Cabernet Sauvignon or Zinfandel, let alone an imperial Number One. Wine is too elusive, human emotion too fugitive.

After thirty-odd years of tasting together, my wife and I will agree on eight out of ten wines, and go opposite each other on the other two. It has even happened, once, with a set of fifteen Gewürztraminers, that her first-placer was my last and vice versa. These opposed votes happen, I think, because remembered smells can provoke strong emotions. Think of how hard it is to begin again to eat a food you believe made you ill. Little matter this, against other, more trying experiences. I know someone who detests the smell of roses for reasons unexplained. For another old friend chocolate is grimmer than silage. Some Pinot Noirs smell faintly like roses, some Cabernets even more faintly like chocolate. Such wines get low marks from the people in question, no matter how towering (and well earned) their reputations. Most times the unhappy tasters do not even stop to recognize the particular aroma.

Wine's other qualities are easier to deal with. Dry or not, tannic or not, tart or not, heady or not—all those questions answer themselves over the span of a handful of wines. But which aromas please and which rouse dislike are questions for a lifetime, and the absolute guarantee that one bibber's unshakable favorite will come in last with an otherwise kindred spirit, and leave a third party altogether unmoved.

The most my lists can do for you is work as a sounding board for your own opinions and provide enough background for you to draw some conclusions. For my choices to be of use to you, we have to do some jockeying for position. I have to confess some prejudices so you can do some discounting.

· The taste of fruit picked fresh from the tree, vine, bush, whatever, comes very near the head of my list of gustatory pleasures. Vegetables and herbs fresh from the garden rank right with them. When scholars at the University of California at Davis sat down to compile a set of flavor associations for individual grape varieties used for table wines, the words they chose included *herbaceous, pepperminty, raspberrylike, fruity-floral, applish,* and *figgy.* Music to my ears.

· The softness of texture and the gentle, mysterious flavors that creep into wine with age in the bottle compete with the tastes of fresh fruit for first place on the list of qualities I hope to find in wine. Bottle bouquet is a bit of an acquired taste. Sometimes an old wine has hints of mushrooms, sometimes damp earth, now and again a faint, faint echo of warm tar. In a California red especially, long age will reveal a tiny reflection of prune or raisin, a souvenir of the summer's heat behind it. Most times there is no exact word for the smells, so *mature* makes do. (Quick aside: In formal work with wine, professionals separate aroma—the smell from the grapes—and bouquet—the smells from every aspect of winemaking. Out of training, I hold to the party line, but it is nothing to worry about.)

· Wine has a hard time being too tart for my taste, which also dotes on grapefruit, wild berries, and young apples. This is a simple, mechanical point of preference. We all perceive fruit acids at about the same levels, but do not tolerate them the same way. Just as dual controls on the electric blanket save a great deal of argument, so do two bottles of wine on some family tables.

The principal acid in grapes, tartaric, is, incidentally, one of the mildest ones in fruit, much gentler than the citric acid that gives grapefruit and lemons their sour edge, gentler even than the malic acid that makes apples taste like apples.

· A little touch of sweet is fine by me, not every time, but in a lot of cases. First, sweet covers tart neatly. Second, it is natural in fresh, ripe fruit, so appropriate in this form of fruit preserves.

Slight sweetness in wine got a bad name when it was used cynically to cover up dumb winemaking, bad grapes, whatever. Some wines still get sweetened for the same low reasons, but a large-enough number end up with a little unfermented, or residual, sugar because it fits in, completes the whole, defines the uses. I know but do not associate with people who categorically dismiss sweet wines but who sugar their tea.

This book dwells not at all on the analytical numbers of wine, but a few statistics on residual sugar may be of use. Almost all of us recognize sweetness when the residual sugar in a wine falls somewhere between 0.5 and 1 percent—the exact point varies with the acid level. Some of us do not want any, some want some, a few want a lot. For my taste, the most comfortable levels are 0.3 percent or less in wines advertised as dry, 0.8 to 1.5 for wines offered as off-dry, and 4.0 to 8.0 percent in the sorts meant as desserts.

· Oak is nowhere near as enjoyable as a prominent flavor in

wine as either fruit or bottle bouquet. Wood has its fascinations as a source of flavor, but not when it has become the most noticeable one. Some American oak barrels make wine taste almost like bourbon, American oak being exactly what flavors bourbon. Native oaks also have made wines taste of dill and varnish. European oak is more apt to summon thoughts of vanillin, but can evoke coconut. It can also remind me of aftershave and other perfumes. One sort of French oak even makes me think exactly of the perfume used in an insect spray. Oaks from both continents sometimes smell exactly like raw wood, just the way boards do at a lumberyard. Few of these are flavors I go out of my way to get. This does not mean I would like to see barrels disappear from cellars. Far from it. But when I wonder more about barrels than grapes, the proportions of a wine have gone screwy.

· Noticeable tannin—the mouth-puckering compound in tea, spinach, and grape skins—is welcome in reds, but it can and often has exceeded my tolerance levels. California has recently been through the era of the inky monster, the sort of wine that would, given a chance, tan cowhides and has wrinkled the insides of human cheeks to the point of pain. Such wines are not complete wastes. Some of them have raised large sums for charity as perennials on the auction circuit.

· Strong flavors of alcohol hold no charms for me at all. When the back of my throat lights up from the heat, the wine is not for me. This is not a feeling based in the currently fashionable game of numbers, in which healthy-food people cut wine off at some arbitrary point, like 11 percent, or 12.5, or whatever. (The healthy-food crowd does not know as many healthy eighty-year-old winemakers as I do, nor has ever failed to keep pace with one of them.) The objection is to clumsy proportion; 11.4 percent of alcohol tastes lousy in a glass of water and does the same in an insipid wine. Contrarily, several wines with 14 percent of alcohol have pleased me as much as wine can.

The short explanation of all of the above is that well-made wines have so deft a balance of acid, tannin, and alcohol and so adroit a touch of oak that the taster never notices any of them. Your sense of the balance point may differ from mine at any or all of the points. Feel free to argue.

In addition to understanding the mechanics of my palate, we all need to understand the rest of a selection process that has winnowed 30 Chardonnays out of some 540, and similar proportions of the other major wines, and also the reasons for listing them in the order they are. Four rules will do it.

Rule 1. The wines on my list are ones we drink often enough to have firm opinions about. A few thoroughly lionized labels are absent because nobody can keep pace with the several thousands of wines released from each vintage, and nobody can love everything. At this point in a long career as a professional judge of wine, I have learned to admire a broader range of styles than I choose for my own pleasure, but this list sticks close to my personal choices.

This has tipped the balance very heavily to the North Coast—Napa, Sonoma, Lake, and Mendocino counties. History favors the region twice: Its wines have been around longer and in greater numbers than those from any other part of the state.

Rule 2: No numerical scores. I know it is all the new rage, but I am already on public record against them, and bound to stay put. Numbers have never explained good wine to me, let alone the ambiguities that make it perpetually interesting to think about.

Rule 3. The wine has to be consistently appealing over a minimum span of five vintages, better ten. One of the lessons explosive growth in wineries has taught is that almost any damn fool can make one good vintage, but that a goodly number of them will follow the winner with four lessers if not losers. All of the equipment is clean at the start. Healthy fear keeps the rookie close to the cookbook. Odds in California heavily favor ripe, healthy fruit. Bingo, a pleasing wine and showers of praise for the new kid on the block. The following years prove a dismal misunderstanding of sanitation, while the first success provokes irresistible desires to do something really great, which often translates as More Is Better. *Pfaugh.* One of the few things in wine I am pretty sure of is that first-rate winemaking starts with an exact sense of style, then operates within the narrowest possible range of responses to the vagaries of vintages, that the slow-moving winemakers are the ones who turn out pleasing wines year after year. Most often, though not always, this means winemakers who have been in the game for a good long while.

Rule 4. Except for White Zinfandel and the other quaffers, the wine has to age well—not to infinity, mind you, just well. Aging well means only that the wine gets better in the bottle over a long-enough time to reward patience. By my standards an age-worthy Sauvignon Blanc hits full stride between three and four years past the vintage, a Cabernet between eight and fifteen. All the rest fall somewhere between those extremes.

The basic reason to look for age-worthiness in a wine is straightforward enough. Every flimsy, poorly made, unbalanced wine goes downhill from low beginnings, while every well-balanced, well-made, and richly flavored one improves with the passing seasons, having been good company from the start. This is the backdoor approach to the most basic fact of them all: Favored vineyards are the irreplaceable root, skillfully managed cellars the necessary branch.

People try to generalize about what makes a great vineyard. This latitude, that slope, whichever soil, dry-farmed or no. Forget generalities. A great vineyard is a great vineyard on the flat as much as the hill, in clay as well as gravel, looking west as soon as east. Look first in the bottle. Find a winner. Try its neighbor next.

In 1973, when Hugh Johnson and I began collaborating on *The Book of California Wine,* the forerunner to this book, both of us had our eyes on geography's part in the proceedings. Throughout we tried to understand the wines county by county, for want of finer shadings. Tighter boundaries have come along since, in the form of federal government—defined American Viticultural Areas. These AVAs have begun to shape the debate about where the superior vineyards are, but they are still trying to catch up with the practical facts.

It is stunning to realize that the 87 Chardonnays we had at

hand for evidence then have grown to more than 450 as of 1987, and that the 9 counties in which the grape excels have fragmented themselves into more than 20 American Viticultural Areas. The other varietal wine types have followed Chardonnay's bewildering example. It is outright daunting to notice that tasting as many as 350 Chardonnays a year means I know less about that one variety now than I did about all white wines together in 1976, and that reds are a more numerous and slower maturing tribe. Still, we must plunge ahead. Things are only going to get worse if we do not finish the prelims and get on with the main event.

THE LAY OF THE LAND

THE TEMPTATION IS TO THINK OF CALIFORNIA as one place because one name is easy. It is—as I keep learning—not a workable idea for much of anything beyond the issuance of license plates, and not worth two hoops in categorizing wines.

California names its finest wines after their dominant grape varieties—Cabernet Sauvignon, Zinfandel, Sauvignon Blanc, etc.—then grows every variety almost everywhere. A blind tasting of, say, Cabernet Sauvignons will show in a few sips that the flavors of the North Coast are not those of the Central Coast, which are not the ones that mark the South Coast, and none of the three tastes is like the Great Central Valley. Within the North Coast shadings get finer, but Napa is not Sonoma, which is not Mendocino. Within Napa, Carneros is not Stag's Leap, which is not Rutherford Bench, and so on. Put another way, to say

California is to say dog; to say Napa Valley is to say retriever, and to say Rutherford Bench is to say golden retriever, or maybe Labrador.

Alas for those who take comfort in certainties, flavors will not hold still for examination the way dogs will. The hints of this place and that are not only fugitive, but mutable and unmeasurable. Those of us who persist in the search have to enjoy the fact that we are on the lookout for a trail of bread crumbs in a hungry forest.

The finest of these shadings of place are, in the main, the latest work of the current generation. Before 1983, according to government regulation, county names came as close to specific identity as a California wine could have. Since 1983, there has been developing an ever-more-telling system of American Viticultural Areas, regions based—somewhat, at least—on kindred growing conditions for grapes. AVAs impose a 75 percent minimum on the proportion of grapes that must grow within an area before its name can go on the label, and so these defined areas have begun to set the terms for whatever debate takes place about which grape varieties should grow where in the state (and the rest of the country, for that matter, but the rest does not concern us for now). AVAs do not have the legal force to say what kinds of grapes can and cannot be grown within them, but they still point toward districts where one variety or another is beginning to outstrip the competition.

And so, on behalf of Cabernet Sauvignon, Chardonnay, and all their kin, this book attempts to chop California into such as the Napa Valley, Russian River Valley, Anderson Valley, Santa Maria Valley, and all their kin.

Now that AVAs exist, it is possible to be surprised at how swiftly the broad outlines had sketched themselves in, and how slowly the details are emerging.

At the beginning of thoughtful grape growing, during the 1870s and 1880s, scholars at the University of California divided the state into two regions based on climate. Much the larger region was the relentlessly warm Great Central Valley. Much the more versatile and interesting was the cooler, fog-kissed Coast Ranges. The original scholarly idea was broad enough that it still works as a rough cut. More surprisingly, by 1882 university researchers had pinpointed some spots for Riesling and the Bordeaux varieties that hold up today.

The two great pioneers at the university—Eugene Waldemar Hilgard, Frederic T. Bioletti—and their co-workers had more than a bit of luck. The Franciscan *padres* could have followed other routes or chosen other mission sites between 1769 and 1825, but did not; the European settlers who followed could have tasted the often vilified mission-made wines and given up hope, but did not.

Although the old *padres* do not seem to have been great vine-yard managers, they hit most of the right spots. Santa Ynez Valley, Edna Valley, Paso Robles, Salinas Valley, Carmel Valley, Santa Clara Valley, and Sonoma Valley are a roll call of mission sites as well as AVAs. The Franciscans missed Livermore Valley by only one row of hills, Napa by the same margin. They ran out of push before they could get into what are now northern Sonoma and Mendocino, or their record might have been perfect.

Their problem was not where they stopped, but what they brought—one dim grape variety later named Mission to make sure they get the blame for it.

The European immigrants who followed the Gold Rush of 1849 quickly added vines to the Napa and Livermore valley landscapes and flooded themselves with varieties before 1885. By the 1880s the University of California had tested more than three hundred varieties and drawn so many useful conclusions that not all of its wisdom was remembered after the long intermission imposed by Prohibition between 1913 and 1933.

During the 1930s successors to Hilgard and Bioletti at the University of California refined the state into five climate regions using total heat as the measuring stick. That system turned most of the Great Central Valley into the warmer Regions IV and V, and carved the Coast Ranges into the cooler and more interesting I, II, and III. Maynard A. Amerine and A. J. Winkler, who devised the scale, recommended varieties by region, basing their judgments partly on local experience, partly on similarities between local and European climates. That is, Riesling was recommended for the coolest Region I, roughly as warm as Germany's Rheingau, while Cabernet Sauvignon got the call for the warmer Regions II and III, with heat summaries near those of Bordeaux. This logical refinement of the original two-zone division has not held up well during the helter-skelter growth in plantings since 1970. Nobody could ever figure out exactly where the heat regions were because they came in small-to-tiny, erratically shaped fragments, so people planted what they wanted where they wanted it. The university has turned out to be right more often than wrong, but it has been wrong. When grapes grew well where they were not supposed to and vice versa, growers began to abandon heat as the lone arbiter.

On an altogether separate line of reasoning growers began to clamor in the late 1970s for a system of appellations based on geographic features, and got it in the form of the AVAs. As of mid-1987, the Bureau of Alcohol, Tobacco and Firearms had agreed to the establishment of forty AVAs in California, three of them in the Sierra Foothills, two in the Great Central Valley, and all the rest in the Coast Ranges.

In attempting to define coastal California's climate for grapes, the single most useful bit of knowledge is that Europe is just no lesson at all for a California grower. It does, however, help some to understand why it is not.

In Europe incoming weather from the Atlantic sweeps across a relatively simple plain inclined toward the Alps. What mountains there are west of the Alps tend to run east-west. As a result, grape varieties are planted in east-west bands. Riesling and Traminer come at the far north in Germany and Alsace. Chardonnay and Pinot Noir come next in Champagne and Burgundy. Chenin Blanc, Sauvignon Blanc, and Cabernet Sauvignon occupy a third band in the Loire and Bordeaux, all of them subtle variations on a climate type called West Coast Maritime. Finally, the Spanish, Portuguese, and Italian varieties are a world unto themselves on peninsulas at the far south, in a weather regime defined not as West Coast Maritime but as the two-season or Mediterranean climate.

California's climate has been defined as Mediterranean too, but with mitigating circumstances. It is, after all, a West Coast state.

Three great factors are at work in coastal California throughout the growing season. One is the Pacific Ocean. Two is a reliably sunny, frequently hot, altogether Mediterranean interior valley. Three is the Coast Ranges, which parallel the north-south shore and operate as the zone of confusion.

First, the Pacific. A great warm-water current, sometimes called the Japanese Current and sometimes the Kuroshio, stays some miles offshore of California as far down as Point Conception. Its offshore course permits upwelling of uncommonly cold water from the deeps just alongshore. Ask any surfer around San Francisco just how cold it is; his answer will be much richer than the thermometer reading, which is 51° to 54°F. As relatively warm eastbound air crosses this band of cold water, a plus or minus fifteen-hundred-foot-deep bank of fog forms.

Now for the land mass. The warm interior works like a vast suction pump, pulling cool, fog-weighted sea air landward. This is the mechanical act that blows flyweight pitchers off the mound at Candlestick Park, causes the bewildered tourists of August to suffer chills in their seersucker jackets at Fisherman's Wharf, and is alleged to have made Mark Twain complain that the coldest winter he ever spent was one summer in San Francisco.

The Coast Ranges balk this airflow most of the time for most of the valleys but rarely halt it for others, which makes them the third and most crucial factor of the three. Only a few gaps—the Golden Gate is the most famous and most obvious among them—allow cold sea fog to overrun warm land. Precisely because the Coast Ranges provide more efficient shelter to the north of San Francisco than to the south, the general run of summer weather gets hotter and winter weather colder to the north than to the south. That much is simple. It is how widely spaced the gaps and how the sea air behaves once it gets through the gaps that make wine growing such an exhilarating occupation all through the Coast Ranges.

On almost any average summer day, the temperatures along the Coast Ranges explain how the old UC system came into being. Taking one hundred miles of US Highway 101 as an axis *north* out of San Francisco through Marin, Sonoma, and Mendocino counties, the following are the high and low temperatures for a run-of-the-mill summer day, August 30, 1987. Contrast them with the temperatures on the same day in European cities spread across five hundred miles:

San Francisco 69/57	Berlin 66/50
San Rafael 78/54	Frankfurt 74/56
Petaluma 83/55	Geneva 77/52
Santa Rosa 78/51	Paris 78/57
Healdsburg 85/55	Lisbon 76/57
Cloverdale 98/55	Madrid 82/66
Ukiah 108/63	Rome 85/62

On the same highway and the same day, the daily extremes going south for two hundred miles through Santa Clara, Monterey, San Luis Obispo, and Santa Barbara counties show similar ups and downs as those north of San Francisco.

Other factors add other complications to understanding how different regions affect their vineyards: Annual rainfall runs upward from thirty inches north of San Francisco, downward from twenty inches south of the city. Most of the wine valleys are folds in the Coast Ranges, which means they run north-south, which means some exposures look to the morning light while others face straight at the afternoon sun. However, several valleys slant, and a couple run true east-west courses. In rough country there is something looking toward every point on the compass no matter what the general trend of the valley.

Thus California has no counterpart to a Rhine or Bordeaux.

Riesling prospers in little islands at the best, freckles at the worst. Cabernet Sauvignon prospers in bigger chunks. What boggles systematizers is that a freckle of Riesling country will crop up inside an island of Cabernet land but not at the cool edge of someplace well suited to Chardonnay. And thus, 130 years after California wine growing's serious beginnings, grape growers still stand about on a harvest morning scratching their heads while winemakers hold theirs between their hands.

Fewer growers and winemakers assume the above postures than did in 1891, or at least they assume them less often. People have begun to make strides, especially where grapes are densely planted, and where they have hung on through thick and thin since the mid-nineteenth century. But enough is confusion that the growers and the university have abandoned the five-region system for more pragmatic approaches.

And so we now have the pleasure of figuring out what AVAs mean. No dusty tramping through the hills to read thermometers. No tedious measuring of sun angles and cloud covers. Just pulling corks, pouring glasses, and recording pluses and minuses as wine falls upon the tongue.

The AVAs are such a new cast of characters that they need introduction by name. They are, most of them, in such old ground that the old names—of towns and counties—are the most familiar way to start. Some—Napa, Sonoma, the Livermore Valley—have been around and vigorous for the whole history. Others—San Luis Obispo, the Sierra Foothills—had long sieges of plucking at the coverlet before their recent recoveries. A couple—Monterey, Santa Barbara—have returned from the grave during the past few years.

California's largest vineyard region is not here at all. The Great Central Valley does a miraculous disappearing act in spite of the fact that its vineyards yield seven of every ten bottles of California wine, because nearly all of the table wines made there are priced and styled for casual, current consumption, while these choices skip over Tuesday's wine in favor of bottles for special occasions.

The sources of special bottles are, at the most general level, North Coast, San Francisco Bay Area, Central Coast, Sierra Foothills, and, perhaps, South Coast. Within them, the broadest divisions are counties. Within the counties are the AVAs.

NORTH COAST

Here is the cradle of coastal winemaking. Within four counties—Napa, Sonoma, Mendocino, Lake—very nearly all of the long-lived dinner wines known to California have been made. This is where there are at least some beginnings of continuity, where third- and fourth-generation members of wine-growing families are in the game in numbers, some of them in monumental cellars dating back to 1880, some in monumental cellars dating back to 1980.

Physically, the region makes a woozy rectangle out of four smaller rectangles. Napa and Sonoma sit side-by-side across the Bay from San Francisco. Lake and Mendocino do likewise, Lake atop Napa and Mendocino above Sonoma. All four counties have surfaces so deeply wrinkled by the Coast Ranges that, among them, they have eighteen AVAs and more aborning.

Though Sonoma had an edge in the early going, Napa is the senior fellow in the group. It had become the more prestigious before Prohibition distorted progress, and got out of the blocks much the fastest of any California wine-growing region after Repeal.

Napa County

For all practical purposes, the Napa Valley and Napa County are synonyms, and so the discussion moves directly to the AVA.

MENDOCINO

potter Valley
Redwood Valley

Navarro Ukiah
NAVARRO RIVER
Talmage
Philo
Boonville
Hopland

OCEAN

Upper Lake

Lakeport

LAKE

Kelseyville

Cloverdale
Middletown

SONOMA
Geyserville
Healdsburg

NAPA
Calistoga
Windsor
Angwin
St. Helena

Guerneville

Forestville
Rutherford
Sebastopol
Oakville
Santa Rosa
Yountville

Glen Ellen
Sonoma
Napa

PACIFIC

NORTH COAST
MARIN

33

NAPA VALLEY AVA

Napa, curiously, is both the keeper of the flame and the cutting edge in California wine growing and winemaking. Since early times, this is where tough competitors have liked to come to try to lead the parade. This is where standards are traditional, and also where tools and techniques reflect the newest thoughts on getting the job done. Money is not no object, but it is less of one than anywhere else.

Napa's long tenure as leader has its graphic side in the lavish architecture of its cellars. The improbable bulk of The Christian Brothers Greystone Cellars dates from 1888–1889. Inglenook's original building comes from the same era, as do the two main buildings at Charles Krug Winery, the great wooden barn at Trefethen Vineyards, and a full score of smaller stone barns. (The early winegrowers did not spare anything when they built their homes either, as witness the Rhine House at Beringer Vineyards and the old Tiburcio Parrott house at Spring Mountain Vineyards.) The contemporary generation of proprietors takes no backseat to the pioneers, Sterling Vineyards, Domaine Chandon, and Robert Mondavi Winery being only the most prominent in a landscape ever fuller of memorable contemporary structures.

Napa's sense of its own preeminence does not show last in the vineyards, some of which are groomed like golf courses— Hollywood farming, one grower from a rival region called it more out of envy than scorn, and the fancy work is undeniably photogenic, but practical goals pay for it.

In the end, as the sages say, it comes down to what is in the bottle. Wines from Napa vines have been California's most formidable contenders for international prizes and praise throughout the state's relatively brief history. But it seems to be this prospect of triumphant quality that keeps the wheels turning, bringing more tough competitors to make the game tougher still. In 1987 a few more than 150 companies are making wine in

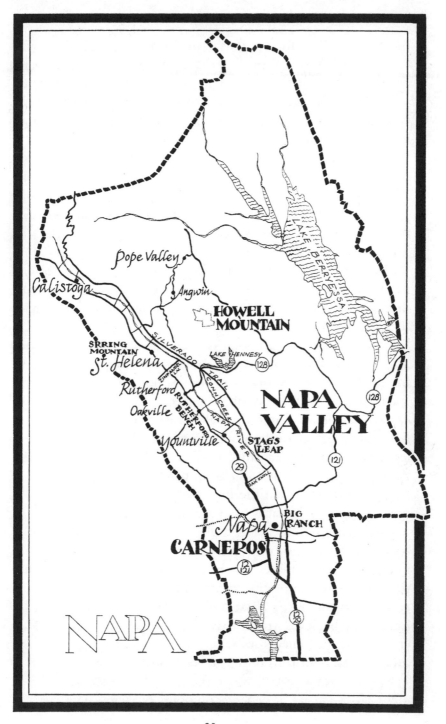

35

the Napa Valley, from a few more than 28,000 acres of vine-yards. The figures are up from 12 companies and 10,000 acres in 1957. In 1895 the figures were 200 companies and 14,500 acres.

What gives Napa its fascination is not just the intensity of the competition, but the density of the plantings. The valley floor is nearly solid with vineyards; the hills are almost as full, at least the plantable parts, and so boundaries begin to be real. Caber-net Sauvignon grows well here, not so well just over there. Riesling's place is limited to these patches. Such things can be said with some confidence because somebody has tried and failed next door to one of the successes. Such things cannot be said yet in many other parts of the state.

Napa's historic power won it the honors of being defined first in the parade of AVAs in California. The blessings might be mixed, having led to a definition that creates more Napa Valley than there is valley.

The valley proper is a long crescent with its foot in the Bay across from San Francisco, its head thirty miles north where Mount St. Helena separates it from Sonoma County's Knights Valley with a long, rocky rib. The steep, thickly wooded Maya-camas Mountains frame the valley neatly on the west, where Sonoma Valley is the neighbor. Barer, rockier hills separate it less cleanly from several smaller upland valleys to the east, where there is no county line to help. In the federal regulations all of this is Napa Valley. In the minds of growers some is, some is not, and some of what is has finer shadings.

Even what is undeniably valley is not all of a piece. From south to north, hills or other natural divisions carve the floor into four separate pieces. At the south is rolling Carneros. After the urbanized interruption of Napa city comes a piece that ex-tends from the north Napa limits to the hills at Yountville. A long, straight, level stretch reaches from Yountville to St. Hel-ena, where the valley goes wasp-waisted. Above the waist, an-other flat straight runs north just beyond Calistoga.

Not illogically, in view of the varied exposures, Napa is blessed—or cursed, it depends on point of view—with versatility. It is best known for Cabernet Sauvignon, but also has grown noteworthy Chardonnay, Sauvignon Blanc, Gewürztraminer, Riesling, Pinot Noir, and more. Plantings reflect the fact: In 1986 Chardonnay had 6,450 acres, Cabernet 5,820, Sauvignon Blanc 3,000, Pinot Noir 2,375, Chenin Blanc 2,030, Zinfandel 2,000, and Riesling 1,015.

Versatility go hang, the Napa Valley has been, is, and probably always will be defined by Cabernet Sauvignon or variations on it. Maybe surprisingly, maybe not, Chardonnay and Pinot Noir were the governing factors behind the first internal AVA boundary, Carneros, but the rest are almost surely to be determined by what is best for Cabernet. Howell Mountain already has official status based on its suitability for Cabernet. In 1987 the Stag's Leap district stands on the brink of official recognition with boundaries drawn for the same purpose. The Rutherford Bench is farther from legal recognition but ever more needful of it.

Rutherford-Oakville Bench Rutherford's historic identity owes especially to Beaulieu Vineyard and Inglenook Vineyards, and more especially to their Cabernet Sauvignons. Later arrivals, including Robert Mondavi, have expanded the fame but kept Cabernet Sauvignon in the limelight. Even the independent vineyards—Martha's, Bella Oaks, Bosché—are famous for their Cabernet and nothing else.

Rutherford has been slow to present itself as a candidate for membership in the club of AVAs, probably because so many of its proponents have exact ideas about where the borders should fall, and so few of them have exactly the same lines in mind. The prevailing wisdom is outlined in detail in the Napa section of the chapter on Cabernet.

Whatever else, the region will continue to be anchored in the village of Rutherford, on the west side of the valley almost exactly at its midpoint. Aside from its virtues for the growing of Cabernet, the bench is, in a quiet way, one of the most beautiful parts of the valley. Almost without interruption, vineyards

37

in well-drained alluvial soils slope slowly up toward steep, wooded hills. The tallest of the hills, Mount St. John, stands directly behind Inglenook's stately old cellars.

Stag's Leap District   The two principal wineries behind the reputation of Stag's Leap are a century newer than Inglenook, but the district has its base in Cabernet Sauvignon just as thoroughly as Rutherford does. Clos du Val Wine Co. and Stag's Leap Wine Cellars are the linchpins, with Pine Ridge Winery, Shafer Vineyards, Silverado Vineyards, and Steltzner Vineyard increasingly in the game. Both of the old-timers are almost synonymous with Cabernet; all their younger rivals focus on it. They have done so well with it that in 1987 the district is on the verge of being granted sub-AVA status.

The vineyards are, like Rutherford's, alluvial, but they are on the east side of the main valley and tipped to the west, the exact opposite of their older counterpart. They sit two miles across the valley from it, and about the same distance south. Their dramatically severe setting seems worlds, not mere miles apart from the gentle charms of Rutherford. The promontory that gives the district its name is the highest of several rocky crags that cap an almost sheer wall of bare rock. That same rock, crumbled, is the vineyard soil below.

Howell Mountain AVA   It is both odd and not odd that Howell Mountain should be Napa's first sub-AVA predicated on Cabernet Sauvignon as a variety. The upland district—its boundary is the fourteen-hundred-foot elevation line—has a long history, but also a long gap. The first modern rumblings of its fitness to grow Cabernet belong mainly to Dunn Vineyards, planted in the 1970s, with a first wine from 1978. The region had been known as a source of Zinfandel and Petite Sirah before Dunn, but pre-Prohibition history suggests that at least a few producers had begun to prize its Cabernet by the turn of the century.

The AVA is almost all a table in the hills east of St. Helena, a little rumpled in spots, but generally tilted a couple of degrees to the west.

Carneros AVA   Carneros loops and rolls incessantly, toes at the foot of the Mayacamas Mountains dipping into chilly bay waters across from San Francisco. It is not an easy place to be comfortable because the wind blows hard day after day, most of the time cooled by sea fogs coming through the Golden Gate. Vines bend in front of that wind even after they have been around enough years to have trunks thicker than a No. 2 Eberhard Faber pencil.

Wineries in the Carneros get their names in the papers for Pinot Noir and Chardonnay. The roster of wineries in the AVA is short—Acacia Winery, Carneros Creek Winery, Chateau Bouchaine, Mont St. John Cellars, and Saintsbury exhaust it—but the list of major wineries with vineyards in it is much longer. The famous Winery Lake Vineyard now belongs to Sterling Vineyards and Domaine Mumm. Louis M. Martini has two sizable ranches. Domaine Chandon, Beaulieu, Inglenook, Clos du Val, Cuvaison, and Sequoia Grove are others.

The two Domaines (soon to be joined by a third, Domaine Carneros) are beginning to make Carneros as noticeable for Chardonnay- and Pinot Noir–based champagne-method sparklers as the other cellars have for still wines from the same two grape varieties.

A good deal of the talk going around these days would make one think that Carneros was invented overnight sometime around 1975. Pish and tosh. The Carneros was a famous district before Prohibition for the presence of Judge John A. Stanly's La Loma Vineyard and the Debret et Priet Vineyard. Louis M. Martini bought most of the old Stanly Ranch in 1942, and soon after had it planted to all of the varieties now causing all the stir. The former Debret et Priet property became Winery Lake Vineyard under Rene di Rosa's ownership in 1961.

Carneros is one of very few AVAs in California to date that straddles a county line. The larger portion, in fact, lies in Sonoma County. The grapes on both sides have dual citizenship; the Napans can call themselves either Napa Valley or Carneros; the Sonomans can go by either Sonoma Valley or Carneros; wines blended from both sides of the line can be Carneros only. Carneros also is the only AVA with two legal names—Carneros or Los Carneros. The name, incidentally, is Spanish for "sheep," an early staple in the local economy.

Other Districts On Napa city's northern outskirt, Big Ranch Road may turn out to be a long-term home of Chardonnay, but it is not ready to be overlooked for its Sauvignon Blanc or Traminer. A subappellation has yet to be discussed let alone formalized. Principal growers in the neighborhood include Beringer, Trefethen, Monticello Cellars, Rutherford Hill Winery, and Sterling. St. Andrew's Winery is smaller, but has contributed to the reputation of the district for Chardonnay.

Calistoga, at the very top of the Napa Valley, has the valley's extreme climate, hotter by day and cooler by night than St. Helena's, and is much more susceptible to spring frosts. Growers in the district for some years lagged behind the movement toward fine varieties. Late in the 1970s, however, they joined the general push toward Cabernet. Some of the go-ahead figures have begun looking seriously at other varieties with origins in Bordeaux, on the grounds that some of them will grow better than Cabernet in Calistoga's particular climate. Sterling and Schramsberg are the great established voices, having both wineries and vineyards in the district.

The rest of the valley floor has more fluid boundaries than any of these. The long, wide stretch running right up the floor from Yountville to St. Helena is the part that won Napa much of its reputation for versatility. Cabernet, Sauvignon Blanc, Chardonnay, Chenin Blanc, Gewürztraminer, even Pinot Noir— all of them grow well. Then there are the eastern vales—Pope, Chiles, and Wooden valleys. The original Napa Valley AVA proposal excluded them. Impassioned pleas by growers in these valleys got them in. Long term, these efforts may be viewed as a probable cause of having slowed down their progress toward individual recognition. The area is big enough, distinct enough to merit its own identity or identities. For now, because of a lack of wineries, it is hard to pinpoint this area by variety, save for its rock-solid performance with Sauvignon Blanc year after year.

Sonoma County

Napa's closest neighbor is increasingly its nearest competitor. History crowds in on the county, especially the Sonoma Valley. Haraszthy at Buena Vista and Gundlach-Bundschu at Rhinefarm are, alas, the only great old Sonoma Valley names to survive. Only Simi is still around of all the wineries farther north, in the Russian River drainage system. For some reason, the county could not keep pace with Napa after 1933, falling instead into long slumber. Perhaps its decline owes itself to a sprawling diversity so pronounced that Sonoma alone was a virtual invitation for the AVA system.

By 1987, just four years into the system, it had 10 AVAs within it and 140 wineries to use them. Because the wineries predate the appellation system, few of them conform exactly to it. Simi, Sonoma-Cutrer, Dry Creek, Chateau St. Jean, Clos du Bois, and other major players reach across lines for grapes without second thoughts. So do wineries as small as Hacienda and Robert Stemmler. The habit seems likely to reinforce itself as new lessons continue to narrow the range of grape varieties within each AVA. For the moment, Sonoma's wealth of varieties remains more evenly distributed than the sun and rain are, but that seems likely to begin changing as vines planted in the early 1970s near replacement planting.

Anyone tempted to ponder what will go where must remember that Sonoma, in general, grows warmer, not only from south to north, but also from west to east.

SONOMA VALLEY AVA

Sonoma Valley is the historic center of wine growing in the county. Buena Vista alone would give it the nod. Not only was it the first major commercial winery in the region, but founder Agoston Haraszthy's promotional genius made it pretty close to the first familiar California label outside the state. Before Haraszthy arrived, Sonoma's Mission vineyard was the first of any kind north of the Bay. First the root louse phylloxera, then Prohibition brought hard times. The valley's roster of wineries plummeted from nearly a hundred to nearly none; Samuele Sebastiani carried the district almost single-handedly through Prohibition and after. Like every other old home to the vine, it began crawling out of the doldrums between 1966 and 1972.

One of the first signs of renewed vigor had every bit as much drama as Haraszthy's performance at Buena Vista. Ambassador James D. Zellerbach founded Hanzell in the mid-1950s with the aim of making Chardonnays and Pinot Noirs that would impress Burgundians. The heart of the idea was to use newly coopered French oak barrels for aging, and Zellerbach came close enough not only to stun wine bibbers of the time, but to inspire first a few, then a score, and finally hundreds of imitators. In 1973 Gundlach-Bundschu returned to life in haunts its owning family had occupied since 1859. Grand Cru, Kenwood, and Chateau St. Jean had already joined in. The roster continues to expand.

The Sonoma Valley parallels the Napa Valley exactly, its virtual twin for length and orientation to the sun. This southeastern corner of the county is fuller of towns and narrower than the Napa Valley, has considerably less arable land, and far fewer acres in grapes. Nearly half of the 6,950-acre total is given over to Chardonnay and Pinot Noir, a fair portion of them toward the southern tip, where grapes have twin patents—Sonoma Valley or Carneros. The valley warms progressively toward the north. At Sonoma town the climate is noticeably hotter and drier than

ALEXANDER VALLEY

DRY CREEK VALLEY

KNIGHTS VALLEY

Healdsburg

128

Chalk Hill

RUSSIAN RIVER VALLEY

Santa Rosa

116

Green Valley

SONOMA VALLEY

Sebastopol

12

Sonoma Mountain

Sonoma

101

Bodega Bay

Carneros

Petaluma

SONOMA

it is a mere two miles south. Just beyond Kenwood its upper end cools again, separated as it is from the Santa Rosa Plain by only a low rise.

It is hard to get a bead on just what does well where. Not surprisingly, Les Pierres and other successful vineyards at the southern end have won their fame with Chardonnay. Northward from there, the calls grow tougher. Sauvignon Blanc comes to mind at Glen Ellen Winery & Vineyards, St. Jean Vineyard, and others well up the valley. Zinfandel of premier quality has come from the Bariccia Vineyard down on the flats south of Sonoma town, from Monte Rosso toward the top of the mountains north of the same town, and from London Ranch in the west hills above Glen Ellen. Cabernet Sauvignon seems to hit its peak in the hills on either side. Gewürztraminer, oddly, seems to do well everywhere. With all of the variations, the valley has—almost predictably—two subappellations within it: Carneros at the south and Sonoma Mountain in the hills that mark its north and west limits.

Carneros AVA   Sonoma has the larger portion of the Carneros AVA within it, most of it overlapping Sonoma Valley, some of it reaching into Napa County. Consistent weather, similar orientation south toward San Francisco, and homogenous soils validate its boundaries.

Were it not for Buena Vista's expansive plantings of Cabernet Sauvignon, Gewürztraminer, Riesling, and Gamay, and some echoes of those varieties belonging to Sebastiani, most of the acreage would be in Chardonnay and Pinot Noir.

Buena Vista's producing winery sits in the midst of its seven hundred (soon to be eleven hundred) acres. The only other winery on the Sonoma County side of the line is the Spanish-owned sparkling wine house of Gloria Ferrer. (Domaine Chandon has a 530-acre ranch straddling the county line; sparkling wines loom as a large and growing factor on both sides.)

Sonoma Mountain AVA   Sonoma Mountain is a second recognized subregion of Sonoma Valley. It echoes the Napa Valley's

Howell Mountain for being all upland slopes and for having had growers of Cabernet Sauvignon lead the campaign for appellation status. It differs for facing east, the opposite direction. In the early going Laurel Glen Cabernets have led the charge. Some Matanzas Creek Sauvignon Blancs say that Sauvignon, too, is a considerable variety on these slopes. Zinfandel from the district has had some great innings at Kenwood.

RUSSIAN RIVER VALLEY AVA

The Russian River Valley is at least as cool as Carneros in most of its sprawling expanses. Much of the valley is also identified to geographers, if not grape growers, as the Santa Rosa Plain. Toward its eastern side, it ranges from virtually flat to slightly rumpled. Its west hills begin to steepen and gather in the plane that links Sebastopol and Forestville. West of them, the hills quickly are truly steep and usually wooded. Sea fogs visit too frequently for grapes to ripen.

West Side Road, a winding two-laner, shows off to perfection just how the Russian River Valley sits at the margin, wandering into the edges of redwood and fir forests, out onto oak-studded grasslands, back into trees, out again to grasslands. It does that for nearly fifteen miles, from its beginnings near Rio Nido until it turns away from the hills toward Healdsburg. A larger-scale demonstration of its diversity comes from the two AVAs within the larger Russian River Valley AVA—Sonoma–Green Valley on the chilly west flank, Chalk Hill on the warmer eastern edge.

Until the mid-1960s very little of the valley was planted to grapes. The prevailing view was that it was too cold and too damp. A few gingerly efforts toward the eastern boundaries of the plain turned out fairly well. From the mid-1970s on plantings pushed west at a vigorous pace until, in 1986, the total acreage stood at 8,375. Chardonnay is the grape of choice, followed by Pinot Noir, then Gewürztraminer. A good half the Chardonnay and well more than half the Pinot Noir goes into champagne-method sparkling wines; Chateau St. Jean, Iron

Horse, Korbel, and Piper-Sonoma all are heavily involved sparkling-wine producers in the Russian River Valley.

Among the still-wine producers that give the valley its right
to a pedigree: De Loach, Dehlinger, Davis Bynum, Louis Foppiano, Hop Kiln, Iron Horse, and Rodney Strong.

Sonoma–Green Valley AVA Out among second-growth redwoods, in the first rolls of hills beyond the Santa Rosa Plain,
Sonoma–Green Valley grows several of the Chardonnays and
Pinot Noirs that have helped the Russian River Valley to eminence. Most of the grapes from a thousand acres go to still
wines. However, and fittingly in view of the cool, foggy climate, a healthy proportion ends up in champagne-method sparkling wines. The two best-known wineries within the sub-AVA
are Domaine Laurier and Iron Horse, but smaller cellars and
several independent growers share the space.

Forestville sits at the hub. The north boundary touches the
Russian River; the south one reaches almost down to Sebastopol. The hyphenated name, Sonoma–Green Valley, distin-
guishes it from Solano–Green Valley, another small AVA on
the north bank of the Sacramento River, where it funnels through
the easternmost hills of the Coast Ranges near Vacaville.

Chalk Hill AVA Most of the Chalk Hill sub-AVA is the west-
facing slopes of Chalk Hill, one of a dozen similar peaks between Santa Rosa and Healdsburg, this one centered on the
hamlet of Windsor. The location puts it where sea air flowing
up the Russian River course still has a bit of force. Balverne
and Chalk Hill wineries and their vineyards help define it. Which
will prove its primary varieties remains to be seen, but Chardonnay has grown well for both Balverne and Chalk Hill and
Rodney Strong Vineyard as well, and Sauvignon Blancs from
independent growers have been stellar for Simi and several others. The 1986 ratio of its thousand acres of vines favored whites
over reds, nine to one.

Dry Creek Valley AVA

Dry Creek Valley is flanked on one side by the Russian River Valley, on the other by Alexander Valley. Its middle position accurately foretells which varieties of grapes do well in it. It shares a boundary with the cooler Russian River Valley for several miles west of Healdsburg and has its downstream end there. Its common boundary with the warmer Alexander Valley runs along the top of a low ridge that divides them. Slow-flowing Dry Creek threads its way south and east down a narrow-stream course for a dozen miles, mostly hills and benchlands and hardly any flood plain except toward its mouth. It ripens Zinfandel as nearly to perfection as Zinfandel will allow. It also is first rate for Sauvignon Blanc, and shows promise with Cabernet Sauvignon. I would hate to see its growers lose sight of Petite Sirah. Among the well-established forces in the Dry Creek Valley: Dry Creek Vineyard, J. Pedroncelli, Preston, and Lambert Bridge.

Alexander Valley AVA

Alexander Valley is the most richly blessed or deeply cursed of all the AVAs within Sonoma for the fact that it grows everything just about equally well. Gewürztraminer, Chardonnay, Riesling, Sauvignon Blanc, Cabernet Sauvignon, Zinfandel, all have been made into wines that demand and get consideration.

As an AVA, Alexander Valley has been carved out of the middle of the Russian River's course, cut off at the north by the Sonoma-Mendocino county line and at the south by the Santa Rosa Plain, or, as the latter is better known to scholars of wine, the Russian River Valley AVA. There is a reason for the boundaries. The Russian River drives through a deep, narrow canyon for several miles north of the county line. At Healdsburg, hills pinch it off from the neighboring Russian River AVA, in the bargain turning it warmer and sunnier than its neighbor.

47

Drive south on US Highway 101 late on a harvest-season night with the windows down and your sleeves up and you will, most times, feel a sudden cooling on your skin somewhere on the long, slow grade between Geyserville and Healdsburg, and will feel it even more somewhere between Healdsburg and Windsor.

Even as a fraction of the geographic Russian River Valley, as distinguished from the AVA, the Alexander is a big valley by Sonoma standards, at twenty-two miles longer than any of the others, and wider than all except its own downstream neighbor. It runs a steady two to three miles wide from Cloverdale south to Healdsburg, where the river takes itself into a sort of cul-de-sac before it begins its run across the Santa Rosa Plain. The cul-de-sac is much narrower, and fuller of wineries and vineyards alike. In all, the AVA holds sixty-five hundred acres of vines.

Considering that the history of the Alexander Valley goes back to the 1880s, the valley is not as well known as it could or should be. However, winemaking there did not make a quick come-back from Prohibition and only recently has made a slow one. There was an abundance of vineyards and a considerable number of wineries early, but most of the wines went east in tank cars to be bottled under merchant names at the other end of the line. The ones that found their way into bottles made little mention of where they came from. In 1972 the serious awakening began. In that year Russ Green bought and began revitalizing a once-great, much-reduced Simi. A corporate owner launched what is now Chateau Souverain. J. Pedroncelli began shifting over in earnest from bulk production. Within the next four years. Alexander Valley Vineyards, Jordan, and Field Stone all had their beginnings.

Even with the renaissance well underway, the Alexander Valley has yet to become a location of many estate wineries, or wineries that operate entirely within its generous bounds. Alexander Valley Vineyards and Jordan Vineyard are the big two in size and reputation. The rest make some Alexander Valley wines, but also reach into other AVAs as well.

Knights Valley AVA

The loftiest of Sonoma's AVAs is also somewhat isolated from the others, handier to Napa by way of Calistoga than anywhere else. It is logical, then, that this small bowl is a sort of Beringer fiefdom at the moment as far as identifiable wines. The Napa winery has had much the largest holdings in Knights Valley since the early 1970s, when it went on an acquisition binge. The winery gets two striking wines: a quick-maturing but neatly balanced and complicated Cabernet Sauvignon almost every year and a richly aromatic late-harvest Riesling every once in a while.

Mendocino County

Mendocino has grown grapes since the 1880s, but its reputation blossomed late, on the heels of Sonoma's. As recently as 1967 the county was a one-winery show, Parducci being the only label with Mendocino written on it. A couple of co-ops helped keep growers in business, but contributed nothing to the reputation of the territory. Only in the late 1960s and early 1970s did new faces begin to appear in the most northerly of the coastal wine-growing counties.

It is tempting to blame transportation for the long silence before Prohibition, and Prohibition for the long silence after. In the 1880s Napa and Sonoma shipped wine across the Bay on scows. Mendocino, one hundred miles north of the Golden Gate, did not have that luxury. After Prohibition the Napa Valley made more than enough to satisfy a sadly shrunken fine-wine market, leaving Mendocino and all the rest to fight over the scraps from 1933 until the mid-1960s.

Now that the northernmost of coastal California's substantial wine-growing counties is up and going, it is as busy fractionating itself as the most active of its peers. At the most fundamental level are two divisions: the cool, coastal Anderson Valley

MENDOCINO & LAKE

and the warm, interior Ukiah Valley. In these climates prosper an intriguing mélange of grape varieties, notably Riesling (325 acres), Chardonnay (1,450), Sauvignon Blanc (740), and, among reds, Cabernet Sauvignon (900), Petite Sirah (360), and Zinfandel (1,330). The total acreage approaches 11,000.

ANDERSON VALLEY AVA

The Anderson Valley is one of those small masterworks of nature that deceives the eye even as it catches it, a small fold in gentle hills that looks expansive because it is always possible to see so far, even from the low spots. Its illusion of size comes because the Navarro River runs a swift, straight course while grassy, looping hills lean away rather than looming up close. In miles, it is only thirteen from Boonville to Navarro, and never more than one mile wide. Its old economic bases, apples and sheepherding, tell all about its climate. No surprise, then, that the first wave of vineyardists came with visions of Pinot Noir, Chardonnay, Riesling, and Gewürztraminer dancing in their heads. Those remain the most-planted varieties among six hundred or so acres, but a powerful force for change is in the wind. Edmeades Vineyards, Husch Vineyards, Greenwood Ridge Vineyards, Navarro Vineyards, and the other early growers were all small, and still are. So are all but one of their newer neighbors. Their not-small new neighbor, Roederer USA, has in mind turning this into a region devoted to champagne-method sparkling wine. Roederer's first wine is not due in the marketplace until late 1988, but speculation is already ripe.

The Anderson Valley, more specifically the hills that frame it on the west, is a hidden treasure on another count. Just inside and just outside the AVA boundary, Greenwood Ridge is a helluva place to grow Zinfandel.

UKIAH-HOPLAND

A high, unbroken set of hills separates the upper Russian River watershed from Mendocino's Pacific shore. The river rises in the hills east of Ukiah and runs ruler-straight through hard country down to the Sonoma county line.

Nowhere is Mendocino's share of the Russian River drainage an easy climate to plant, nor is it easy to live with once planted, because it is more violent than any of its peers along the coast. In spring frosts are a threat after the tender shoots have poked out eight inches, even a foot. Hailstorms are not unknown. Summer is hot and dry enough to produce thoroughly ripe fruit, but short. Autumn rains start early. Winter is chill and vigorously rainy enough to carve the west hills a little deeper each year. Because the growing season is potentially hot and incurably short, vintages in Mendocino bear closer watching than districts that give growers more comfortable margins.

Local growers and winemakers used to think of the upper Russian River watershed as one place. Now they think of it as Redwood Valley, Potter Valley, McDowell Valley, and Ukiah and Hopland. In the usual topsy-turvy of development, Potter Valley is an AVA without a full-fledged winery in it; Cole Ranch is a single-property AVA, also without a winery; and McDowell Valley is a one-winery, one-vineyard AVA, leaving all the rest with the great majority of wineries and vineyards but no pedigreed name to call their own. The unpedigreed parts hold the greatest interest. For purposes of clarity, the subsections are presented here from north to south.

Potter Valley AVA   Potter is the easternmost and highest of the valleys that, together, make up the Russian River watershed in Sonoma County. It has no winery that it can call its own and only occasionally yields a wine with its name blazoned on the label from a thousand acres of vines. But Sauvignon Blancs from here have already established themselves as contenders.

Redwood Valley   Just to the north of the town of Ukiah, Redwood Valley is a small flat hemmed on all sides by steep, incurving hills. None of the gentle rolls of Anderson Valley here. Quite the opposite, these loom craggy, deeply cut by narrow canyons. In the shade of some of those canyons are Fetzer Vine-yards–owned plantings that have yielded memorable Cabernet Sauvignons and Pinot Blancs. From my perspective a couple of Cabernets challenge Napa's. Several small, new wineries also call the valley home.

Ukiah The river valley from Ukiah at the north down as far as Talmage stays narrow. A majority of the grapes are on the wider shelf east of the Russian River, especially on steepening, west-facing slopes near Talmage, but grapes grow in every quarter. From lower-lying vineyards near Talmage, Simi Winery's Zelma Long has made deeply flavored, durable Chardonnays. Richard Arrowood of Chateau St. Jean coaxed some first-rate Late Harvest Rieslings out of the same neighborhood in the mid-1970s; Hidden Cellars has taken up the task with even more success in recent years. Husch Vineyards can look back on several attractive Sauvignon Blancs and Cabernet Sauvignons from its owner's La Ribera Ranch. And all of this where plenty of Petite Sirah and French Colombard hang on from Mendocino's bulk-wine days.

The Parducci family's pioneer winery is in Ukiah, as are Cresta Blanca and Parsons Creek Winery. Hidden Cellars has its winery at Talmage, and Husch Vineyards has one of its two there.

Cole Ranch AVA The ranch has one hundred acres of vines in its own mile-long valley up in the hills west of Ukiah. Fetzer Vineyards has given it most of its public attention with a series of vineyard-identified Cabernet Sauvignons of more than passing interest.

Hopland Hills pinch tight against the Russian River just downstream from Talmage, and never do widen out much in the remaining miles to the Sonoma county line. However, the narrow valley floor is supplemented by several more narrow canyons leading west into steep hill country. Fetzer's Sun Dial and Valley Oaks ranches and Parducci Wine Cellars's Largo

Ranch take up most of the available space in the main valley. Two generations of the Tijsseling family have planted a two-mile-long, east-west canyon to grapes for their Tijsseling, Tyland, and Mendocino Estates labels. Jepson Vineyards has a smaller but similarly oriented vineyard, as does Milano Winery.

Chardonnay (Fetzer Sun Dial, Tijsseling, Milano Sanel Valley) has had the best of it in the district to date.

McDowell Valley AVA   For all practical purposes, Richard and Karen Keehn own the sub-AVA. Their 360-acre vineyard and modern winery are the only ones in it. The Keehns grow a bit of everything for the McDowell Valley Vineyards label in a small, bowl-like depression in hills above and east of Hopland. Syrah and Zinfandel have been the most promising wine types.

Lake County

Lake County winemaking had a wonderfully romantic early history, with Lily Langtry in a leading role, but all went under during Prohibition. Only since the late 1970s has it begun the noticeable parts of its revival, though the first vineyards go back a few years more. And still, a powerful majority of the hints to date point to Sauvignon Blanc and Cabernet Sauvignon and their kin as the ways to go.

CLEAR LAKE AVA

Close to half of the surface of Lake County is Clear Lake, the lake. Another 10 or 15 percent is Clear Lake, the AVA; its vines crowd onto a narrow shelf between the lake and high hills farther west. In 1987 vines do not press the AVA, with some 3,000 acres of them scattered throughout 170,000 acres of eligible terrain more given to pears and tourist resorts. Konocti Winery is the old hand, and the only winery in the AVA entirely devoted to making wine from it. The larger Kendall-Jackson Vineyards

& Winery draws from this and other districts as well. Both wineries steadily reinforce the notion that Sauvignon Blanc is meant to grow here, and Cabernet probably is.

GUENOC VALLEY AVA

Lily Langtry's old ranch is now home to the Guenoc Winery and its 250-acre vineyard, and a one-property AVA. The rolling property, mostly rangeland, touches Napa County to the south, just across the line from the upper reaches of Pope Valley. The AVA supports nearly the whole spectrum of familiar varieties, Zinfandel and Chenin Blanc being two of the leaders among them.

SAN FRANCISCO BAY AREA

Mainly, the San Francisco Bay Area is two separated and disparate AVAs: the Livermore Valley and the Santa Cruz Mountains. In other eras it has been more. But now, it is just these two, and without hope of being much more for lack of places to plant vines. Silicon Valley and other developments have eaten up the rest.

Wines from both regions differ from those of both the North and Central coasts, sometimes in small ways, more often in marked ones. The two AVAS also differ from each other in every way.

LIVERMORE VALLEY AVA

The Livermore Valley nestles between two rows of steep hills east of San Francisco Bay, about level with San Francisco International Airport. Most of it has filled up with suburban homes, but an irregular old arroyo still is given over to vineyards that have been around since the 1870s and earlier. The soil in it is

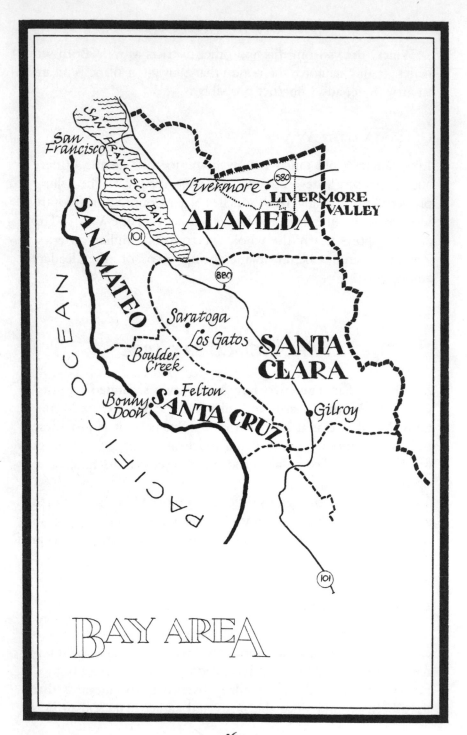

BAY AREA

rocks, golf-ball size up to about cantaloupe, and is said to run six hundred feet deep. The imagination balks at the thought of anyone digging a hole to find out. Almost two thousand acres of vines are planted in the stuff.

Wente Bros. and Concannon Vineyard, which face each other obliquely across Tesla Road east of Livermore town, are the old names. The Wentes got a one-year jump on their neighbors, with an 1881 founding date. Before the turn of the century they had a couple of dozen competitors in the valley. All of the other pioneers are gone. Three tiny wineries flesh out the current roster.

Sheltered as it is by hills both east and west, Livermore is one of the warmest of the coastal AVAs. Its great fame has rested with Sauvignon Blanc, but plantings are dominated by Gray Riesling, and also include Chardonnay, Cabernet Sauvignon, and Petite Sirah.

It falls, quite incidentally, within the much larger boundaries of Alameda County, but the county name never has had as much currency among wine drinkers as Livermore. Further, it has no other district to confuse the issue.

SANTA CRUZ MOUNTAINS AVA

The long, rugged ridgeline separating San Francisco Bay from the Pacific runs south forty miles to Santa Cruz, much the most of it encompassed by a sprawling AVA with hardly more than one hundred acres of vines scattered throughout its length. If it were not for some riveting wines from these parts, the AVA could be taken almost as a joke: a patch of vines, ten miles of grasslands, another scrap of vineyard, ten miles of trees, and so on. But there are those riveting wines, a handful of them Cabernets, a smaller handful Chardonnays, a smaller handful still Pinot Noir. The flesh-and-blood Paul Masson started in these hills around the turn of the century. The current familiar names include Congress Springs Vineyards, Felton-Empire, Thomas Fogarty Winery, and especially Ridge Vineyards. Latterly, a blithe spirit named Randall Grahm has launched Bonny Doon Vineyard with the express aim of growing the great varieties of the Rhône, particularly Syrah, Marsanne, and Roussanne, and commanded attention with the early results. As fanciers of Condrieu well know, volume ain't everything.

CENTRAL COAST

Except for a thin to outright fragile thread of Zinfandels around Paso Robles, the Central Coast is a whole new game. The old-timer, forgetting those Zinfandels, is Chalone, which struggled toward an identity from 1919 until 1969, when the current proprietors caught hold.

In the new game are, from north to south, the counties of Monterey, San Benito, San Luis Obispo, and Santa Barbara. With the advent of AVAs, they have already subdivided. Monterey is Arroyo Seco, Chalone, and Carmel Valley. San Luis Obispo has Edna Valley, Paso Robles, and the latter's subdivision, York Mountain. In Santa Barbara, it is Santa Maria Valley and Santa Ynez Valley.

To what end all of this, I have only a few sketchy ideas. It is not easy to think about places that do not yet have a fifteen-year-old wine to show for their efforts. With rare exceptions the vineyards still grow their first generation of vines. New vineyards continue to spring up so rapidly, in such unexpected places, that today's guesses are unlikely to amount to much for very long anyhow. The track record of these vines is, in fact, so short that the first ambiguities are still to come. The wineries are newer yet.

Monterey County

Five wines leap to mind with the mention of Monterey: Wente Bros. Spätlese Johannisberg Riesling, Jekel Vineyard Johannis-

San Francisco

SAN FRANCISCO BAY

SAN MATEO

ALAMEDA

Livermore

Saratoga
Los Gatos
Boulder Creek
Felton
Bonny Doon
SANTA CRUZ

SANTA CLARA

Hollister

Paicines

Salinas

Monterey
Carmel
Carmel Valley Village
Soledad
Greenfield
King City

SAN BENITO

SALINAS RIVER

MONTEREY

San Miguel

Paso Robles
Templeton
Shandon
Creston

SAN LUIS OBISPO

San Luis Obispo

Arroyo Grande

Santa Maria
Sisquoc
Los Alamos
Lompoc Buellton Los Olivos
Solvang Santa Ynez

SANTA BARBARA

PACIFIC OCEAN

CENTRAL COAST

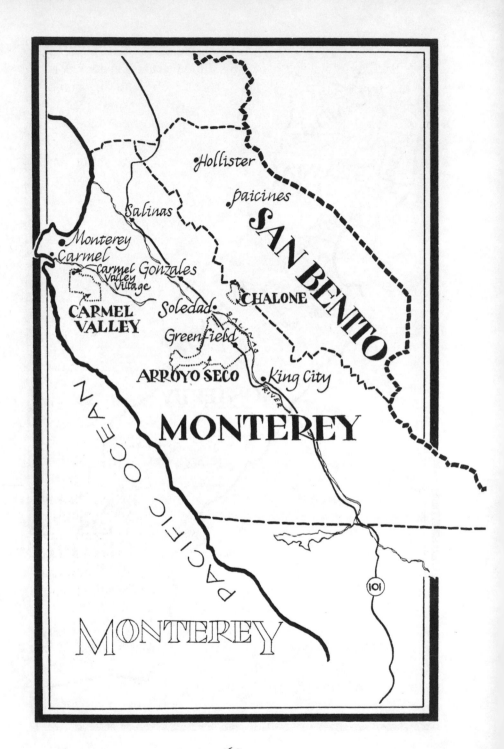

berg Riesling, Chalone Vineyards Pinot Blanc, Chalone Vineyards Pinot Noir, and Durney Vineyard Cabernet Sauvignon. It is a short list for a parade that started off all banners and bugles in 1972, and not a list that shows signs of exploding in numbers any time soon, and yet Monterey is more a newspaper story than a book these days. Revolutionary change would seem to be its ongoing fate.

Chalone hides away in its own AVA, a fold high up in the Gavilans, low mountains that form the east side of the Salinas Valley. Durney grows Cabernet Sauvignon in a location just as separate. William Durney's ocean-facing vineyard lies in Carmel Valley AVA, beyond the ridge tops forming the Salinas Valley's west hills, closer to Carmel than Greenfield. The two wineries between them grow fewer than three hundred acres out of a county total that peaked at thirty-seven thousand. All the rest is in the long, wide trough of the Salinas Valley.

Salinas Valley is a most curious place. Rainfall is almost non-existent, but the north end is one of the coldest, dampest places in all of California because the low, wide mouth offers no resistance at all to sea fogs sweeping in from Monterey Bay, while the far-distant south end is relentlessly sunny and warm. Even Riesling will not get ripe up north at Chualar; Tinta Madeira for port types does just fine down south, near King City. In between the extremes, several of the valley's pioneer growers have marked out the Arroyo Seco AVA, where Riesling has done particularly well, and Gewürztraminer and Chardonnay have given glimpses of an improving future. Almost everything else, but especially Sauvignon Blanc and Cabernet Sauvignon, has earned the territory an unwanted fame for an unwanted flavor known as the Monterey veggies.

Grapes came to the Salinas Valley because of urban pressures on vines elsewhere and so did not bring many wineries with them. (The pioneer planters were Mirassou Vineyards, Paul Masson, and Wente Bros., all with wineries farther north in the Santa Clara and Livermore valleys. The next wave included San Martin Winery and J. Lohr Winery, also with cellars elsewhere.)

The swiftness of Monterey's coming left no room for measured thought. The county had fewer than one hundred acres of bearing vineyard in 1970, and more than twenty-five thousand in 1974. The total peaked at thirty-five thousand in 1980, then fell back to thirty-one thousand by 1986. However, these numbers give weight to the old saw about there being lies, damnable lies, and statistics, because the relatively steady numbers since 1976 hide an almost perpetual revolution in the plantings.

The 1976 figures included a very substantial acreage from Gonzales northward that now has reverted to strawberries, broccoli, asparagus, and the like. More recent figures include a heavy investment by Almaden in vineyards ranging south from King City, plantings which Heublein, the new owners of Almaden, planned in 1987 to lease or abandon.

The stories of the wineries resonate with similar tales of shifting fortunes. The Monterey Vineyard was founded in 1973 to be a showcase for Monterey. A series of interlocking partnerships owned ninety-six hundred acres of vineyard and the winery. The winery still exists under other owners, but very few of the original vineyards outlasted its 1975 sale by more than two years. Another two owners later, the winery still takes Monterey grapes for some of its whites but looks elsewhere for its reds. But it is the outlanders who made the biggest waves. Almaden, from a headquarters in Santa Clara County, plunged in with twenty-two hundred acres in 1972; now the label has no property in either place. Paul Masson was one of the earliest investors in the 1960s, with a fermenting winery and one thousand (later forty-five hundred) acres. In the late 1970s Seagram built a larger winery for Taylor California Cellars (TCC), and later still moved Paul Masson into it. Now new owners have relocated Paul Masson in what started out as TCC, have the original winery on the block, and are still making decisions about the vineyards, some of which are dying of phylloxera, none of which yielded the sort of red wines desired. (Masson reds in recent vintages have come from Sonoma.) The San Martin

Winery once was tied to thirteen thousand acres of vineyard. After its sale to new owners, the acreage reverted to other crops.

And still the acreage is substantial. And still the hopes are there for this to emerge as one of California's great wine-growing regions. And still some of the wines say it may well be so.

Arroyo Seco AVA

Growers and wineries together took a long look at the short history of vineyards in the county and drew a line around the midsection for their principal AVA, Arroyo Seco. It is a cross-valley belt anchored in the towns of Greenfield and Soledad. Even within it the currents of change flow hard, especially for the pioneer growers. Mirassou Vineyards has sustained its vines, but, like Paul Masson, looks elsewhere for reds. Wente Bros. has hung on with an almost-all-white wine vineyard, but, even here, there has been considerable adjustment in varieties.

The later arrivals, Ventana Vineyards and Jekel Vineyard, have both wineries and vineyards in the territory.

In 1987 it comes down to this: The purely native bearers of the standard for the Salinas Valley are but two, Jekel and Ventana, if one looks for a range of wines. The list goes to four only with the inclusion of two specialists, Morgan in Chardonnay and Smith & Hook in Cabernet Sauvignon. The Monterey Vineyard and Paul Masson produce Monterey wines in some but not all varietal types. A few small starts are in the wings, but even with them the roster will remain very short indeed.

Made-on-the-spot wines do not exhaust Monterey by any means. Mirassou Vineyards, J. Lohr Winery, and Wente Bros. produce substantial volumes of Monterey wines from their vineyards in the Arroyo Seco AVA, the former two in San Jose, the latter in Livermore. A dozen or more small wineries spread all over the state make wines bearing the Monterey or Arroyo Seco appellation.

As if the Arroyo Seco did not have enough other worries, phylloxera threatens the area. Many of the early growers planted the great wine varieties on their own roots rather than resistant stock, on the two assumptions that pre-phylloxera wines were greater than modern ones and that phylloxera-free Monterey could be kept that way. Wrong on both counts. The French have conducted scores of studies showing no difference in wines from vines on resistant roots versus vines on their own roots, and Monterey made no better case. Within a decade of the first plantings, Monterey had plenty of phylloxera. Like the rest of the story, this chapter has yet to play itself out.

CHALONE AVA

From almost any part of the hills east of Soledad a summer visitor can bake in strong sunlight while the valley below hides in thick mists. At Chalone the contrast is almost a given. Surprise, then, that this one-vineyard, one-winery slope has focused on such cool-climate grapes as Chardonnay, Pinot Noir, and Pinot Blanc and—typically—grown them with more authority than the far cooler precincts below.

The proprietors of Chalone Vineyards credit their quartz-rich soils for the character of the wines. It will take another grower in Chalone, but out of the quartz belt, to prove the point. Meanwhile, Chalone is so unlike the Arroyo Seco AVA a couple of miles down the hill that no one can balk at its separate existence.

CARMEL VALLEY AVA

Carmel Valley is as separate from the Arroyo Seco as Chalone is, perhaps more so. It faces west toward the Pacific shore from the seaward slopes of the hills separating the Monterey Peninsula from the Salinas Valley. To date, it has two vineyards and three wineries. Durney Vineyard is the elder statesman on both counts, owner William Durney having planted in 1968 and built his cellars in time for the 1973s. Robert Talbott is the other estate winery. Chateau Julien rounds out the roster of cellars.

To this point the small plantings have not declared themselves thoroughly.

San Luis Obispo County

Somewhere on the planet there may be an odder couple than the Paso Robles and Edna Valley AVAs, but I doubt it. Nowhere that comes to mind do so few miles make such startling differences to grapes.

One of the most familiar visions of California is William Randolph Hearst's San Simeon swimming in misty sea air against a backdrop of steep, high coastal mountains. Paso Robles, town and AVA, is on the other side of that wall of hills, some twenty-four miles east as the crow flies but a world away in climate. Edna Valley, forty miles downcoast from San Simeon but no more than thirty miles south of Paso Robles, shares the sea air with Willie's castle. On a summer's day Paso Robles will bake at a dry, still 110°F while the Edna Valley struggles to reach 80°F before the afternoon breezes kick up.

Paso Robles AVA

Paso Robles has one of the strangest physical situations in California. It is fewer than twenty-five miles from the sea, but one of the hottest valleys in the Coast Ranges and at the head of their longest river, the Salinas, which drains into Monterey Bay more than a hundred miles north, not San Luis Bay some twenty miles south. Throughout July and August the afternoon temperature will hit and pass 100°F far more often than it does not. September is not immune. Elevation is the culprit and the saving grace. The town sits at eight hundred feet. Higher hills to the west and south block every hint of ocean air out of the entire, huge AVA. However, the resulting clear, dry air cools enough at night to keep grapes from going straight from green to raisined.

65

A handful of vineyards range up wooded hills to the west of Paso Robles. Most of fifty-four hundred acres stretch east across rolling terrain that is grassland where it is not vines all the way to the ridgeline that separates this valley from the great San Joaquin Valley.

Small as it is, the hilly country west of Paso Robles town is a venerable and, by fans of heavyweight Zinfandels, venerated area. Ignace Paderewski, the pianist and president of Poland, grew Zinfandel hereabouts in the early 1900s and won prizes with it; he is still the best-known vineyardist in regional history. Unfortunately, his timing was lousy in everything but music. He bought his Paso Robles ranch not long before Prohibition and became president of Poland just about the time Hitler's German armies turned in his direction.

York Mountain Winery goes back farther, to 1882 (and did the hard work for gentleman-farmer Paderewski when he came along). A few plantings of other grapes have crept into the modern landscape, but Zinfandel holds the center. Among local wineries, Mastantuono is the first name to look for in a hunt for a typically large, sunny Zinfandel, and the easiest one to find outside of the region. More than a dozen other small to tiny cellars pursue the variety in and around Paso Robles town and Templeton.

The growers east of town have pretty well turned their backs on Zinfandel. All newcomers since the 1970s, they have their caps set for Cabernet Sauvignon and Chardonnay, with fallback positions in Sauvignon Blanc, Chenin Blanc, Syrah, and a few others. Through a short history, Martin Brothers Sauvignon Blanc has been our measuring stick for that variety. Eberle Winery Chardonnay stands at the head of its line. Eberle and Adelaida Cellars tell the story best for Cabernet Sauvignon. Other wineries in the territory include Estrella River, Arciero Vineyards, and little Creston Manor.

EDNA VALLEY AVA

The Edna Valley is an altogether different sort of place among the Central Coast wine-growing districts. In a small, oval bowl

San Miguel

Paso Robles

PASO ROBLES

Templeton

Shandon

• Creston

**SAN
LUIS
OBISPO**

San Luis Obispo

**EDNA
VALLEY**

Arroyo Grande

Santa Maria

Sisquoc

**SANTA MARIA
VALLEY**

SANTA BARBARA

Los Alamos

Lompoc

Buellton

Los Olivos

Santa Ynez

Solvang

**SANTA YNEZ
VALLEY**

PACIFIC

OCEAN

S. CENTRAL COAST

directly south of the town of San Luis Obispo, it has fewer than seven hundred acres in vines within boundaries encompassing hardly more than ten times that area. All of the vines grow in the bottom of the bowl.

Four young wineries spread themselves about as far apart as they can without going over one of the lines. Of the four, Edna Valley Vineyard is jointly owned (with Chalone) by the dominant grower, Paragon Vineyard Co. The smaller Chamisal grows its own Chardonnay. The other two—tiny Claiborne & Churchill and substantial Corbett Canyon Vineyards—buy their grapes. Claiborne & Churchill is all local and specializes in Gewürztraminer. Corbett Canyon has an Edna Valley Chardonnay but, perforce, acquires most of its grapes from other parts of the Central Coast.

To this point, the valley's reputation is for Chardonnays, less on the strength of its home wineries than on the wines of Ahern, Leeward, and other outsiders with longer track records. Pinot Noir, the other major variety in acreage, has yet to prove itself.

In its miniaturism the AVA leaves out at least one vineyard of more than passing interest. André Lallier of Deutz & Geldermann scouted for a long while before he settled on a slope south and east of the town of Arroyo Grande as the place to plant the first 150 acres of vines for his Maison Deutz California sparkling wines. The first results are not yet in, and may not be expected before 1990. In the interim the grapes come from a few miles south, in the Santa Maria Valley.

Santa Barbara County

It takes a long time of looking around to come to grips with all the ways Santa Barbara County differs from its peers as a home to vineyards. The rounded grassy hills that are everywhere in coastal California are here too. Same oaks. Same eucalyptus trees. Same sun. Same coastal fog bank. Finally, the point sinks in. It is what is not here. No thickly wooded slopes. No conifer woods at all.

Along about sunset, and feeling pretty dim for other reasons, one realizes that the sun is going down at the foot of the valley and not behind hills to one side or the other. The county is not in the Coast Ranges but the Transverse Mountains. Santa Barbara has the only east-west running valleys in California, in fact along the whole Pacific Coast of North America.

Santa Barbara County is beyond the southern tip of the range of any of the major conifers. It is just at the tip of the coastal fog bank, not because of mountains but because the great Pacific current turns west exactly at the bulge called Point Conception.

Just thirty miles downcoast from Point Conception the splendid small city of Santa Barbara is all tropical gardens and warm-water beaches and no grapes at all.

In terms of climate and orientation and all the other basics of grape growing, it is a question, still, of just how closely allied Santa Barbara might be to the counties farther north. It is, at the very least, at the margin, a fact that does not seem to harm its wines at all.

In some ways it validates the old University of California climate region system better than any of the places it was designed to fit. Santa Barbara has two AVAs—the Santa Maria and Santa Ynez valleys—with gradual changes so regular that they can be plotted on a map without much or any of the back-and-forth that is epidemic everywhere else.

It will take a while to know much. An old vineyard here is one that was planted in 1972, when winemaking made an absolutely fresh start in the county. In mid-1987 the county had about ten thousand acres of vineyard and twenty wineries.

Santa Maria Valley AVA

Within Santa Barbara County, the Santa Maria Valley is unique in being the only true, unbent east-west valley, and the only one with a wide-enough mouth to let sea fogs roll in unchecked. So bleak is the shoreside climate that grapes will not grow anywhere west of US Highway 101. Thus, in spite of its being almost at Los Angeles's doorstep, it competes with the Anderson Valley in Mendocino and the Russian River Valley in Sonoma for the title of coolest grape-growing region in California. Otherwise, it is as unlike its rivals as can be. Most of the soils here are sandy; rain is a mild novelty, even in winter; a frost after budbreak would cause the local newspaper to interview the oldest living local on the rarity of the event. Loam, rain, and spring frosts are rules of life in the Anderson and Russian River valleys.

The other way in which it differs from the Anderson and Russian River valleys is its youth. For wine, history began here in 1972, when the first vines went into the ground. The first winery, Rancho Sisquoc, came along in 1977. In 1987 its only companion was Byron, a third winery having folded its tents a year earlier. The figure misleads; most of the twelve wineries in neighboring Santa Ynez draw grapes from Santa Maria.

The valley grows some of all of the familiar varieties. The two that have piqued the most interest in a short career are Pinot Noir and Chardonnay.

Santa Ynez Valley AVA

Physically, the Santa Ynez Valley is an interesting hybrid. It starts out east-west at its lower end, around Lompoc, then makes a climbing turn north at Solvang, the sort of dogleg that makes even the Jack Nicklauses of the world go wobbly at the knees. Clear at the top, it runs right into the inland end of the Santa Maria.

The local rule of thumb is, the temperature goes up a degree a mile from Lompoc all the way to Solvang. Down low, the primary hopes rest with Pinot Noir and Chardonnay, as in Santa Maria. The climate is so different from the upper reaches that some growers and winemakers are thinking of establishing a maritime AVA that would embrace the lowest parts of the Santa

Ynez, all of the Santa Maria, some shoreward parts of the land separating them, and the part of San Luis Obispo County where Maison Deutz struggles along without an AVA.

The major bearing vineyards in the marine end of the AVA in 1987 are Sanford & Benedict's pioneer piece, Santa Barbara Winery's Lafond plantings, and the estate vines of Babcock Vineyard. A small cellar called Vega Vineyards and Winery also has vines in the lower end of the valley.

Meanwhile, the upper part of the Santa Ynez has gotten and still gets its greatest plaudits for Sauvignon Blanc, though it grows a diverse range of varieties well. The Brander Vineyard shows all the rest the way in Sauvignon Blanc; Gainey is one to watch.

Plantings are larger and more numerous east of US 101, above the bend in the dogleg. The Firestone Vineyard and Zaca Mesa have the largest holdings (and the well-made wines of both are useful benchmarks for all the others).

The upstream countryside broadly resembles the lower valley, but in detail they differ. Down toward the river's mouth, vines are few and share space with seed-flower farms. Upstream, the principal alternative to a modestly greater supply of grapes is horses; this is serious breeding country.

The little chunk inside the U formed by the two AVAs has several substantial vineyards. The most-prized plantings in this, the Los Alamos Valley, are of Pinot Noir.

SIERRA FOOTHILLS

The Foothills, California's historic Gold Rush country, point a mildly accusatory finger at the public these days. The territory seems wonderfully well suited to its historic variety, Zinfandel, but growers and wineries alike are clamoring to turn it to Cabernet Sauvignon and Sauvignon Blanc, more in response to the marketplace than shortcomings in its Zinfandel vines.

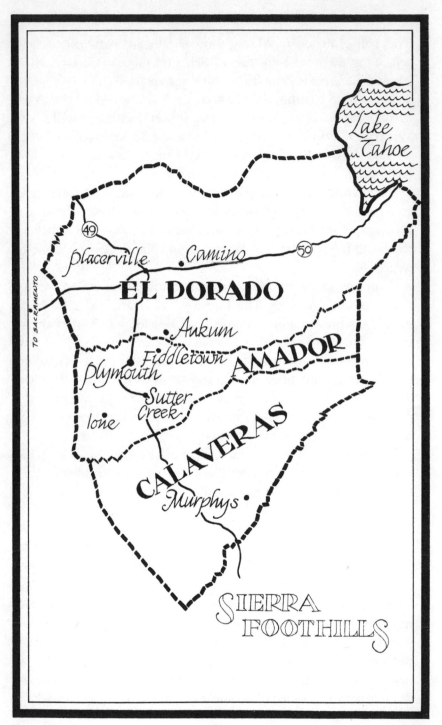

In 1971 Amador and El Dorado counties between them had four hundred acres of Zinfandel and precious little of any other varieties. By 1986 Zinfandel had increased to 1,200 acres, but had 365 of Sauvignon Blanc and 100 of Cabernet Sauvignon offering competition. It is not that Sauvignon Blanc and Cabernet Sauvignon are poor ideas, mind you. In fact the roster of wineries has grown from five to thirty-five while the acreages of Sauvignon Blanc and Cabernet Sauvignon were going up. It is just that Zinfandel does not want crowding out of a territory in which it has performed so well for so long.

Zinfandel is a big wine grown in these parts, big enough to tackle venison and even the tomato sauce from Teresa's restaurant in Jackson Gate. There are not many like it, while the Cabernet and the Sauvignon Blanc from here are so normal they never stick out in any crowd.

Vineyards freckle a landscape that alternates between woodlands and meadows for more than twenty miles along a north-south axis from Placerville, in El Dorado County, down to Plymouth, in Amador County. The former sits at the intersection of US Highway 50, the route to South Lake Tahoe, and State Route 49, the quickest way to Plymouth. Nearly the whole of the grape-growing territory lies parallel to and just east of the state route, in two AVAs: El Dorado in the county of the same name and California-Shenandoah Valley in Amador.

SHENANDOAH VALLEY AVA

The heart of Amador's vineyards, if a heart can be at an extremity, is due east of Plymouth, in a broad, shallow bowl known locally as the Shenandoah Valley. To the Bureau of Alcohol, Tobacco and Firearms, and thus to label readers everywhere, it is known as California-Shenandoah Valley out of deference to Virginians. The general exposure is west, toward the afternoon sun, in a region that gets sun just about every day from May until October. It has no trouble ripening any variety, but can be hard put to hold back. Zinfandel is the proven quantity.

Locals have considerable hopes for Sauvignon Blanc, and some evidence to back it. The first faint stirrings of interest in dessert wines have an independent vineyardist growing several traditional varieties of Portugal's Douro for the Quady Winery, a specialist in ports and Muscats. (Quady's winery is down in the San Joaquin Valley at Madera.) Several Muscats also grow well in the region.

Of the current roster of wineries, the ones that persistently make strong cases for properly large, handsomely polished Shenandoah Valley Zinfandel are Karly Wines and Baldinelli Vineyards. Monteviña, Santino, and Shenandoah Vineyards push them. The latter has begun to produce some intriguing Muscats.

FIDDLETOWN AVA

At a back corner of the Shenandoah Valley and ranging uphill from it, Fiddletown has been certified as an AVA, mostly to give added emphasis to some ancient plantings of Zinfandel. All of the grapes go to wineries in the larger AVA or out of the county.

EL DORADO AVA

A map of El Dorado County vineyards looks like a long, tenuous comma, with its head on the westerly side of Apple Hill at Placerville and the tail curling down the length of County Road E-16, most often but not always on slopes tipped toward the afternoon sun. El Dorado's growers itch more to work with Cabernet Sauvignon, Merlot, Sauvignon Blanc, and Chardonnay than they do with Zinfandel. The two old-timers—Boeger Winery and Sierra Vista Winery—give good account of locally grown fruit. Here too the roster of growers and producers is expanding.

SOUTH COAST

The South Coast only begins to emerge as a wine district. Its centerpiece is a small AVA called Temecula, in the southwest corner of Riverside County, right where it abuts San Diego County. The latter, and Ventura County to the north of Los Angeles, have tiny plantings of grapes to supplement Temecula's seventeen hundred acres.

The first vineyards were planted in 1968–1969; Ely Callaway bonded the first winery in 1974. In 1987 there were another dozen cellars to share the crop.

At this early hour the vineyards hold a bit of everything. Chardonnay, Chenin Blanc, Riesling, Sauvignon Blanc, and Traminer are among the whites; Cabernet Sauvignon, Petite Sirah, Pinot Noir, and Zinfandel all are represented among the red varieties. To date, Sauvignon Blanc has been the most reliable producer of attractive wines, with Chardonnay close behind. Neither type has struck me as having the depth of flavor or the richness of texture that repay keeping, but regional history is too short for last words.

CABERNET SAUVIGNON

TWENTY-FIVE YEARS LATER I CAN STILL REMEM-
ber the instant Cabernet Sauvignon got me. We were living in
student digs in Palo Alto; it had been a good day at work for
both my wife and me; we decided to pamper ourselves with a
bit of beef and our one and only bottle of ten-year-old Cabernet, a 1952 Louis M. Martini Private Reserve.

It was the second glass that did it. The first one had been all
silk and polish, and had carried the suggestion of herbs that is
supposed to be Cabernet's marker. The start of the second glass
was still all silk and polish, but the flavors rang truer to some
berrylike fruit for a couple of sips, drifted back to herbs for a
moment, then took off on a new tangent altogether. That was
the instant. That was when I could begin to imagine that keeping wine for a long time was worth the trouble, and that Cabernet would pay particular dividends. Some thousands of bottles

later I still feel the same way, but the reasons grow ever more complicated.

Cabernet Sauvignon ought to be easy. Its varietal flavors are so pronounced that soil and climate hardly ever disguise them. Many of the wines last so long and evolve so slowly that any diligent taster can build a history of consistent opinions about each one. Why, then, does most of the outright flapdoodle I have written about wine concern Cabernet? Where have the old certainties gone?

Well, nothing will stand still for twenty-five (in fact thirty) years to have its picture taken.

Now that Cabernet Sauvignon is playing chocolate to Chardonnay's vanilla, it is hard to remember how small its fan club was three decades ago, and how short the roster of vineyards. Coming out of Prohibition, Cabernet plantings were so meager that Louis M. Martini, the man, had to hunt for grapes as far afield as the old Rixford vineyard at Woodside, twenty-odd miles south of San Francisco. George Deuer bought Cabernet in Sonoma County to augment Inglenook Vineyards's tiny supply, though the old winemaker never would say exactly where. Only Beaulieu Vineyard seemed to have enough vineyard to take care of its needs. The exact total acreage of the day is lost, but it did not take long, or much, to catch up. In 1950 all of California had fewer than two hundred acres of Cabernet, a long half of that in Napa, and it was too much. As late as 1960 people who knew went to the cellar door at Inglenook, bought half-gallon jugs of IVY Red for a dollar, and went home with pure Cabernet. The uppity went to Martini or Beaulieu and bought ten-year-old bottles for less than three dollars, and now you know where we got ours. Collect those three and Charles Krug Winery and Napa had given its all. Get some Concannon Vineyards and the occasional Martin Ray and that was about it for age-worthy Cabernet for the whole state.

It was a great time for being certain. Not only was the list short, but there were not many complications. No one had plantings of Merlot or other blend grapes in the 1950s, and no plans for any because real Cabernet was all Cabernet. French oak barrels were not in play. More than that, barrels of any kind were rare things to see. Redwood tanks did for most. The really serious producers had ancient six hundred- to fifteen-hundred-gallon oak ovals for special lots.

By 1980 California had twenty-five thousand acres planted to Cabernet Sauvignon, little more than a fifth of the total in Napa, almost a third of it in places that did not grow grapes at all in 1970, forget 1950. Merlot has climbed to twenty-eight hundred acres; Cabernet Franc is on a roll. Petit Verdot and Malbec are getting tryouts. Along with blend grapes have come barrels made of oak from every forest in Europe and several in North America. At least three hundred producers clamor for attention, more than one hundred of them from Napa.

As early as the mid-1970s all of the wines I had spent twenty years getting to know were, suddenly, a minority report amid dozens, then scores of Allier/Limousin/Nevers/Troncais-aged, Merlot-blended newcomers from where did he say?

Merlot was supposed to soften tannically austere Cabernet so it would be enjoyable sooner. Oak was supposed to add grace notes. As the huge crop of rookie winemakers rushed to be in the vanguard, Merlot flattened more Cabernet than it softened, and oak made too much of it taste overpoweringly like industrial perfume, varnish, or raw wood, all qualities hard to define as grace notes. As a breed Cabernet became so distorted it was hard to recognize, was in fact ruined, or so I thought.

A few wines that Merlot and oak hurt early, they helped later. The first raw enthusiasms for both have been tempered. As masters of the newer styles begin to pull ahead of the pack, all of the foofaraw about blending and wood aging begins to look like what it should have been all along—a source of subtle points of style—and emphasis is sliding back to the vineyard.

And so it is coming down again to the old rules for picking a winner, the rules that make the old ways look very good indeed, but not the only game in town. I go hunting with the following checklist:

· Look for explicit herbaceous or tealike notes, but be sure they are hard to find behind a screen of fruity flavors. Really fine, really durable Cabernets balance between the two for years, slowly leaning farther toward hints of leaves and stalks, but never quite losing the opposite quality of fruits and flowers.

As a word, *herbaceous* has been in trouble of late. Back in the old days when all of the Cabernet came from the North Coast, both herb and tea worked perfectly to distinguish the variety from Petite Sirah and/or Zinfandel. Then came the outright vegetative Cabernets of the Central Coast, and latter-day critics took *herbaceous* as a curse word to dismiss them, leaving themselves with nothing useful to pinpoint the essence of Cabernet. In the old list of flavor associations from UC-Davis, Cabernet also was called "olivaceous," but that is too oblique for most tasters, so it has never caught on. Herbaceous is, damn it, the correct key. Pungently vegetative is not the same smell at all.

· A new corollary, imposed by aging in new oak barrels, is to make sure a young wine tastes of Cabernet and not wood at the finish. At first impression a new bottling can taste oaky as all get out and still may recover to become a balanced, harmonious bottle, but it has almost no chance of outgrowing its oaky flavors if they are the last ones in a sip.

· Bright ruby color comes next. Don't trust anything that is outright pale; don't trust anything too inky. Above all, guard against a young wine with any hints of amber at the edges. The browner a wine is, the closer it is to the end of its trail no matter what the date on the label, and many of the fiercely oaky reds show brown tones early.

· The corollary of staying away from inky-dark Cabernets is: Stay away from ferociously tannic examples, unless tannin is one's own catnip. Many rookie collectors in the 1970s bought up tannic monsters by the truckload. They still have tannic monsters. They will always have tannic monsters until they put the things into a charity auction to take their places as perennials on the circuit.

The assumption behind inky-dark, tannic monster Cabernets was that tannin is what allows wine to age, and so the more the better. If things were as easy as that, Sophia Loren would be more beautiful if she were seven feet, four inches tall and Schubert's Trio No. 1 would be more sublime as an octet, and so on.

Well-made, properly balanced, harmoniously styled California Cabernets drink well as soon as they come on the market, then again while they are between eight and fifteen years old. For the first year in bottle the wine has enough fruit to charm its drinker and enough baby fat to hide the hard edges. Then it goes into a funk for a while. The first hints of bottle bouquet signal the end of the funk, after which the wine launches into a long, almost level aging curve that can last until the wine is twenty, thirty, fifty, whatever. However, the very best part of the curve is that stretch from eight to fifteen, while something of youthful vigor remains to give an extra dimension.

It takes a case or more to see what benefits age confers. A couple of bottles reveal the youthful charms. Two or three more at stately intervals show that the funk has come and gone. Most of the rest go in quicker succession to catch the peak. However, if the last two or three bottles get into an unreachable corner, the owner will have a chance at one of the few satisfying consolations for diminishing range on the backhand side, thinning hair, and all the allied indignities.

Because Cabernet has a tendency to be tannic, it is the classic red-wine drinker's wine. Its herbaceous side does nothing to mitigate the reputation. For all of that, the variety matches up with most of the national diet. Some of the smaller scaled ones do very well indeed with roasted chicken, especially if the bird has been seasoned with rosemary, tarragon, or one of the other pungent herbs. Juicy steaks make readier companions, especially with the bigger styles of the wine. Mature Cabernet is the right stuff with sweetbreads, whether they are in Madeira sauce or *printanière*. Lamb is a classic pairing—bring on the rosemary but forget the mint. The pinnacle for us, though, is duck, especially duckling with figs. When we really want to show off a bottle, that is our first thought.

And so, on to individual wines and the vineyards from which they come. The chapters in this book lean heavily on geography for their internal logic, but only up to a point. Wine is not all logic. For Cabernet and all the wines that follow, the first region listed is my favorite. The rest follow along in descending order. Within each region, the AVAs (or, sometimes, counties) follow the same pattern. The sequence varies with each variety. North Coast is the whole of it for Cabernet, and Napa much the most.

NORTH COAST

It was something of a shock to old eyes to see that the North Coast's thirteen thousand acres amounted to only 62 percent of the state's total 1986 plantings of Cabernet Sauvignon. Back when the Big Four—Beaulieu, Inglenook, Charles Krug, and Louis M. Martini—were forming my taste for wine, the region's meager acreage amounted to very nearly all there was. One thing has not changed. Every vineyard I treasure is in one of the four counties: Napa, Mendocino, Sonoma, or Lake.

Growing conditions are far from homogenous, and so are the wines, but the basic requirement—that Cabernet veil its herbaceous side in fruit—comes from almost every corner of all of these counties. The living proof of it has been the regular bottling of Louis M. Martini Cabernet Sauvignon, which brings together grapes from a minimum of two, sometimes three, of them, in the process legitimizing the sometimes-disparaged notion of "North Coast" as a statement of origin.

LOUIS M. MARTINI

Way back when we were just beginning to buy more bottles of wine than we could drink within the week, I came across a magazine piece that said Louis M. Martini Cabernet Sauvignons were good, but always silver medalists at the old state fair, never gold.

All of these years later we find many of our long-term favorites among the silver medalists, few among the gold. The golds, too often, are too showy. Wines have to be a bit like the courses they accompany at dinner. Hors d'oeuvres can be outlandish. So can first courses, and certainly desserts. But the entrée has to be something you can stay with long enough to fill up. Silver medal kinds of wines seem to be the ones that can keep pace with entrées.

On such grounds we have downed more Martini than any other Cabernet, and by far. We got started because of student economics. We have kept the preference because the wines taste so good. With beef, lamb, pork, chicken, cheese, and pasta they taste good. Young, old, and in between they taste good. Old, they regularly outduel the gold medalists of yore in head-to-head confrontations over dinner, causing most of this whole list to be made in their image.

One other thing they do. They epitomize assembled wine, wine drawn from several vineyards. Assembled wines have a bad name in Europe because all of the outstanding properties are reserved for estate bottlings and only the ragtag stuff gets assembled, except in Champagne, where assembling is a cardinal virtue.

The European shadow keeps assembling from being a cardinal virtue in California nowadays. Social ramble notwithstanding, a long half of the state's most-praised Cabernets are assembled wines. They excel for the simple fact that quite a few of them are assembled from properties of the first rank, Martini Cabernets being Exhibit A. Two of the legendary red-wine properties of pre-Prohibition California winemaking were the Goldstein Vineyard, toward the top of Sonoma Mountain, and the Stanly Ranch, right at the heart of Los Carneros. The Goldstein property, now called Monte Rosso, turns out deep, dark, ripe Cabernet; Stanly Ranch, now La Loma, yields lean, tart, aromatic Cabernet. Together the two are the heart and soul of all Martini

Cabernets, sometimes the entirety of Special Selections (S.S.), though almost never the whole corpus of regular bottlings.

California collectors have had to be agile to keep up with everything Martini Cabernets are. The regular bottlings are anchored in Monte Rosso and La Loma, but supplemented by grapes from other sources—Alexander Valley, Chiles Valley, and Napa Valley most commonly. For a brief while the regulars even had a proportion of grapes from the Central Coast, but that day ended in the early 1970s. Private Reserves have been only the regular bottling held for extra aging in bottle at the winery. Special Selections have been the ones that wanted careful scrutiny. In most years they have been outstanding lots held out of the regular blend, but it also has been a Martini habit to share the results of research with loyal customers under the S.S. rubric. Twice, in 1958 and 1968, there were five separate S.S. bottlings. The 1958s tested various wood-aging ideas, the 1968s different appellations within the master blend. Lately, Private Reserve has disappeared, and Special Selection has been joined by individual vineyard wines from Monte Rosso and, more rarely, La Loma.

Through all of the variations, the striking fact is how consistent are the wines. Some Special Selection lots have stood out as bigger, tougher wines than the regulars. A few of the intentionally instructional bottlings have stood apart. But in the main, vintage after vintage, the Martinis deliver balanced, graceful wines with understated but persistent echoes of Cabernet grapes the way they taste picked fresh from a vine.

The tasting notes for Martini are going to take off from 1951. Some apologies are in order because of that. I hate writers who go on and on about how they had an enchanting 1893 at Adolphe's (three Michelin stars, naturally), and how Adolphe had whipped his kitchen to produce just the terrine to complement the fading but still memorable charms of the wine. One fills in the details to satisfy envy—how Adolphe had also peopled the rest of the table with film stars and dukes—or cynicism, how Adolphe had footed the bill. In any case, the implication is that the hapless reader will never enjoy the privilege, and *nyah, nyah, nyah*. And here I am touting the 1951s and 1952s, unseen in commerce for, lo, these thirty years? Absolutely. Prohibition having interrupted our studies, we are, all of us, still trying to get a handle on when to drink California Cabernets to our maximum profit. The long records of Martini (and Beaulieu as an estate counterpart) are the best evidence I can offer.

Year after year the Martinis say that balance and harmony matter much more than size. Their Cabernets please early for their gentle fruit flavors and polished textures, then please later for astonishingly durable flavors of Cabernet hedged about with a dusty flavor we have always ascribed to old oak cooperage, and a mysterious, intriguing hint of tar that dwindles away as the level lowers in the bottle.

1951 Not quite the equal of 1952, but so close it has always taken diligent attention to choose between them. Still a bridesmaid in 1987.

1952 Rich early. Perfect example of silken maturity by 1962, but still vital and tasting clearly of fruit today. Perhaps the single greatest California Cabernet of the 1950s, to judge by how it tastes in 1987.

1953 No recollection.

1954 Good, solid performer in its time. Long gone from our cellar.

1955 Lean, firm, more powerfully varietal in its salad days than most Martinis. The regular went a shade weary in the 1970s; the third- and second-to-last bottles of S.S. in our cellar showed youthful color and firm Cabernet aromas in 1985 and 1986.

1956 Always ran in the pack.

1957 Either this was an overlooked vintage or they all are good. The wine was understated, even blurred early, but the regular drank almost as well as the 1955 S.S. in 1986.

1958 Exactly the measure of its vintage: all light and agreeable charm early, then surprisingly durable, but not as full of stuffings as several other years of the decade. It flattened its old rivals in a blind tasting in 1981, but all were easing onto the downslope.

1959 Good solid vintage. Showed some slightly overripe flavors, but otherwise in good form as late as 1984.

1960 No recollection.

1961 Early, concentrated varietal flavors marked a wine from a year in which spring frosts cut the crop to a quarter of normal. A bottle opened in 1987 was all bouquet—engaging, but more an ancient Tuscan red than a Cabernet.

1962 In the pack; from a vintage of early, prolonged rains.

1963 Lightly regarded early, the vintage nonetheless aged fairly well. Still drank agreeably in 1984.

1964 Early, a powerful vintage much along the lines of 1955. It still could give pleasure as a fully mature wine in 1983, but seemed nearer the end of the line than the 1955.

1965 Good sound vintage that lasted nicely into 1985, though it was older then than a Charles Krug Select from the same year.

1966 We were dubious about this vintage early and bought little. A last bottle in December 1983 says we were wrong. Still young in color and lively in flavor then.

1967 A bit pallid early, it has shown the virtues of balance ever since. Drinking as a fairly young wine in 1986.

1968 Early and late, an exact echo of 1958. Fully mature by the early 1980s, but hanging in there in 1986.

1969 No note.

1970 Regular bottling uncommonly herbaceous for a Martini, and also uncommonly soft. Much touted early, it has been agreeable, but a bit of a plodder. The S.S., meanwhile, was living up to the reputation of the vintage as of 1986.

1971 No note.

1972 From a rain-plagued year, a balanced, stylish wine in its youth, and a better-than-average one at ten. Darker and firmer than almost any other wine from the vintage.

1973 Attractive, complete wine from its first days; now showing its heels to many a tannic monster from the year.

1974 Atypically slow to get going, the wine was still a bit hard in early 1979, but had become all silk and polish by 1985; it is still in top form in 1987.

1975 Lean, tart, reserved for a Martini. Still evolving.

1976 Among its own, a drought-concentrated wine seemed hard and unbalanced; against others, it shone and shines. The S.S. goes the regular one better.

1977 Regular bottling a typical underplayed but durable Martini; S.S. very hard and pungently herbaceous as of 1984.

1978 One of the most harmonious, deft wines of recent vintages early, and still gaining in 1985.

1979 More pungently herbaceous than the 1978, and a bit leaner or firmer, but still readily appealing as early as 1984. Shows signs of being an ager.

1980 Regular bottling typically polished and appealing early, but not so full of stuffings as some of the longest agers have been. Vintage also saw the introduction of vineyard-designated Monte Rosso (rich, ripe, utterly Californian, though the first Martini to show recognizable touches of oak) and La Loma (lean, tart, intensely scented of Cabernet) at their introduction in 1984.

1981 Regular bottling immediately pleasing. The La Loma promises the earth.

1982 The vintage gave delicacy every advantage, and the Martini regular appears to have taken them all. A Monte Rosso wine had definite bouquets of oak early, but the stuffings say it will come around.

1983 Spot-on Martini in the regular bottling; perhaps the sturdiest of the last several vintages.

1984 Enigmatic early, when it seemed very forward.

Napa Valley AVA

In the 1950s Napa truly was an easy place. Napa Valley Cabernet Sauvignon meant Rutherford Cabernet Sauvignon, and Rutherford meant Beaulieu Vineyard Georges de Latour and Inglenook Cask. Anything else measured itself by their rule.

The vineyards that produced these two wines sat (still sit) side-by-side on the Rutherford Bench, tipped ever so slightly to the morning sun, shaded early in the afternoon by the bulk of Mount St. John and moistened by its dwindling supply of ground water right up until the eve of harvest. Seasoned tasters looked for the distinctive note they call Rutherford dust, calibrated its presence or absence on their palates, and identified which wine they were drinking from a very short list of possibilities. The real keepers of the flame numbered just four, Charles Krug and Louis M. Martini being the other two.

It was not just Rutherford that kept life easy for a learner. Real Cabernet meant pure, unblended Cabernet. Wood was not a confusing complication, or at least not a recognized factor. Wines that were going to age particularly well gave off all the signs early, a vexation only because they tasted so good in the freshness of their youth it was hard to wait.

In truth, the simple truth was not as simple as all that. Some of the Inglenooks came from John Daniel's other vineyard, Napanook, clear down at Yountville. A distinctive factor in Beaulieu's personality came from American oak barrels. With these chances to go wrong, in blind tastings I was able to pick Napanook wines as quintessential expressions of Rutherford dust, and fuddle the American oak-tinged Beaulieus with non-Rutherford Louis M. Martinis that never saw a barrel. But compared to the mistakes I can make now?

Napa acreage planted to the variety has gone from two hundred to sixty-two hundred acres scattered all the way from Carneros to Calistoga. Not just Merlot, but also Cabernet Franc and Petit Verdot have crept into blends. The choice of wood has become a subject unto itself. While that and all kinds of other hell have broken loose, Rutherford has remained a solid anchor point, the place to begin understanding not just Napa, but all California Cabernet Sauvignon, because the track record stretches back to 1934 and because some of Napa's senior statesmen have been on the track most or all of that time, helping post an uncommonly consistent record with grapes that do what they ought: yield durably fascinating wines.

Nobody has ever drawn an official boundary of the Rutherford Bench. The winemakers who use it have differing notions, mostly having to do with the easterly limits. The hard physical facts of Mount St. John and its lesser neighbors draw a sharp line on the west. There is a sturdy consensus in favor of Zinfandel Lane as the northerly limit. John Daniel's old Napanook vineyard near Yountville has pretty much been accepted as the southerly extreme. But the east side knows no such boundary. André Tchelistcheff always favored the St. Helena Highway. Louis P. Martini has a wavering line that keeps a certain distance from the Napa River. A lot of growers draw a line that puts their place inside the limits and wanders after that.

Now that AVAs exist, the idea of a legal definition has gathered steam. The mood in 1987 is to draw the lines around two related, well-drained soils series called Bale Loam and Pleasanton Loam. If that idea prevails, the bench will stretch from Yountville to Zinfandel Lane, and will reach east across the Napa River in a few places and stop well short of it in a few others. By a handy margin it will take in all of the vineyards that have made the name what it is.

The vineyards that now define the bench for people who wish to taste Rutherford dust go into Beaulieu Vineyard Georges de Latour, Inglenook Vineyards Cask Reserve, Heitz Cellars Martha's Vineyard, Robert Mondavi Winery Reserve, and Freemark Abbey Winery Cabernet Bosché. These parcels all go back fifteen years and more, long enough to show their colors in all weathers, long enough for their wines to tell all they know. The cast is listed in order of its first appearance.

BEAULIEU VINEYARD GEORGES DE LATOUR

When Russian-born, French-trained André Tchelistcheff arrived in the valley in 1937, he had a fresh canvas on which to work. Cabernet Sauvignon hardly existed, and a style for it did not. What he designed during his first few years was and remains a Napa original.

His starting point was fully ripened grapes. The last step was three years, sometimes more, in American oak barrels. What he got out of those major steps and some subtler ones was a silky wine full of sunny flavors as well as the seamlessly joined tastes of Cabernet and oak. Sometimes the singular personality was easy to spot in a crowd, occasionally for the ripe grape taste, more often for the fugitive note of varnish that American oak can contribute. When people identified a BV blind, they would say, "Sure bet." When they missed, they could not imagine how.

It was no easy balancing act. A good many other people have imitated it with less success, but Tchelistcheff could dance on the head of a pin. Nearly every one of his De Latours has stayed welcome on the dinner table for twenty years and up. I have managed to get my nose into glasses of the 1941 and 1945 during the 1980s and come away glad not for the abstract experience but for the pleasure of the drink. The 1951 and 1952 still have some spring left in them, the 1954 a lot. This durability is doubly intriguing because the wines seemed so complete young. They did not seem, they were complete, the least changeable Cabernets over ten or twenty years of any I know, save a couple made along the same lines.

Tchelistcheff stayed at his old last through the vintage of 1971, leaving shortly after it to teach a new generation as a consulting winemaker. At this point I cannot know whether the De Latours dipped during the mid-1970s, or I got too preoccupied with noticing their characteristic overtone of American oak, or they grew too familiar in a time when the revolution forced my attention elsewhere. I think they dipped. According to my tasting notes, they grew older faster; they did not have the old depth of color early or late; the flavors seemed less distinctive; finally, the wines felt less lively on the tongue.

However my self-debate finally turns out, the first few vintages from the 1980s have all of the old form. The colors are young and deep, the flavors of Cabernet far in front of any perfumes from oak barrels. The silky textures never left.

Tchelistcheff's successors at Beaulieu never did tinker with his design, or the source. In the early days nearly all of the grapes came from the vineyard sometimes called De Pins, sometimes BV No. 1. It sits straight across the state highway from the winery, sandwiched between Inglenook on one side and the Bosché vineyard on the other. (Bosché grapes used to fill an occasional corner in a De Latour.) For more than twenty years a second vineyard, the sixty-six-acre BV No. 2, has been an added source (and will be the main source through the late 1980s while BV No. 1 is replanted). BV No. 2 adjoins Robert Mondavi's winery property on its north side, in the same soil and at the same orientation as its illustrious older brother.

Because the history is so constant, the tasting notes begin in 1958 as an index to what performance can be expected from a single source—or virtually that.

1958 Intense Cabernet character accompanied the traditional flavor of American oak early, late, and in between. Still specific of its variety in 1987, but never all of the depth or complexity of flavor of some other vintages.

1959 No recollection.

1960 Not quite the equal of the 1958, but close; like the 1958, still full of Cabernet aromas in age, so said our last bottle in 1985.

1961 Dense wine, like many from a frost-reduced vintage. No recent notes.

1962 Steady wine in the vein of 1960.

1963 No recollection.

1964 The entire vintage was released as De Latour. A wine of huge dimensions and powerful flavors early, it dwindled somewhat with age, and was only modestly appealing in 1979 and again in late 1983.

1965 Subtle and charming rather than full of power in youth. No recent bottles to test its maturity.

1966 A burly vintage that aged much as the 1964.

1967 Many of the same appealing qualities of the 1965 early.

1968 A shade fuller and riper than the run of 1968s, the wine was appealing early, dipped a bit, then got an impressive second wind that took it as far as 1983. Bottles in 1985 and 1986 seemed wearier.

1969 Early, well-above-average vintage, with a bit more stuffings than the 1968. No recent bottles.

1970 Classical De Latour, perhaps the finest of the two decades leading up to it. To date, all polish and harmony at least once a year throughout the 1980s.

1971 Smaller than typical in the early going. No recent bottles.

1972 Always a shade paler than the run of De Latours, and a bit overripe to taste.

1973 Powerfully aromatic early, reflecting its vintage. Never seemed to have the depths of the 1970 or 1968, but still in the upper tier.

1974 Did not quite come up to its vintage early. By 1982 a bit tawny, with bouqueted flavors to match.

1975 Much along the lines of 1965 early in its career.

1976 Typically concentrated wine of a drought vintage.

1977 Fragile, along the lines of 1972.

1978 Soft, easy, perhaps a bit simple. Fully mature by 1987.

1979 Lean and hard, in the vein of the vintage. Well marked by oak, but even more so by Cabernet. Drinking very well in 1987.

1980 Deep color for the first time in several vintages, but the flavors fall a bit short. In the pack.

91

1981 Probably a near-termer, but, in 1987, still crisp and lively on the tongue, and layered with flavors.

1982 Dark-hued, full of Cabernet flavors, less full of oak. Has the spine to last as long as the flavors do.

1983 Follows the style laid down in 1982. Appears firmer, structured for even longer aging.

One side note: The regular Beaulieu Cabernet Sauvignon, now subtitled Rutherford, is a delicious, reliable, altogether price-worthy ten-year wine made on a slightly smaller scale than the De Latours.

INGLENOOK VINEYARDS RESERVE CASK

Inglenook has been far the most changeable of the original Big Four. Several changes of ownership led to wholesale changes in vineyard sources, winemaking technique, market strategy—all of the variables.

The Inglenook of owner John Daniel and winemaker George Deuer was a purist's delight. Both men were in winemaking for the long haul. They made wine with no compromise toward time, human frailty, or their own pocketbooks. Much of what they did was admirable, if not always lovable—mixtures of pleasure and penance. When Hugh Johnson and I were tasting our way toward the forerunner to this book in 1973 and 1974, we elected the winery the official purveyor to Sword Swallowers International. We had no idea that it was only a mild precursor of the dark, tannic wines of later times. Still, the 1949 would be a salutary lesson for a lot of the vintners who tell their patrons not to drink their wine until twenty years later. It was advertised that way for twenty years. The last time I saw a bottle of it, in 1971, all was crumbling except the tannin.

All of the grapes for old-style Inglenook cask wines came from Daniel's own vineyards, two at the winery plus Napanook at Yountville. Deuer fermented in open-topped redwood, and aged the wine in ancient oak ovals from Germany's Spessart forests.

By the time real inky monsters came along, Inglenook was a

mild-mannered, thoroughly commercial kind of Cabernet, which it remained through most of the 1970s. Now the Reserve Cask wine is regaining some of Inglenook's old eminence, this time in a style leaning more toward understatement than main strength.

Daniel sold to grower-owned United Vintners in 1964. The Inglenook of these proprietors veered fairly sharply toward purely commercial avenues between 1965 and 1975. By the time the real inky monsters came along, not many Inglenook Cabernets could compete with the merely modest. Heublein, Inc., bought that Inglenook, and, after a period of reflection, turned it back in directions Daniel could have understood.

The Cask Cabernet of 1977 first served notice that Heublein was turning Inglenook back toward the earlier paths. However, the winery has not gone back to square one with either vineyards or style.

Throughout John Daniel's long reign, recall, the difference between Inglenook and Inglenook Cask was merely selection. The wines all came from the same vineyards, and were made the same way. Daniel just enjoyed picking one or two of his old German oak ovals as having slightly superior wine and bottling it that way. After he sold the winery in 1964, the designation lost definition as the new owners brought in grapes from all over the valley. With John Richburg as winemaker, Inglenook's regular bottlings come from a broad spectrum of vineyards while the Cask Reserves represent two or three selected properties on the Rutherford Bench or within hailing distance of it, depending on who sets the boundaries. His wines do not carry cask numbers as the old-timers did—the casks are gone in favor of barrels, and the government has said, "No casks, no numbers"—but the aim is as high.

Richburg's style puts more flesh on Cabernet's bones than George Deuer's did—or else starts with smaller, less knobbled bones. A hint of new oak flickers in and around definitive aromas of Napa Cabernet. In short, the wines have come to be silver medalists in the same sense as the finest Martinis.

The run of tasting notes here goes from 1958 through 1964, then picks up again with the 1977.

1958 Spectacular early—lean, tannic, packed with the flavors of Cabernet. By 1980 it had become a bit too tannic and heady for what remained of the fruit.

1959 More approachable than the 1958 all along, and ultimately more pleasing to drink.

1960 Close kin to the 1958 early, and more agreeably balanced later. As late as autumn 1986 it had enough Cabernet and other flavors to do battle with both smoked duck and spicy lamb chops at Mustard's Grill, an eater's mecca in Yountville.

1961 Always a shade too lean and hard after frost cut the crop to a quarter of normal size.

1962 Outstanding in youth and has yet to flag. Delicious flavors combined with unaccustomed succulence to do the trick. In autumn 1986 the wine had more layers of flavor than an onion has skin. For our taste, *the* Inglenook of the decade, perhaps of the whole series since 1955.

1963 Not quite the 1962, but close.

1964 Split the difference between 1958 and 1962 in the early going. No bottles recently.

1977 The regular was regular, but the cask bottling signaled a return to the top ranks. Balanced, subtle, and full of fruit early; still at peak form in 1986.

1978 From a vintage that dealt in charm rather than power, and an accurate reflection of it. In my book, competed at the top in a 1983 blind tasting of big names.

1979 Like most of the vintage, a lean, hard, austere wine for texture, and a fascinating one for the depths of flavor. Still growing in the bottle.

1980 Has yet to blossom. In 1987 one of the lesser vintages of the decade.

1981 On release, distinct Cabernet flavors in a wine of light, polished, but decidedly firm textures. Began to show bouquet in 1987, but still young, and long of fruit then.

1982 Enigmatic early. By 1987 decidedly older wine than its running mate from 1981. In the pack at best.

1983 Excellent varietal flavors and a supple but solid structure suggest a long career. Handily the wine of the decade to date.

HEITZ CELLARS MARTHA'S VINEYARD

André Tchelistcheff taught a large number of young winemakers their trade during his long tenure at Beaulieu, none of them more adept at the lessons than Joe Heitz. While Heitz is no clone of his mentor and Martha's Vineyard is no carbon copy of the De Pins patch, the underlying similarities between a Martha's Vineyard and a De Latour are not figments of the imagination either.

Martha's Vineyard belongs to independent growers Tom and Martha May. Their property sits at the heart of the Rutherford Bench, hard against the west hills about two miles south of BV No. 1 and, like it, tipped just slightly toward the morning light, so Heitz did not have to think many new thoughts about grapes after his tenure at BV.

Heitz's predilection for long aging in wood makes his Cabernets similar in weight and texture to old Beaulieu De Latours. However, differences weigh as much or more than similarities. Rather than relying entirely on American barrels, Heitz uses an ever-shifting, seemingly intuitive mix of new and used French and American woods to arrive at an overtone, a bouquet, a whatever you want to call it, that is definitely not from Cabernet Sauvignon, but not definitely the taste of oak. The shorthand for it is *spice box*. Heitz himself says that wood should be like the seasonings in a sauce, apparent but never identifiable. The results bear him and the shorthand out.

Heitz wines resemble Tchelistcheff wines in another way, and that is they are very nearly complete as soon as they are released. For all their size, the wines are not only ready to drink but richly laden with bouquets and polished smooth. Four or five years in bottle bring a few more grace notes, but the changes are harder to notice than the ones that come to wines harvested less ripe and aged less long in barrel.

In the end Heitz Cabernet Sauvignons are very particular wines, ones that are almost impossible to miss in blind tastings no mat-

95

ter how hard one tries not to think of who, what, where, when, and why. They are pungently scented of spice box, well perfumed by Cabernet Sauvignon, recognizably marked with something reminiscent of eucalyptus (or mint), further complicated by their mixed bouquet of oak, and lightly touched by a few other, less identifiable characteristics. And that is only what one gets by smelling the glass.

Even if the prices were less, Martha's Vineyards would not be bottles to haul out on a whim. Wines of such dimension obliterate foods with a deal more flavor than chicken or veal. There are times, in fact, when food seems like a heckler from the boxes. The proprietor loves to serve them with plain roast of beef, and it is almost impossible to argue. The beef goes by, the wine commands attention, and nobody complains. At the other pole, its spicy side recommends it with spicy beef dishes. A Greek stew called *stifado* sings the harmony part with a Martha's Vineyard. So do *chimichangas* and a lot of other Mexican shredded beef dishes not cloaked in *salsa verde*. Marinated rack of lamb has been another welcome companion.

Beginning with 1976 Heitz added a second vineyard-identified wine to his roster. The Bella Oaks Vineyard of Dr. Bernard and Belle Rhodes sits just about halfway between BV No. 1 and Martha's. Intriguingly, it has less spice box and more Rutherford dust than the Martha's, though the two are made identically. Heitz also makes a wine straightforwardly identified as Napa Valley; it has all of the family traits but not the stuffings of its superiors, which sometimes makes it the more versatile of the three at table. The notes apply to the Martha's in particular, but can be extended to the others unless otherwise noted.

1965 Not labeled with the vineyard name, but dominated by the first crop from it. A foretaste, but never quite the equal of later vintages, and well past its best days by 1980.

1966 Sturdy but comparatively plain early; quick to reveal a warm growing season later.

1967 A cool year running counter to the proprietor's best hopes. The wine fell short early, but has aged particularly well among the early vintages, small by Heitz standards, but quite agreeable.

1968 Another cool season, but Heitz managed to get ripe fruit out of Martha's, and made the first of a series of huge wines exactly to his liking. It held very well into the 1980s, but has crumbled slightly since 1982 or 1983.

1969 Not so dramatic early as the 1968, but rigged better for the long haul. Still a vital, richly perfumed wine in mid-1987, when it was drinking better than any other of the first eight vintages.

1970 Has fallen between the 1968 and 1969 from day one, and holds that position in 1987.

1971 Difficult, rainy vintage. No Martha's Vineyard.

1972 In the pack early. Perhaps an echo of the 1967 as it develops.

1973 Overshadowed early by the 1974, it has lived on as one of the finest evocations of Heitz's style, much as the 1969 has endured to outshine the 1968.

1974 The epitome of what Heitz strives for early, and still cruising as a huge, ripe, complicated mouthful in 1987. The whole Martha's Vineyard crop was bottled as such.

1975 Smaller and slower to develop than typical.

1976 Big and forward on release, having been concentrated by drought. Not holding as well as most.

1977 Always in the pack.

1978 Strikingly delicate among the Martha's at release, and has remained ever thus. Quite mature in 1987.

1979 Spot-on Martha's Vineyard in style and substance. Early firmness helps put it among the most attractive of recent vintages for aging. No Bella Oaks from the vintage.

1980 The same firmness as its immediate predecessor, and richer Cabernet aromas.

1981 Appears to have not quite the stuffings of 1979 or 1980, but still a wine of considerable proportions. The Bella Oaks is running well off the pace of the Martha's.

1982 Early the Martha's showed some of the delicacy and refinement of the 1978.

1983 At its debut, showed some of the restraint that marked 1973 and 1969.

Freemark Abbey Winery Cabernet Bosché and Napa Valley

Vineyards matter beyond doubt, but nature sometimes gets the credit or blame for man's doing. California has not been around long enough to see many examples, but when John Bosché stopped sending his grapes to Beaulieu and started sending them to Freemark Abbey, the change turned more upside down than it left alone.

While Bosché sold his grapes to Beaulieu, they went most often into the regular bottling, but, in short years, into the De Latour. For Beaulieu, adding them to the De Latour meant only jumping across a tractor row, Bosché flanking BV No. 1 on its north boundary, 30 acres nestled against 130.

Whichever wine the Bosché grapes joined, they fell into line without a murmur, tasting exactly like Beaulieu. In 1972 Bosché began selling to Freemark Abbey, and, in a trice, the old leopard had new spots. Under the direction of Brad Webb, every aspect of the winemaking reversed field. Gone the lush textures and plummy flavors of a Beaulieu. In their place a firm, lean feel and flavors much more in the herbaceous direction of less-ripe Cabernet. Gone the now-varnishy, now-bourbonlike tastes of American oak in favor of the more vanillinlike smack of French wood. Gone the softness from three years in barrel in favor of the fresher but rougher feel from two years or less in wood.

The result is one of the few Cabernets that fight the typical Napa aging curve, a wine that gives little pleasure to drink early, but compensates more than enough later. Once time does turn a Freemark Abbey Cabernet Bosché silky and perfumey, the wine offers new flavors born out of the marriage of Cabernet and oak, scents that keep people thinking ever-shifting thoughts until the wine is gone. I am not crazy enough to try to explain them, or crazy enough to pass a chance to hunt through them again.

The long discussion of Freemark's Bosché does not mean to sell short the Napa Valley edition, which is made in much the same way from grapes grown in three Rutherford-area vineyards belonging to partners in the winery. It has as many fruit flavors or more, and not quite so definite a bouquet of oak. In many vintages it blossoms earlier, then lasts as long as its more pedigreed running mate. In all truth, I would just as soon have one as the other. In most vintages I have a hard time telling them apart.

As mature wines, either will keep company with the whole familiar roster of dishes, but lamb seasoned with rosemary is the one that lets both show off everything they have.

The tasting notes bear particularly on the Bosché. As a generality, the Napa Valley bottling is almost identical in good years and a bit more successful in the off vintages.

1970 Rousing introduction. Still full of Cabernet flavors and still youthful in 1986. One of the finest of the series.

1971 Always a little weak, but still pleasant and harmonious in spring 1986.

1972 Meager among its siblings. Quite weary by 1984.

1973 The wine of the series thus far. Polished, refined, subtle early and late. The clear winner of a retrospective of them all.

1974 Rather hard and austere, even among wines meant to be just that. The color in 1985 said it has plenty of time to tame itself.

1975 Fruit flavors never have caught up with the woody ones. In the lower rank.

1976 Typical drought-concentrated, somewhat unbalanced wine.

1977 Small and supple, as the vintage tended to be. Drinking in peak form at ten years.

1978 All delicacy and subtlety early. With age, it has gained layers and layers of flavor. The challenger to 1973 among all the wines of the decade.

1979 Typical of its vintage, a firm, intensely flavorful wine just beginning to round into form in 1987. Promises long life.

1980 Promising, but at the depths of its sophomore slump early in 1986.

1981 Strikingly forward vintage. Always supple and understated. Probably a near-termer among the Boschés.

1982 Very well balanced and full of Cabernet flavors early. Ahead of the 1980 in development, but still miles from the end of its road to judge by an enticing bottle in mid-1987.

1983 Spot-on Freemark Abbey—understated fruit, elusive bouquets from the winemaking, and the beginnings of supple textures.

ROBERT MONDAVI WINERY RESERVE

Ask any Napa winemaker which is the most experimental winery in the Napa Valley and the answer will be Robert Mondavi.

Taste a sequence of vintages of the Reserve Cabernets, and there is no need to ask.

Robert Mondavi Reserve Cabernets have become, slowly, the French-oaked equivalents of BV's American-oaked De Latours: big, lush, full-bodied wines unmistakably marked by the barrels in which they aged and unmistakably from fully ripened fruit. This after they started out (under the identity of Unfined or Unfiltered) as the purest possible expressions of Cabernet's grape flavors in 1966, and gravitated to a lean, tannically firm, oak-tinged style by 1970. The current trend set in with the 1978.

For my personal taste, the pinnacle was the period from 1970 through 1977. Sometimes accurate echoes of that style still show in the regular bottling, which is welcome not only to my palate but also to my pocketbook.

Whether weather gets the credit or one of the Mondavis does, the leaner, firmer wines are the ones that have repaid long keeping, especially when put out against lamb or duck, or any other meat that wants a firm, cleansing wine to keep it on the rails. The fat wines have had their best days earlier, and against juicy beef.

These tasting notes begin with the first Reserve, 1970. Counterpart wines from 1966 through 1969 (labeled Unfined or Unfiltered) have aged in good health but without anything like the complexity of vintages that followed the coining of a specific reserve style: an amplified oak-aging program, a narrowing of grape source to the winery's own Tokalon Vineyard (particularly the blocks adjoining Martha's Vineyard), and fuller ripeness than the regular bottling.

1970 One of the best of an excellent vintage, and one of the greatest of the Mondavis. Lean early and lean late, but always with whole galaxies of aroma and bouquet. A stunningly delicious wine in 1984, whether on the judge's table or the dinner table.

1971 Typical of a difficult vintage, it was pallid in the series.

1972 After hot 1971 delivered a frail wine, wet 1972 produced another of the same.

1973 Close challenger to the 1970. From its earliest days supple without being soft, and full of a deft interplay of flavors from Cabernet and aging in oak. Gained steadily at least through 1980, and may be gaining still.

1974 Fatter than the 1973 and a little more definitively marked by its time in oak, but still one of the finest wines from its decade. Still developing in 1985.

1975 Exact opposite of 1974: light, delicate in textures and flavors alike, but so well balanced that it still has all the earmarks of youth in 1987. All pleasure to drink.

1976 Rather more deft than most wines from the drought, but still blocky by the winery's standards.

1977 Typical of the vintage, a small wine of dim flavors in the early going. Always in the pack.

1978 Big, ripe, and strongly marked by its time in oak. A questionable ager as early as 1983; a fading, noticeably raisiny wine by 1985.

1979 Typical of its vintage, intensely aromatic of Cabernet and a bit hard. Just coming out of its adolescent funk in 1985. A wait-and-see wine.

1980 Early, showed considerable kinship to the 1973. Quick to develop—an unmitigated pleasure to drink in 1985 and since. Poised to be one of the finest.

1981 Agreeable, but without the stuffings to be an obvious great ager.

1982 Early, was well balanced for feel but seemed to want a bit more fruit or a bit less oak. Remember that it was a Mondavi that taught how much oak could disappear with time in bottle.

1983 Just after bottling, very fleshy and forcibly marked by the flavors of aging in new French wood.

If soil becomes the definition of Rutherford Bench, Caymus and Raymond will be part of it. If old, empirical habits prevail, Caymus will be outside the zone to the east, and Raymond will be just inside or just outside the northeastern corner.

CAYMUS VINEYARDS

Some wines get your attention right now and will not let go. Cabernets that do that are hardly ever the ones to put up against chicken or veal. They are the ones that must have the more pointed and fatter textures of duck or lamb or juicy steak as foils.

Caymus Cabernet Sauvignon is one of them. If the definitive

note of Cabernet is herbs or tea, this is the textbook example, but the wine is also packed full of berrylike flavors or, maybe, the often-cited cassis (nobody can drink everything; cassis is not on my list; here is a clear case of why describing flavors gets a body into a deal of difficulty and out of none). Sometimes it takes real concentration to find the herbs behind all of the berrylike perfumes.

Whatever the precise recipe for grape flavors, the sum of them is intense enough that father-and-son owners Charley and Chuck Wagner give the regular bottling three years in mostly new oak, the Reserve even longer, all in the name of keeping the grape aromas from shouting too loudly. My own preference is for the regular estate bottling, the Reserve being too dark, too tannic, and too woody for my taste, but several skillful judges tell me this is just a sign of *my* general decline.

Reserve or regular, oaky or not so oaky, all of these wines are polished and supple even in youth. The long sleep in wood takes the rough edges away before they go to bottle.

Caymus Cabernets are not yet through being different in my mind. One of their other characteristics is a deeper, longer funk than almost any other Napan. Through their first year in bottle their powerful fruit aromas and polished textures give them instant appeal. After they are eight or nine, they mix youthful aroma and mature bouquet in enticing, appetizing ways. In between, I'd rather wait. This loopy aging curve is common to most Napa Valley Cabernets of quality, but the swings are not so wide in any of the others we follow closely.

Perhaps the dip owes itself to the intensely herbaceous flavors from Caymus's vineyard, which shares Bale loam with the Rutherford Bench but tips the other way, from a gentle slope on the east side of the Napa River between the end of Rutherford Cross Road and the Silverado Trail. It may be that the tilt toward the setting sun has as much to do with how the grapes behave as the soil. Two similarly inclined neighbors to the north yield similar flavors. So does Beringer's State Lane vineyard, though it is miles south, in the angle formed by the Silverado Trail and Yountville Cross Road.

Not incidentally, the winery added a non-estate Cabernet called Napa Cuvée with the vintage of 1984. The debut was impressive.

The tasting notes, atypically, apply primarily to the regular estate bottling.

1973 Almost overwhelmingly intense in youth, it settled into fine form along about 1978 as a pungently varietal but well-balanced advertisement of what was to come. Drinking very well in 1987, and with years to go.

1974 As its predecessor, impressive for its depth of herbaceous Cabernet flavors and its richness of texture. Hardly a day older late in 1986 than it was early in 1980.

1975 Bigger and riper than most from its vintage, but still small among its siblings.

1976 The usual problems of the drought year.

1977 Far surpassed its vintage, but still in the pack among Caymus Cabernets.

1978 Very near the peak—ripe, full of flavor, and very sturdy, yet somehow balanced at all of its points. In mid-1987 cruising in splendid form.

1979 From the beginning, extra intense in flavor. The longest and gloomiest sophomore slump, and thus the most glorious recovery beginning late in 1986.

1980 Restrained power from the beginning; all finesse and polish. Perhaps the vintage of the series through its first five years and promising for the long haul.

1981 Of all the Caymus Cabernets, the silkiest and subtlest early, and the slowest to dip into adolescence. Seemed polished and complete as early as 1986.

1982 Pleasing, lively, full of fruit in youth.

1983 In youth, more forcefully flavored by oak than its forerunners, and slightly harder or harsher, but still full of the usual promises for the long term.

RAYMOND VINEYARD & CELLAR

Everyone remembers some doughy little kid who disappeared then reappeared years later looking like a Greek statue. Raymond Cabernet Sauvignons are never doughy little kids, but they make me think the thought for changing more along the way to statuehood than many of their peers.

In one vintage after another the young wines manage to muffle the herbaceous side of their varietal character with baby fat, fruit, and the sweet, vanillalike perfumes of new oak. I had, I must confess, settled so deep into a rut of thinking of them in that way that I did not find out about the Greek statue part of their aging curve until late spring 1987, with a bottle of the 1975 chosen specifically to bridge the gap between my wife and me and a couple of friends who think red wine is a leftover from the Inquisition. What we got was a classical Napa Cabernet Sauvignon, somehow grown rich in overtones of tea or herb that played off against fading echoes of oak on one hand and blossoming notes from its time in bottle on the other. With all of that it had just enough tannin to keep a fine dish of duck from weighing too much, not so much as to cause wounded cries from the innocents, who demolished their half of the bottle and a little bit of our share.

In the early going all of the grapes came from Raymond's own vineyard, on the south side of Zinfandel Lane between the state highway and the Napa River, which is either the southernmost limit of St. Helena or the northernmost reach of the Rutherford Bench. The reserve bottling still does come from the home ranch, but the regular one is now supplemented by a minority portion from three small vineyards in the immediate neighborhood.

By style and substance less separates the Raymond regular and reserve bottlings than at most wineries. The Reserve has a scintilla more of everything, but the family resemblance is profound.

1974 The debut Raymond rather falsely promised a sequence of small, supple wines meant for early drinking.
1975 Spot-on Raymond. A wine of fleshy textures and understated Cabernet flavors early, it turned supple, polished, and distinctive for its taste of the grape by the time it was ten.

1976 Like so many from the drought year, a ponderous wine early, and a ponderous wine later.

1977 Well constructed and sturdy from a vintage that yielded few such. Performed very well against 1978s and 1979s in blind tastings in 1986; still had plenty of room to grow.

1978 Light of flavor and texture by the standards of a vintage that leaned that way; markedly gentler than its own kin, except for the 1974.

1979 Always an enigma to me. The usual understated varietal early, but dark and harder in texture than most.

1980 Close to if not the vintage of the series. The quintessential Raymond: understated for herbs, supple, refined, but with plenty of stuffings to last.

1981 A bit soft and out of focus, much along the lines of both the 1974 and 1978.

1982 In the early going the tastes of oak seemed to outweigh the tastes of Cabernet in a wine otherwise supple and easy to drink. By 1987 the Cabernet had gained the upper hand.

1983 Contends with the 1980 for top honors for all the same reasons—supple textures and delicate but indelible flavors.

Rutherford Vintners

Proprietor-winemaker Bernard Skoda spent nearly twenty years working for Louis M. Martini, and it shows in an instant in his Cabernet Sauvignons, although his come from his own vineyard between Rutherford and Oakville while the models are assembled from such varied points as Sonoma Valley, Alexander Valley, Carneros, and the upper Napa Valley.

What Skoda learned from his longtime employer was to pick the fruit and make the wines with balance and harmony in mind. He gives his a little firmer touch of oak, but the rest of the style is familiar to any old Martini hand—to include the rare capacity to drink well on the day they are released, and for who knows how long thereafter. The debut 1974 continues on the top of its form, as do all of its successors.

The Stag's Leap district came to the party late, but made a spectacular entrance when it did. Stag's Leap Wine Cellars brought swift attention to the neighborhood when its 1973 placed first in the oft-cited Paris tasting of 1976. Clos du Val kept the lamp lighted when its 1972 ranked first in a reprise in New York in 1986. In the interim the same Clos du Val placed first in another tasting in France, the Gault-Millau Wine Olympiad.

The achievements are all the more amazing for the fact that Bernard Portet planted Clos du Val in 1972, and Warren Winiarski bought what is now Stag's Leap Vineyard in the same year. Nathan Fay, who planted in the 1950s, and Richard Steltzner, who followed in the 1960s, almost qualify as pioneers. And still, in mid-1987 the two are the reasons for its being on the brink of becoming a subappellation in the Napa Valley.

With the 1982s, Clos du Val and Stag's Leap Wine Cellars started their second decade of Cabernets, shafts of light in a large darkness, sources of what must pass for historical perspective. Because of these two, Cabernet Sauvignon from this little patch, almost enclave, established not only a distinct reputation well before the decade was out, but even began to show a particular character. Wines from here seem to lean just a degree or two farther in the direction of fruit than their more herbaceous peers from the Rutherford-Oakville Bench, and to show their tannic side a shade less. The differences are not on an unmistakable scale, especially after winery styles come into the equation, but are enough to give the practiced a chance to pull off coups in parlor-game blind tastings.

The area is neatly defined, a bench tipped from east to west at the foot of the east hills and stretching from just north of Napa city to just south of Yountville. It is bigger than it looks at first glance because two of the Yountville hills hide a wide band of plantings behind them, almost directly beneath the pinnacle of a tall palisade that gives name to the place.

CLOS DU VAL WINE CO.

From the very beginning Bernard Portet has not sought to define Clos du Val by varietal character, but rather by what he calls completeness. What he wants, he has said over and over, is a wine that starts out feeling to the mouth like rough velvet and ages from there to smooth velvet, then raw silk, and finally polished silk. While it is doing that, the flavors should progress apace from fruit to flowers to perfumes.

Ten years' worth of tasting notes suggest that he is an accurate poet as well as a formidably skillful winemaker. Time after time, in blind tastings as often as at the dinner table, the three-word echo shows up: subtle, polished, finessy. The balance is impeccable good years and bad. "Appealing fruit" is the most frequent note about flavors. Only now and again does "herbaceous" show up as a particular descriptive, usually only after the wine has several years in the bottle, and always in the way of a grace note. Almost inevitably a Clos du Val, young or old, draws some sort of remark about bouquet; almost never is it possible to get specific about oak, let alone what sort. In short, the wines are complete.

Portet brought new thoughts to a new place when he began developing Clos du Val in 1972. The son of a longtime director of winemaking at Château Lafite-Rothschild was drawn to the Napa Valley by its Cabernet Sauvignons. For all of that, he had decided before he made a single bottle that he would do something different, would steer away from the weight and power of traditional Napa Cabernet and toward delicacy and finesse. To Portet that meant behaving as a Bordelais in the cellars, and, more than that, finding a slightly cooler spot than Rutherford to grow the grapes. When he felt a touch of cool air on his skin one day, on the way down a gentle grade on the Silverado Trail, Stag's Leap became the place. The first vintages came from Steltzner, the next several from a blend of Steltzner and Clos du Val. Since 1977, the source has been the estate. Only in droughty 1976 has Portet reached outside Stag's Leap for grapes, and only that wine gets the back of his hand when he talks of vintages.

Portet prefers cool growing seasons for a variety of reasons, but mainly because they seem to allow him to build a tiny bit more austerity into the wine, and it is that little fillip, he believes, that pays the greatest dividends in aging.

1972 Almost self-effacing early, but so neatly balanced it continued as a supple, graceful, altogether admirable wine approaching its fifteenth birthday.

1973 Fuller, riper than its predecessor, but still reined in and subtle among others of the vintage. Aging particularly well.

1974 The biggest of the Clos du Vals in the early going, it has never changed its spots. First-rate with beef in 1986.

1975 Lean, firm, a whole tapestry of understatements; shows no signs of weakening as of 1987. The winemaker's own favorite.

1976 Portet saw drought-stricken leaves shriveling, picked early, and made the wine of the vintage. Still well down in the pack among his own. Showing some age in 1986.

1977 One of the two or three finest Cabernets from a difficult year. Understated but still well built enough to age for some time yet. Drank very well in 1986.

1978 From a vintage that favored delicacy, it takes full advantage. All subtlety and polish in 1980, unchanged in 1987.

1979 Has the austerity typical of its vintage, and the polish typical of Clos du Val. Looks a superior long-term bet.

1980 Every bit as lean as the 1979, but perhaps not quite as much depth of aroma. Drinking well in 1987, but wants watching over the next few years.

1981 Firm, straightforward, well balanced. May age longer than most from a vintage that seems to have been a bit weak.

1982 All charm early. Probably lacks the stuffings for long age, but surely will remain appealing for ten years.

1983 Spot-on Clos du Val, much like the 1973.

STAG'S LEAP WINE CELLARS

Warren Winiarski provides as complete a contrast to Bernard Portet as one could hope to design, so completes a perfect test of what is man and what is sun and soil in a wine from this sharply defined district. Through a decade of startlingly various weathers, the results of that test score one point for man: The vintages differ from each other, but not quite as much as the wines do.

The proprietor-winemaker of Stag's Leap abandoned a scholarly career in classical Greek in favor of Napa Valley winemaking, but he never lost his academic turn of mind, and it shows up in the gripping but splendidly abstract images he sets as models for his Cabernets. Notes from a 1977 interview already include the two main ones: iron fist in a velvet glove, and the Golden Rectangle—yin and yang in western clothes, as it were. He has added to his phrase book since, but sees, always, the virtues of creating harmony by using opposites. His wines do, indeed, give concrete expression to the picture he has of them. They are subtle and polished, but on a bigger scale than the Clos du Vals: a shade darker, distinctly fuller or fleshier at first, then with more tannic spine underneath. A good deal of the difference may be explained in approach to vintages. Winiarski likes warm-season wines in the glass, likes to work with them in the winery. The 1974 and 1976 appeal to him most in the late 1980s for their extra amplitude (his word). When he makes a Cask 23, it is for the same added dimension, which almost always tastes to me like an extra touch of ripeness. It is not, however, an extra intensity of flavor. Rather, it is an added dimension of texture, another Winiarskian opposition, maybe. Whatever, it makes his favorites most intriguing at my table when the fare has something of the same character. Lamb and duck always come to mind first, with rare roasts of beef not far behind, and skip the funny sauces. My own favorites tend to come from the cool years for reasons that make sense to me if not Winiarski, the main one being that they seem to show more facets.

If Winiarksi's intellectual approach was formed in the halls of Chicago University, his winemaking is entirely a product of the Napa Valley. He started his apprenticeship with Lee Stewart at the original Souverain Cellars, and extended it with Robert Mondavi. Stag's Leap Wine Cellars Cabernets carry unmistakable signs, take more cues from exactly the wines that Portet admired but decided not to copy. And yet Stag's Leap Cabernets go in directions of their own. With his neighbor to the south, Winiarski does not go out of his way to emphasize varietal character, may indeed work to temper it with Merlot, oak aging, perhaps some of each. Here, too, ten years' worth of tasting notes only occasionally remark herbaceous as the main flavor; here, too, oak is almost never a specific.

1972 No recollection.

1973 Brilliant beginning in the first full-scale vintage. Full of flavors, but polished fine at the same time. Still youthful and firm in 1987.

1974 Very ripe and full of flavor early. Held well until 1983 or so, but has tottered a bit since.

1975 All of the complex flavors of the 1973 but lighter and more lithe. Much my favorite when all from the 1970s were tasted together at dinner in 1987.

1976 As all others from the vintage, big and a bit blocky, but this one has balance few did or do. Agreeable in 1987 if in the pack.

1977 Seemed as weak as most in a difficult vintage early, but found a second wind. Supple, flavorful in 1987.

1978 All lighthearted charms, as the vintage generally was. It has held its edge into 1987, but seems to have done all it can.

1979 Has concentrated Cabernet flavors—one of the few Stag's Leaps that has provoked "herbaceous" as a description—and firm textures to match. A wine for keeping by the signs in 1987.

1980 Not sure about this one. Seems a shade forward, and not quite as well balanced as many in the series. Perhaps still in its funk in 1986.

1981 Forward, agreeable. Not an apparent long-keeper.

1982 Of all the series, the wine for early drinking because of its wonderful suppleness. But has depths of flavor and spine to age too.

1983 Exact opposite of 1982, a lean, hard wine powerfully marked by the herblike side of Cabernet. One to lay away.

1984 Splits the difference between 1982, 1983.

Napa does not stop, does not even come close to stopping, with the Rutherford Bench and Stag's Leap. There is Calistoga. There are the mountain vineyards on either side. There is Chiles Valley. Not least, there are the assembled wines from all of the foregoing and all the rest of the valley floor. The names of appealing wines flood to mind—Tudal Winery, Monticello Cellars, Cakebread Cellars, Silverado Vineyards, Rutherford Hill

Winery, Pine Ridge, Johnson Turnbull Vineyards, Frog's Leap Winery, Dunn Vineyards—all of them and another score besides have made at least one wine to compete with the very finest Napa has to offer, usually more than one, but they are young or migrating between styles or sources. Besides, this has to stop somewhere. Beringer Vineyard Private Reserve is going to be that somewhere, a stand-in for all the others because its progress from single-vineyard to (just barely) assembled wine has shown so well what is possible.

BERINGER VINEYARD PRIVATE RESERVE

At the outset, the proprietors of Beringer Vineyard thought of Estate and Private Reserve as one and the same, no surprise given the history of fine wine, and so the first several vintages were from either of two individual vineyards.

Lemmon Ranch, alias Lemmon-Chabot and Chabot, hides in a little, rolling side valley east of St. Helena, at the foot of the high hill from which the St. Helena Sanitorium looms over town. It yields wines of rich textures and impeccable balance but with a tendency to have a hole in the aromas.

State Lane sits on a slight, west-facing slope between the Silverado Trail and the Napa River, a few yards north of Yountville Cross Road. It produces dazzlingly intense, specifically herbaceous Cabernet aromas in wines a deal leaner and tarter than the Lemmons.

Myron Nightingale, Ed Sbragia, and the rest of the Beringer staff waffled back and forth until 1981, when they said, in effect, two heads are better than one, and began blending Lemmon and State. It is some measure of their success that difficult 1981 turned out the wine of the series to that point.

1977 *Lemmon* Full-bodied and polished smooth on release, but wanted more stuffings and more specific aromas from the grapes. It is still healthy, but still wanting.
1978 *Lemmon* Very ripe, a shade over full of tannins and a bit heady.

Still, the richest and most flavorful of the Lemmons, and a pleasing Cabernet in 1987.

1979 *State* Powerful Cabernet leaning toward herbaceous, but leaning toward soft for textures. Much more intriguing for flavors than its forerunners. Developing well in 1986. Perfect flavors for lamb with red peppers.

1980 *Lemmon* Richly textured. Good flavors depending much on wood aging, less on grapes. *State* More fruit, less herb than the 1979 in another pneumatically soft wine.

1981 *Lemmon plus State, plus a tiny dollop from Knights Valley* The wine of the series at release—definite Cabernet aromas in a firm, structured wine showing some signs of age-worthiness from a vintage that offered a few such.

1982 *Lemmon plus State* Excellent Cabernet aromas tightly allied with a distinct note from oak aging. A bigger wine than typical of the vintage, but perfectly balanced and already showing polish that should carry it through a long life.

1983 *Lemmon plus State* Has a certain lightness or delicacy of texture to go with fine varietal flavors and sturdy underpinnings. Suspect an ager in this one.

Sonoma

Thinking about Cabernet Sauvignon and Sonoma causes the mind to dart all around an expansive countryside but never light for long. One vineyard comes to mind in Alexander Valley, another in the Russian River, a third and a fourth in Sonoma Valley, and then the screen goes blank for a while. A pattern is a hard thing to find when thoughts are as rabbity as that, but rabbity thoughts are the only kind that seem to come along.

I am probably all wrong about Sonoma. I am making plans for being all wrong, mostly in the direction of building a high wall around the house and not opening the door to anybody who does not know my mother's middle and maiden names. But the sense will not go away: Sonoma has not yet found the single area that can compete with Napa Valley in Cabernet Sauvignon. Individual wines can charm birds out of the trees, but such charmers never come in clusters, and seldom from the same place three and four times in a row, let alone year after year.

The time may come. Sonoma already has tiny leads in Chardonnay and Pinot Noir, and is right on Napa's shoulder in Sauvignon Blanc. But, for now, in Cabernet it is not even close. One of the reasons for being less than dead certain about the long haul is that, as a grower and producer of Cabernet Sauvignon, the county is still (or maybe again) toddling. Look for a ten-year-old vineyard—a mere ten—and the list is not long. Look for labels that have been using the same vineyard for ten years, and the roster does not reach double figures, though quite a few can now lay claim to seven and eight consecutive vintages from one spot. Look for a set style, and the roster shrinks back to a small handful. Look for memorable wines, and they come from shifting sources, here in this vintage, there in the next, and somewhere altogether different in the third. Look for long-agers, and something goes agley somewhere, in spite of the fact that the Simi 1935 continues in rude good health, or at least did through its fiftieth birthday, when we drank our last three bottles in celebration of assorted milestones.

Sonoma, to go back to ground zero, is several different places for Cabernet. Some of the regions differ so markedly that it is far harder to think of them together than it is to chew gum and walk. Only one, Alexander Valley, has developed enough to show what it probably is going to be. The rest keep shoving contradictions at tasters, or else do not offer enough specifics to allow a generality.

Alexander Valley separates itself from the rest of the pack in two particulars. First, its wines press the vegetative side of Cabernet to a fault. Second, tannins hardly seem to exist in Alexander Valley Cabernets, though they are there.

Exceptions exist in the matter of regional flavors, but, take the vineyards all around, their grapes persistently evoke thoughts of pungent herbs, especially dill. At the extreme, Alexander Valley Cabernets can be mistaken for some of the ferociously one-dimensional examples from the Central Coast.

As for the hard-to-detect tannins, the technicians have an explanation. Tannins, it seems, come in various sizes, while the receptors in human mouths are pretty much of one caliber. If the tannins fit, they really pucker a body's cheeks. If they are too big for the receptors, they drift on by without making an impression. (The picture that comes to mind is of a whole mouthful of little tiny Allen wrenches looking for nuts to twist tight.)

ALEXANDER VALLEY VINEYARDS

With the appearance of a dark, richly scented, altogether appealing 1984, Alexander Valley Vineyards became the first of the valley's wineries to reach the decade mark with an estate-bottled Cabernet Sauvignon.

Hank Wetzel's wines are and are not typical of their region. They are spot-on for their round, big-molecule tannins. They differ from their peers for tasting more of fruit, less of herbs than the norm. The fruit flavor is fresh and berrylike, a taste that sometimes brings Zinfandel to mind quicker than Cabernet until the underlying current of herb makes its presence known. It is subtly different from any other regional characteristic, and pretty rare but not unique in Alexander Valley itself.

The location of the vineyard explains nothing. It starts on the flats along the east bank of the Russian River, almost due east of Healdsburg, and ranges up onto the first set of east-side knolls. Neighbor ranches on either side yield typical, dilly Alexander Valley Cabernet. Rock-steady fermented-in-steel, aged-in-French-oak winemaking is conventional enough in these parts that it does not seem to hold the key either.

Whether the vineyard holds the riddle or not, it should be at its peak throughout the 1980s. The Wetzel family planted it between 1964 and 1973. Vintages before 1975 went to Simi.

1975 Sound, well balanced, but always wanting just a bit more depth than it had. Still lively in 1986, but short of later vintages.
1976 Sound but pallid; off the pace from the beginning.

1977 From a weak vintage, a weak wine.

1978 Appealing berry flavors early; more typical Alexander Valley herbaceous aromas by 1986; always a deft touch of oak. Still a young,
lively wine in 1987.

1979 Supple, but with firm underpinnings. Fine berry aromas complicated by an appealing, faintly earthy note. Easily the winner matched
head-to-head against several of its mates in 1986.

1980 A few wayward notes in the nose detract only slightly from a
well-balanced wine still dominated in 1987 by its grape flavors.

1981 Dark and quite hard among the series. Still seeking its level in
autumn 1986.

1982 A bit weak from the beginning and seemingly forward. A wine
for now from its performance in 1986.

1983 Very well balanced just after bottling, but still closed.

1984 Perhaps the vintage of the series to date. Richly flavored, firmly
structured, altogether inviting when it went to bottle.

JORDAN VINEYARD AND WINERY

Jordan, meanwhile, has reliably provided almost the textbook
example of Alexander Valley's regional flavor. Vintages through
1980 would have been the essence of it, I think, if the winemaking had not done such a splendid job of camouflaging. Vintages
since have tempered the quality noticeably.

It has become one of my habits of mind never to think what
any one wine might be in blind tastings. The minute a name
flashes across one's mind, the tasting stops being blind. The
wine gets itself saddled with all the virtues and vices of that
name, whether it deserves them or not. That said, Jordan is—
has been, at least—one of those rare wines that will not stay
anonymous, mainly because its forceful regional flavors are hedged
about with so many subtle other ones that the sum of the parts
is hard to mistake for anything else. That it is so smooth and
silky on the tongue helps identify it in a lineup.

Right at the beginning owner Tom Jordan gave his winemakers the task of making a wine that would be ready to drink
early, what in the trade is loosely called a restaurant wine. He
could not have picked a better place than the Alexander Valley

to make a wine naturally soft and round and smooth, but he could not have known it at the time for lack of other evidence.

The vineyard is close to two miles north of Alexander Valley Vineyards. It stretches across a little flat between the river and a settlement called Jimtown, hardly four feet above the winter river at its high spots.

1976 Markedly pruney or raisiny right from the outset; the only non-estate wine in the series, though all from Alexander Valley.

1977 Closer picture of the wines to come than the 1976, but always a shade weak and indistinct. From a difficult vintage. Starting the downslope in 1984.

1978 Too pungent of the herbaceous side of Alexander Valley to slip down quietly. By 1985 seemed a bit overripe, and finished a bit hot.

1979 Much the same flavors as the 1978, but more deftly balanced.

1980 Adroit use of wood aging tempered the regional flavors to perfection in a balanced, polished wine. For me, the finest in the series to date.

1981 Close kin to the 1978 in the early going, and still that in late summer 1987.

1982 Almost jammy as a very young wine; seems a hint heavy for a long pull, but plenty of charm coming out of the box.

IRON HORSE VINEYARDS

Forrest Tancer and his family own a small hillside vineyard on the east side of the Alexander Valley, almost due north of Alexander Valley Vineyards and due east of Jordan. As a partner and winemaker at Iron Horse, Tancer elicits from his grapes a dark, full-bodied, ripe Cabernet that he then marks firmly with flavors from wood aging. I have come to it only in its last two released vintages, 1982 and 1983, but both suggest that it bears watching.

The rest of Sonoma is more contradictory than the Alexander Valley in sum, and far more so in its parts. There is a lot of territory here: Carneros, Sonoma Valley, Russian River Valley, Chalk Hill, Dry Creek Valley, and Knights Valley. All have yielded wines that command our attention, none consistently, and those mainly from single vineyards somewhere off by themselves.

The lack of a favorite from Dry Creek Valley startles me. I have the persistent notion that its north- and east-facing benchlands may be some of the county's most promising terrain for Cabernet Sauvignon. Certainly wines from this valley have had intriguing Cabernet flavors—intense notes of berry mixed up with hints of cedar and I do not know what all else. I suspect that a favorite is about to emerge under the J. Pedroncelli label.

The Pedroncellis have made sound, agreeable, occasionally exciting Cabernets for twenty years. The early ones were blended with Zinfandels, for lack of Cabernet in the region. The middle years blended Dry Creek and Alexander Valley grapes and showed greater turns of speed. In them, it seemed as if the Dry Creek grapes played a lean, firm Laurel to Alexander Valley's fat Hardy. But it is the Pedroncellis' pure Dry Creek wines from the as-yet-unreleased vintages of 1984 and 1985 that have stirred my soul the most.

Other wineries have caught the flavors but not the balance. I remain hopeful.

While Dry Creek Valley continues to warm to its task, Carneros, Sonoma Valley (especially Sonoma Mountain), and Russian River Valley turn out three cellar-worthies, not one of them suggesting that they will have company anytime soon.

Buena Vista Winery & Vineyard/Carneros

Buena Vista's Carneros Cabernet Sauvignons come as almost complete shocks among all of the North Coast's red wines: at once fleshy and tart, intensely varietal, without any of the sunny ripeness of their peers from either Napa or Sonoma. Especially, they are tart.

Foggy, windy Carneros does not make life easy for those who would grow Cabernet Sauvignon on its gentle but persistent slopes, but it does not make the dream impossible either. The variety ripens late, and it stays tart, but it delivers concentrated fruit flavors that balance betwixt delicately herbaceous and richly fruity, almost jammy. Or so the wines from Buena Vista have said in their youth, and—except for a similarly impressive Louis M. Martini Cabernet from the La Loma Ranch—they are the only measure as of 1987.

Winemaker Jill Davis seems to have found an appealing balance point for the grapes, and now is honing and sculpting the fine points that add up to style. Each of the vintages from 1981 through 1984 has been a step forward in that process; otherwise the wines have been remarkably consistent in balance and depth of fruit flavor.

LAUREL GLEN VINEYARD/SONOMA MOUNTAIN

Patrick Campbell has coaxed a couple of stunning Cabernet Sauvignons out of his sloping property up in the Sonoma Mountain section of Sonoma Valley—subtle, well-proportioned wines that balance adroitly between the fruity and herbaceous sides of Cabernet's character. Everything about them says they are agers, but it will be a while before we know. Including two homemades, the series goes back only to 1978 (still youthful at the beginning of 1986). The 1981 has been the most convincing spokesman for Campbell's commercial releases to date, though the 1984 and 1985 both seem poised to outdo it. His homemade 1979 remains the wine of the lot to this point.

The vineyard began yielding with the vintage of 1972, but the wineries that took the grapes before Campbell opened his own cellar did not make anything like the wines he has.

It was Cabernet that caused the several growers on these east-facing slopes to form their own Sonoma Mountain AVA, but everything beyond Laurel Glen is a hope, not an accomplishment. Other wines from the territory have tended to be extremely ripe, ferociously tannic, or both.

DEHLINGER WINERY/RUSSIAN RIVER VALLEY

Tom Dehlinger's Cabernet Sauvignons, at this point, have to be taken even more as freaks than the Laurel Glens, and are much more likely to stay that way. Dehlinger's neighbors look on in disbelief as his grapes grow dark and plump every September. Few grow Cabernet; nearly all who have tried have had poor luck with maturity. With Chardonnay and Pinot Noir firmly at the forefront all over the valley, Cabernet's chances of making headway do not appear fat.

Dehlinger does not care. His Merlot-tinged Cabernet is a dark, ripe wine, but not a sun-burnished one. He got his first crop in 1975, from vines planted in 1972. In all the vintages since, his Cabernet has been among the leaders in Sonoma.

1975 Richly herbaceous flavors and rough for texture. Perhaps always to be a bit homemade.

1976 No note.

1977 Flavors like those of 1975, but more polished early. Long and complex in late summer 1986 and still miles from the end of its road.

1978 Seemed a bit troubled early and not quite so well balanced as its forerunners. No recent bottles.

1979 Steady, but in the pack in the early going.

1980 Sturdy, rather tannic wine with strong varietal aromas. Best prospects for aging since 1977.

1981 Handily the wine of the series on release. Rich fruit flavors balanced by beginnings of appealing bouquets. Fuller bodied than the 1980 yet more polished.

1982 On release excellent prospects for aging. Much in the vein of the 1977.

1983 Surprisingly light and supple in texture. Straight-ahead flavors of Cabernet match the weight.

BERINGER VINEYARDS/KNIGHTS VALLEY

As with all of these wines, now is no time to make final judgments. Thus far, every vintage in the series has been complex, supple, outright enjoyable to drink in youth. All, in fact, have seemed at the top of their form from their third to sixth years. The first few, from 1976 on, seem to be edging onto the down-slope, little hints of varnish having supplanted the fruit flavors in them, not disastrously but not to their benefit. Even if they end up as wines for early drinking, few if any serve the purpose as well. Their scale makes them versatile dinner companions as well as pleasant ones. The absence of a single off-vintage adds luster to their name.

Mendocino

Just two wines give me faith in Mendocino's prospects as Ca-bernet country, but, my, how they give me faith, because both balance between fruit and herb as effortlessly as the most adept Napans and because both have lasted twenty years without a tremor.

One came from the Fetzer Home Ranch in Redwood Valley in 1968; the other was made in the same year by John Parducci from an independent grower's Anderson Valley grapes. If any other Cabernet from the county would make a patch on these, I never got to taste it, but the same two wineries keep coming close, and mainly from sources in the same territories. It is a little early to start closing the books on Mendocino at large, but the sneaking suspicion is that the variety is going to deliver its richest wines from vineyards in the hills that separate Ukiah and Boonville. I think this primarily on the evidence produced by vines in an upland valley known as Cole Ranch. The valley floor from Ukiah down to Hopland turns out pleasant young Caber-nets, but I cannot think of one that did not go soft and a little raisiny before it turned ten. The Anderson Valley is so cool and damp that late-ripening Cabernet has a tough time getting dark enough to make a sturdy rosé in a lot of years, and only gets fully ripe in about one out of ten, in John Parducci's long ex-perience. A couple of ridgetop vineyards, up out of the fog, ripen more often but have yet to produce a memorable Cabernet. The intervening hills, meanwhile, moderate both extremes and build memorable flavors while they are at it.

FETZER VINEYARDS

It is the two ends of the rope that make Fetzer Cabernet Sauvignons interesting to think about and agreeable to drink. The winemaking went south not long after the 1968 and stayed there until Paul Dolan signed on as winemaker in 1978. The 1979s showed the new beginnings; the vintages since have gained more ground.

The 1968 taught all of California's lessons. It started out all easy and appealing with its abundance of fruit, dipped into the sophomore slump for a couple of years, then climbed to new heights when it had been around long enough for some bottle bouquet to develop. By 1985 it was passing glorious.

The winemaking, to hear the Fetzers tell it, was close to unconscious. The family had the cookbook recipe—ferment in stainless steel, age in barrels, bottle when ready—and followed it. The barrels were new, of American oak, and the wine stayed in them for the prescribed two years. As soon as it got to bottle it promised to deliver over the long haul. The Cabernet flavors came out of UC's textbook. A little earthy note gave them something to play against. The balance could not have been better. We never had it in mind to keep anything that tasted so good early, but we lost a few bottles in a back corner. Came 1985 and came the revelation.

To this point, Dolan's contributions have not had a chance to turn twenty, but the early signs are hopeful. The 1979s through 1982s were made along the general lines of the sainted 1968s, though with more deliberate intent. With 1983 came the first shift toward French barrels. The 1984 aged only in new French wood. Also, the source began to shift. Private Reserves from 1982 through 1984 are wholly from Cole Ranch.

Fetzer Home Ranch, the sole source of the 1968, is in a little box canyon in the hills that form Redwood Valley's west side. Its walls trend east-west. The vines in Cole Ranch occupy a mile-long, north-south upland valley almost due west of Ukiah.

The vintage notes apply only to the wines designated as Private Reserve or the equivalent. The Fetzers make several Cabernet Sauvignons each year, most of the others designed for early, casual consumption. Only the Reserves are meant to run a long course.

1979 In the first strong mark of the renaissance, separate Home Ranch and Cole Ranch bottlings both competed very well against top-flight Cabernets early. In 1987 the Cole Ranch bottling seemed to be at the absolute height of its powers, a delicious mouthful of wine. Hints of brick at the edges say it has done all it can do, except hold form for years to come.

1980 No note.

1981 No note.

1982 *All Cole Ranch* Well balanced, agreeable wine from a difficult harvest.

1983 *All Cole Ranch* All delicacy and finesse in its early days, but balanced to last for a long time.

1984 *All Cole Ranch* Fuller of fruit than the 1983 and more clearly marked by French wood, but tart and lively. Very unlike the 1983, but just as likely to age.

CHARDONNAY

WE DO LOVE A CHARDONNAY AROUND THIS place, which is a partial confession that our diets are not all they could be in an era when *skinny* and *fit* have become synonyms. Chardonnay is what one wants with lobster and drawn butter, or salmon, or sweetbreads—a wine of riches for times of blissful excess at the dinner table.

Such it has been for quite a few years now, going back to a Hanzell 1956 that never appeared in public and a 1957 that did. Both were the kind of wine that made a body lean back, confident that there was nothing better to do with the evening than stay put in happy contemplation of their honeyed aromas and flavors. Connoisseurs of honey insisted it was sage honey. Maybe. Whatever, it could not wear out its welcome. Although I have learned to admire other sorts since, "honeyed" is still the loftiest compliment I can pay a Chardonnay.

What the Hanzells proved was that, together, ripe Chardonnay and fresh-coopered oak barrels from French forests could produce a luscious, rich, intricately complicated wine. Almost everybody seized upon the Hanzell model in one way or another beginning with the early 1960s. Ripe grapes and French oak continue to be the points on which first decisions of style in California Chardonnay depend today.

All by itself Chardonnay is supposed to taste something like apple, according to the set of flavor associations devised by Dr. Maynard A. Amerine and his colleagues at the University of California at Davis, and sometimes it does. Sometimes fully ripe ones smack of something closer to peach. With the proliferation of clones in recent years, it is possible to wander through vine rows of Chardonnay with tastes more reminiscent of strawberry than either apple or peach. Any of these may have the faintest undercurrent of something vegetative, to my mind an elusive hint of garden-fresh asparagus. When I mention asparagus in connection with Chardonnay, people look at me as if my last hinge had just come loose, but it has been a most successful key in the parlor game kind of blind tastings wine nuts inflict on one another. Chenin Blancs and Pinot Blancs often suggest apples or peaches, but never asparagus.

Regional character abets the confusion in sly, small ways. Logic says pungently aromatic varieties like Sauvignon Blanc and Gewürztraminer might pull more wool over one's eyes. In fact, large-scale flavors magnify regional differences while subtle, understated Chardonnay hides them well enough to drive tasters daft. Put a little group of Chardonnays out for blind tasting, especially if it has been assembled to make things easy, and separations may be evident. Permit yourself to judge one hundred samples and more at a national competition and, *pffftt,* the distinctions dissolve. The only distinction I have been able to cling to consistently separates the North Coast from the Central Coast. The latter, especially Monterey, tends to have a soft texture and straightforward peach flavor not found north of San Francisco.

It takes a deal of concentration to get at any of the flavor associations for Chardonnay because Chardonnay is rarely allowed to be itself. More than any other, except champagne-method sparklers, Chardonnay is a winemaker's wine. Something in its quiet but indelible nature challenges people to change it. What might have tasted of apple or peach, or strawberry or asparagus, often ends up hinting instead of pineapple or vanillin or toast or butterscotch, or some variation on those themes, because the wine fermented in oak, with or without the complication of malolactic fermentation, and aged in wood as well. On just these points the permutations are endless, and there remains the matter of where the oak grew and how it was coopered—both mighty agents of change in the flavor of Chardonnay. Then there are the subtler variations of how many new barrels and how many seasoned ones, and so on and so forth.

It was a sorry day when technique began dominating the consciousness of us other benighted drinkers of Chardonnay for one clichéd fact: Talking a good game and playing one are not the same thing. What it comes down to is that wines of quality never let the drinker know how the work was done while meager stuff broadcasts the method of its manufacture.

The simple way to define Chardonnays is to string them like beads, with powerfully fruity ones at one pole and not-at-all-fruity titans at the other, leaving subtlety to hold the center.

It helps to eat "Californian" if you are going to have the richest, fruitiest California Chardonnays. Packed full of flavor as they are, they match up with the most flavorful of the fresh foods, including most all of the Central and South American and many of the Asian sorts, though not the fieriest Mexican and Hunan dishes. Large-scale Chardonnays are just about the right size, for example, to take on a chicken, tomato, and avocado salad sprinkled liberally with sesame seeds. The fat, fleshy ones take some of the dryness out of turkey white meat and taste good alongside it too.

The large-scale toasty, buttery, other-than-fruity Chardonnays are the ones for lobster and salmon and sweetbreads, as well as for white meats swimming in traditional French cream, butter, or mushroom sauces.

At the center of the stick, the subtle wines—whether subtly

fruity or subtly woody—find their matches with oysters, white-fleshed fish, plain chicken, and the like. They also go well with a surprising number of the foods noted with the polar extremes.

In all, I stick my nose into a few more than two thousand glasses of Chardonnay a year and so am surer about Chardonnay than any other sort of wine. Of two things I am very sure: There are no absolutes, and the ambiguities are the best parts.

Of the 540 or so Chardonnays currently on the market, a long third would be welcome on my dinner table, but the 35 singled out in the following pages run well ahead of the pack. They, like the Cabernets, are divided into longer and shorter entries. If I had to sit down at a judging table, some of the wines consigned to short entries would come out ahead of their ostensible betters—and so would some wines left off the list. It happens that way at the table too. The dintinction, again, is how often the wines of a particular label have given pleasure and how seldom they have failed to do so.

NORTH COAST

To repeat a point already made in the Cabernet Sauvignon chapter and to be made again in later sections, the North Coast has all the edge in Chardonnay because it has all the history. "All the history" is a narrow edge, Chardonnay having blossomed much later than either Cabernet Sauvignon or Sauvignon Blanc. To be specific, historic edge means that dozens of winemakers have used the same vineyards for a decade and more, and a few have been on the track for three. With that, people, styles, and properties all crowd close enough together for the mosaics to begin to make sense. Further, Chardonnay grows in almost every nook and cranny in three of the four counties, so that the weak spots can be located too.

Also as in the Cabernet chapter, the sequence of regions begins with my current favorite and descends from there. Unlike Cabernet, Chardonnay makes me want to put the Russian River Valley, Napa Valley, and Carneros as equals, and to make tiny steps down from there, but typography does not permit.

California's system of AVAs is still young and disorganized enough that reliable acreage figures for them hardly exist. Counties are still the statistical unit. As of 1986, Sonoma led with 6,900 bearing acres, followed by Napa at 6,700, and trailed by Mendocino with 1,500. Lake had only 210 acres bearing in 1986.

Russian River Valley AVA

The Russian River Valley's particular gift to Chardonnay is a vitality that comes easily from one after another of its vineyards, but only rarely from a scattering of properties in a few other places. Wines from here almost vibrate with varietal character, not just in the first bloom of youth but for years. This quality seems truer of the eastern reaches of a broad, almost plainlike valley than the western ones. The grapes seem to ripen a shade fuller to the east, and so to deliver richer aromas. Vineyards toward the western edge of the region are more likely to yield up tart, appley Chardonnays—a fact not lost on an expanding community of sparkling-wine producers. However, this, like all truths about wine, seems to have notable exceptions.

Just how long it is going to take for the richest Russian River Valley Chardonnays to grow too old remains open to debate because the valley began to be planted only in the 1970s; the wines I would choose to test the limits have come only from the 1980s.

The valley came late to grapes because two gaps in the Coast Ranges allow chill and foggy marine air to spill into it morning and night all summer long. Old-time growers used to getting fifty-five dollars a ton for mixed blacks were not about to waste money planting grapes in such uncertain climes when they could ripen everything every year from Healdsburg north to Clover-dale. A number of veteran growers in those precincts tried to save Brice Jones from himself in the early 1970s when he started tracking after properties west of Santa Rosa all the way to Forestville. His blithe ignorance and general bullheadedness brought about Sonoma-Cutrer Vineyards. Cecil De Loach, Tom Dehlinger, Jacob Shilo, and Rodney Strong were out there planting with him. Herds have followed since.

DE LOACH VINEYARDS

In the past six seasons I have come to De Loach Chardonnays ten times in competitions, offered them eight golds and a silver, and never come close to guessing their identity. And yet when my wife and I sit down to dinner with a bottle, it seems about as hard to identify as a brass band with seventy-six trombones and a piccolo.

Cecil De Loach is not a shy man, and his Chardonnay is not a shy wine. And yet, and yet. It always has a certain rightness of proportion about it and a capacity for showing itself in facets, for holding something in reserve. De Loach takes a good deal less than all the aromas his grapes would give him, instead chipping away a bit here and there until all the parts fit. In the seasons since 1980 he has moved his harvest forward by a couple of small increments, increased the proportion of wine he barrel ferments, begun to leave some of the newly fermented wine on the lees, and otherwise tempered the aromas in a series of controlled steps, and his wine still heaps Chardonnay in the glass.

When the wine is ready to bottle, it is ready to drink, and then it lasts. De Loach bottles each vintage before the next harvest rolls around and releases the wine on his birthday in mid-September. Two years in bottle adds some extra polish. Four years has not been too much.

At each of these ages the wine commands attention as soon as its aromas start filling a room, but it is curiously adaptable to foods that might seem at first glance too delicate to be paired with it. De Loach likes to put it out with sautéed abalone; one taste explains why. It is at the top of my list for Monterey Bay prawns sautéed in butter and brandy, for lobster tails fixed any way lobster tails can be fixed, but especially boiled (à la Trader Vic) or broiled and served with drawn butter. I would never turn it down with juicy, buttery roast chicken. The presence of all this butter is no accident. What sets a De Loach Chardonnay apart from most of the rest is its apposition of rich flavors and cleansing textures.

Not much in De Loach's background suggests the source of his sense of wine—his boyhood was spent with a grandfather who was a southern Baptist preacher; his last career before wine was as a San Francisco firefighter—but it is a background that has allowed him to turn out a rock-steady string of Chardonnays during a sequence of wildly variable growing seasons between 1980 and 1985.

The first two vintages were estate wines from his vineyards on Olivet Road, several miles west of Santa Rosa. Those vines remain the heart of the wine, but they are supplemented now by grapes from three other properties ranging three miles west, always close to River Road.

1980 Fine balance and rich Chardonnay flavors called immediate attention to a then-newcomer.

1981 Richly flavored and beautifully balanced early; drinking in peak form at the end of 1985 with such as stuffed quail.

1982 Right on form early; still youthful in autumn 1986. Subtle enough for salmon, flavorful enough for chicken in a Thai coconut sauce.

1983 First vintage to show overtones of honey and spice along with subtler but still definitive Chardonnay fruit flavors. Splendid with buttery dishes, but deft enough to provide adept counterpoint to herbed chicken and polenta.

1984 Again the honeyed, spicy overtones that mark a perfect marriage of fruit and wood, and again subtle enough to provide countermelody to a lemony sauce.

1985 Full of the flavors begun with the 1983, and more. An early hint of austerity quickly gave way to opulent textures. In all, a glorious demonstration that giants can be perfectly proportioned too.

1986 On release, seemed much in the vein of the ever-more-admirable 1983.

SONOMA-CUTRER VINEYARDS

One night in Dallas, a group of us, in town to judge at the *Dallas Morning News* wine competition, went to a restaurant called Oasis West to warm up our palates. We ordered some of everything from the menu and a bottle of Sonoma-Cutrer Chardonnay, Cutrer Vineyard. When that was gone, we looked through a long wine list and ordered another one. When that was gone, etc. . . . We judged well in the competition too.

Although Sonoma-Cutrer and De Loach are near neighbors, and the broad outlines of the winemaking are similar, Sonoma-Cutrer is not the same wine. The two do share fruit aromas so vibrant and so inviting that both wines are at once accessible and durable, but the Sonoma-Cutrer is reined in a good deal more and has been from its first vintage onward.

Sonoma-Cutrer had a settled style at its debut because Bill Bonetti makes the wine, and Bonetti goes back, in an improbably straight line, to the beginnings of the sort of Chardonnay people now identify as Californian.

The winery goes back only to 1981, its vineyards to 1972. But Bonetti's first Chardonnay was a 1963 at Charles Krug. That wine and all its successors have been influenced by the legendary 1957 Hanzell, which, Bonetti says, turned on the light for him. Up to the day he was introduced to it, his estimates of California's potential for white wine started at below average and ranged downward. He has gladly made a liar out of himself in nearly every vintage from 1963 on.

To do it, he has built three wineries, of which Sonoma-Cutrer is by far the most particularly designed. All the others were wineries; this is a Chardonnay winery with no compromises. Arriving grapes ride through a chilling tunnel so they may begin fermentation at exactly the temperature Bonetti believes to be ideal; the winery does not even own a stemmer-crusher, only Willmes tank presses that minimize oxidation; barrel fermentation takes place in a humid underground cellar. The list of particulars continues.

Four vineyards produce its two Russian River Valley wines. Cutrer Vineyard is bottled separately under its own name. Shiloh, Kent, and a bit of Mirabelle go together as the Russian River Ranches (RRR) bottling. (The third and most expensive bottling, Les Pierres, comes from a Sonoma Valley vineyard described on page 152.) Cutrer flanks the winery, which is dead parallel with the De Loach cellar and about a mile north of it. Mirabelle is well west, near Rio Nido; Kent is not far east at the village of Fulton; Shiloh is east of Kent in the Chalk Hill district, all three of them in a line traced by River Road. Bonetti puts Les Pierres as the most age-worthy wine of the three, followed closely by Cutrer. Russian River Ranches is designed to be ready early; age-worthiness is not a prime goal. In the early going they are of much the same flavors, but not quite the same textures and certainly not the same depth.

To date, none of the Cutrers has been sorely tested by time. The notes refer to them unless a separate comment on the RRR bottling is added.

1981 Lovely fruit with all sorts of grace notes. Fat and rich for texture, but obviously endowed with spine to age. The RRR comparatively overstated for fruit flavors, but still a joy to drink.

1982 Much like the 1981 for flavor, but not quite so firm. Exactly the flavors to go with salmon. RRR toned back here and henceforth to more closely resemble its running mate.

1983 All of the flavor and almost all of the spine of the 1981. Again, has matched perfectly with salmon.

1984 Equals or exceeds the 1981 on all counts. Fills the mouth with flavors and texture instantly, but still has a delicacy.

1985 The early released RRR promised that this would be the vintage of the series to date. The Cutrer has kept that promise.

DOMAINE LAURIER

Like a majority of California's most memorable Chardonnays, the Domaine Laurier is almost a work of architecture. Proprietors Jacob and Barbara Shilo and winemaker Steven Test draw on three vineyards planted to two different clones, then ferment some of the crop in tanks and some in barrels to amplify the original complications.

What they get almost exactly bridges the gap between a De Loach and a Sonoma-Cutrer for flavor, but goes off in its own direction in having lighter textures and a need to age in bottle for a year or more to round itself out. As a result of all of the foregoing, the Domaine Laurier is one of those wines that keep calling one back to the glass for another sniff, another sip, and keep gathering esteem. Every time we have a bottle, it seems, we think of a different reason to have another one soon, to see how many more colors there are in the chameleon.

Trying to pin down the differences among such as the Domaine Laurier, the De Loach, and the Sonoma-Cutrer is exactly what makes wine nuts hunt among the techniques. They hope that understanding how will also explain why. It does not, it will not.

One fine spring day in 1986 the Shilos and Test gave my wife and me a chance to see why. They set out a tasting of all of the separate components of their 1985, plus the final blend. Somebody with hay fever could have spotted the difference between the clones. One was astoundingly perfumey of some unknowable mélange of fruits, probably including strawberries. The other traditional California clone tasted very much like an apple, just as the professors at UC-Davis say Chardonnay does. In the proportion Test finally used, with help from a whole chorus of French oaks, the blended clones tasted deliciously like neither and both. I figured out how to enjoy the final blend right away. A little surreptitious kitchen blending of the others showed how easy it would be to get something altogether different.

1980 Fairly pale, but firmly marked by toasty notes from wood aging; Chardonnay became a grace note early and has stayed such.
1981 Graceful balance of fruit and wood in this one; deftly balanced on the palate as well. In mid-1986 still drinking very well, the wood by then showing as a toasty or buttery note.

1982 More richly flavored and more complex than earlier vintages, yet crisper and firmer on the palate. All grace and refinement.

1983 Great Chardonnay early—riper than apple, less luscious than peach. All enjoyment through 1985; in 1986 seemed to be fading.

1984 Buttery and toasty notes dominate early, as in the 1981.

1985 Close kin to the 1981 for flavors and textures. Seemed polished and mature in mid-1987.

IRON HORSE VINEYARDS

For once in the world of wine, pure logic rules without error. Forrest Tancer gets all of the grapes for the still wine from the same estate vineyard that yields all of Iron Horse's understated champagne-method sparkling wines, and the results are the palest, most delicately light-bodied and tart of all the Russian River Valley Chardonnays. They always seem readier to do duty with white-fleshed fish and some of the plainer chicken dishes than with anything remotely hearty in flavor or heavy in texture. We seem to pull them out of the cellar most happily when they are two to four years old. A couple of bottles have rewarded greater patience in surprising degree, but still kept company with delicate foods more readily than richer ones.

1980 Pale, delicately structured, but full of the apple flavors of Chardonnay in youth. By December 1984 it had darkened in color and filled out for texture, but still tasted freshly of apple. (A separate barrel-fermented lot seemed older at the same season.)

1981 Pale, more clearly marked by oak than its forerunners. Still a fresh, lively wine in 1985; by this time richer in fruit than wood flavors.

1982 Crisp, tart, cleansing in youth. Applelike flavors nicely balanced against sweeter wood. The quintessential Chardonnay for white-fleshed fish, to which we sacrificed our entire supply by early 1986.

1983 Spot-on the pale, tart, fresh house style. Perhaps a bit less forceful of fruit than usual.

1984 Enticing flavors of apple all through. Pale and crisp, as always; a bit more austere in the finish than earlier vintages.

1985 Much an echo of the 1983 in the early going.

DEHLINGER WINERY

The closest competitors to Iron Horse for delicacy among Russian River Chardonnays come from Dehlinger. In youth, some have seemed understated to the point of being plain in the midst of the many intensely varietal wines of the neighborhood (a mild astonishment in view of proprietor Tom Dehlinger's richly flavored Pinot Noirs, Cabernet Sauvignons, and Zinfandels). Indeed the Chardonnays are not as mild and plain as they first seem; they just take a couple of years to get going. Once in stride, they come fairly close to Iron Horse Chardonnays for lightness of texture, but carry a more definite note from their time in wood. The 1985 lifted the level over earlier vintages.

Napa Valley

Maybe, a hundred years from now, the Russian River Valley will have all of the Chardonnay, and people rummaging through ancient books will wonder what they missed in Napa. If such a thing happens, they will have missed some treasures.

I am not sure yet why it is so, whether it owes to the vineyards or the winemakers, but for whatever reason, where the Russian River Valley gives us three or four outstanding wines, the Napa Valley presents those of us living in the current edition of the good old days with fully a score of memorable Chardonnays.

Napa, as usual, is anything but a monolith. It has at least three distinct zones for Chardonnay. The most southerly (leaving Carneros to speak in its own voice) flanks both sides of Big Ranch Road, which runs north from the city of Napa between the state highway and the Silverado Trail. The second, smallest, and most distinctive is the hills of the morning light, which frame the west side of the valley from St. Helena north almost to Calistoga. The third zone is the valley floor beginning directly north of the Big Ranch area and extending north at least as far as Oakville, maybe as far as Zinfandel Lane, a crossroad about halfway between Rutherford and St. Helena.

Of the first ten Napa Chardonnays on my roster, three—Trefethen Vineyards, Beringer Vineyard Private Reserve, and St. Andrew's Winery Estate—come from vineyards on Big Ranch Road or very near it. Silverado Vineyards lies within hailing distance to the north.

In the west hills Stony Hill Vineyard has been joined by Smith-Madrone Vineyards, credentials enough for us to have pushed vineyards on those steep slopes toward the front of our lists. After these, most of the rest of my annual want list is anchored on the valley floor between Yountville and St. Helena, but spiced with grapes from farther south. The risk on the valley floor is too much of a good thing—too much flesh, too ripe a flavor, too heady a wine. Temper those qualities with leaner fruit from the cooler territories to the south and very few Chardonnays can outrun the results. Freemark Abbey Winery, Raymond Vineyard & Cellar, Robert Mondavi Winery, and Folie à Deux Winery are particular examples.

There is no ranking these wines top to bottom. They are gathered here within the three districts, from south to north.

TREFETHEN VINEYARDS

Sometimes the search for distinctions between one Chardonnay and another gets down to such fine points that I cannot keep them in memory from one glass to the next. Not so Trefethen. Its dominating fruit flavors can be confused with several others, but its succulent, almost juicy textures set it apart from all of its peers.

Almost any food that threatens to taste dry profits from a bottle of Trefethen, but the real test is white breast meat from roasted turkey, the part that comes closest to chewing like cardboard and is most likely to make white wine taste a little bit like wet fur. A Trefethen of any vintage turns the meat succulent while keeping its own ripe, almost peachy fruit flavors fresh.

The source of the juiciness lies first with the vineyard, which has been the sole source from the beginning. However, David Whitehouse's winemaking does everything to keep both fruit flavors and juicy textures intact: fermentation in stainless steel, a polishing few months in seasoned oak, and thence to bottle.

Even by Napa's strict standards, the Trefethens are long-lived Chardonnays. In the summer of 1985 John and Janet Trefethen staged a blind tasting of their first eleven vintages, beginning with 1973. Only two of the wines put themselves firmly at the older end of the spectrum, and only one at the younger. Not one was overaged to see, to smell, or to taste. The voting results of a dozen assembled tasters argued firmly, as usual, against vintage charts.

1975 Among the riper and heavier wines of the series from the outset, but aging well at ten.

1976 An unexpected star from a drought year. Though slightly heady, had enticing Chardonnay aromas early and still had them in autumn 1986.

1977 One of the lesser lights in the series.

1978 Not as rich in flavor or texture as some others, but still a vintage of considerable substance and staying power.

1979 Right at the top of the lists. A wine filled with ripe flavors and plush textures, and still one with ample backbone. Aging beautifully in mid-summer 1987.

1980 Rich, honeyed fruit in long finish by mid-1985; still aging on a very slow curve in mid-1987. Wood never more than a faint echo, a grace note. For all the riches, good with sea bass in a creamy sauce.

1981 Not quite so rich in fruit flavors as the 1980, but almost. All finesse and polish late in 1985.

1982 Much of the ripe, honeyed fruit flavors of the 1981, but seemed a shade softer in texture than that wine late in 1985. Still on the up-slope then.

1983 Honeyed again—the perfect, seamless marriage of fruit and oak. Outstanding balance for the long haul; still fresh and lively on the tongue at the end of 1986.

1984 Again, rich, honeyed, and yet polished and subtle enough to keep perfect company with Hubert Keller's most delicate mousse-

line of sea scallops at Fleur de Lys in San Francisco in mid-1987.
1985 All of the family features, but one shade subtler for fruit than
most, and one shade firmer or more tart. Doubtless ager.

BERINGER VINEYARDS PRIVATE RESERVE

Beringer's is the non-fruity member of the big, ripe school of
Napa Chardonnays, at the opposite end of the pole from Trefethen. For us, its style is the primary choice for salmon, especially salmon in sorrel or other herbed sauces. To my way of
thinking, salmon does not mate all that well with the broader
perfumes of fruit, yet needs flavors of some authority to match
its own richness. For similar reasons, the Beringer Private Reserves are able companions for sweetbreads in almost any way
sweetbreads can be fixed.

One searches for a way to explain why a wine can taste so
much without tasting of anything exactly identifiable. It carries
shadowy hints of fruit and even more shadowy suggestions of
oak, especially the toasty notes (portions are fermented in barrel, and malolactic has a role too). But it is definitively not of
the fruity sort, and almost as distinctly not one of the toasty
school of Chardonnay either. No point in straining for effect.
The idea is, this is a wine for people who like body and strength
in a wine but want it to stay a little bit in the background so
the food can make a clear case of its own.

Nearly all of the Private Reserves have come from a small
block of Chardonnay the Beringer winery identifies as Salvador
Ranch, though other properties have contributed to some of
them, mainly the early ones. Just off Big Ranch Road not far
south of Trefethen, Salvador has yielded beautifully balanced,
age-worthy wines vintage after vintage. The winery launched
the series in 1977 and spent the first three vintages settling into
stride. Since then the course has been arrow-straight.

1980 Dark gold, well marked by toasty oak but even more marked by
ripe Chardonnay. Early fleshy textures masked a considerable firm-

ness, but it always seemed a shade too much for any meal.

1981 Pulled back just enough from the 1980 to become a memorable wine, especially with salmon, sweetbreads, and other rich dishes not much enhanced by lively fruit flavors. Still drinking at peak from in spring 1987.

1982 Much in the vein of the 1981 for its rich textures, complex bouquets, and subdued taste of Chardonnay. In early spring 1987 a perfect match with salmon fillets in an orange, herb, and butter sauce.

1983 More pronounced Chardonnay aromas than its predecessors, but still true to its style. As usual, mostly reserved for salmon in flavorful sauces (shallots and tarragon braised in butter, for example). Drinking so well late in 1987 that we are saving a few bottles to see how it does at six and eight.

1984 Paler and leaner than the 1983 in the early going, and more restrained in its fruit flavors. When we have had it, we have had salmon to go with it. Or is it vice versa?

1985 Virtual twin of the 1982 for subdued Chardonnay and rich but not weighty textures.

ST. ANDREW'S WINERY ESTATE

St. Andrew's estate-bottled Chardonnay is that rare breed of wine that disarms a body going in. The first sip is pleasant both for fresh fruit flavors and gentle textures. The second is more so. By the fourth or fifth sip the wine begins to command some attention. How, one begins to wonder, can a wine be this pleasant to drink without having a single obvious quality? Therein, I begin to think, lies the charm. It is, pure and simple, complete. All the pieces of the puzzle fit to make an engaging, in fact seamless, whole. One of these days we will test their durability, but the pleasure these wines give at three and four keeps depriving us of experimental materials.

In thinking about the St. Andrew's wines together with their near neighbors from Beringer and Trefethen, it comes sharply to mind that none ever has the pineapple or tropical notes that creep into Chardonnays from almost every other part of the North Coast. The range is from apple to peach, never further. Whether this owes to vineyards or winemaking I cannot think.

Incidentally, a second, similarly styled non-estate Napa Chardonnay gives fine value for not much money.

The tasting notes speak only to the estate wine.

1980 Ripe Napa Chardonnay neatly buttressed by wood; balanced and polished on the tongue. Altogether appealing in the finish.

1981 The same understated elegance and polish of the 1980, and a still subtler touch of wood. A wine for similarly underplayed foods.

1982 A little riper and fuller in fruit flavors than its forerunners, but just as harmonious. Again, an enticing set of fruit flavors in the finish.

1983 A return to the restaint of the 1981. So polished it drank well as an appetizer in early 1985, but also had enough stuffings to go perfectly with poached salmon a year later.

1984 Much in the vein of the 1980 in the early going.

1985 Again, all polish and elegance and perfection of flavor right through the finish.

SILVERADO VINEYARDS

By this point you will have gotten the drift: that I am heavily prejudiced in favor of the fruit flavors of Chardonnay and not so fond of the taste of oak (which strikes me as a reasonable outlook; from childhood I have eaten fruit and left the trees alone and felt pretty wise about it). Silverado sometimes makes me wonder if I have been missing something.

Of all the wines on this list, Silverado Chardonnay infallibly calls attention to its time in barrel, but it does so without a single strident note. From the debut vintage of 1981 on, winemaker John Stuart has run an elegantly poised juggling act in a wine that hints first at oak, then at Chardonnay, then at an even more elusive interplay of the two together. And then it starts all over in some other order.

The vineyard runs west toward Yountville from the foot of the knoll on which the winery sits, about a mile north of Trefethen Vineyards.

1981 Well marked by new oak, but well balanced and promising for the future of the winery.

1982 Again, a plentiful dose of oak, but richer in fruit than its predecessor and again well balanced.

1983 Splendid fruit deftly supported by a note from aging in new barrels. Much the most appealing, polished wine of the series to date.

1984 All polish and refinement from distinctive but underplayed flavor of grapes to restrained toasty note from barrel aging. One of the impressive wines of its vintage.

1985 Challenges the 1983. Fine fruit flavors neatly joined to subtle, toasty notes from oak. For all the subtlety, plenty flavorful enough to handle an extremely tart turkey *piccata* in spring 1987.

FREEMARK ABBEY WINERY

If pleasure could be measured in units, like heat is measured in BTUs, Freemark Abbey Chardonnay would be the hottest property in our collection. We have put away more bottles of it than any other Chardonnay over a longer span of years, and with it provoked more sighs of contentment and never a serious disappointment.

A curious sidelight to our enthusiasm for the Freemarks is that we keep them for ourselves. Most of the wines we like we trot out for guests at the drop of a hat. Not these. Sometimes I dream of sitting down in a room with the blinds drawn, with a large jar of fresh caviar and a big spoon, and eating the whole lot. The Freemarks do not cost anywhere near as much and are not so difficult to find, so they often stand in for the caviar.

Getting at the flavors of these wines would be a lifework for a poet. Rich, ripe, almost honeyed fruit is the first impression. Oak never comes to mind exactly, but the wines always give a sense of having been aged in barrel. All of this sounds exactly like tasting notes for a couple of dozen other Chardonnays. What sets a Freemark apart is its fugitive note of garden-fresh asparagus, something that shows up fairly often in smaller scale Chardonnays, but not often in the ripe, honeyed ones.

Better still to go after the way the wines feel in the mouth:

Freemarks have a texture all their own. While most Chardonnays have almost a silky feel on the tongue, Freemarks are cut from a rougher fabric. Which I am not sure, but one with a noticeable nap. It is their combination of rich flavors and firm texture that makes them the quintessential wine for lobster and drawn butter. The flavors match up. The textures provide welcome relief from the embarrassment of riches.

The man behind the wine is Brad Webb, the same spirit who designed the original Hanzells, but not exactly the same winemaker. At least the Freemarks behave differently from Webb's earlier efforts, especially as agers. The first year in bottle, they tend to be just slightly out of sorts, a little rough and raw. Then all the pieces come together and stay together for four, five, six years. At some mysterious moment they plunge over a veritable cliff. The color darkens. The flavors become old ones, not completely gone but sharply different from those in the wine at full form. When that day comes, we hasten through the last bottle or two of our supply.

Two vineyards contribute to the wine. Both belong to owning partners in the winery. One, called Connolly-Carpy, lies directly east of Rutherford. If others in its neighborhood are any indicator, it provides the bold ripeness of flavor and the ample body. The other vineyard, called Jaeger for short, is at the north end of Big Ranch Road, in an angle formed by Trefethen to the west and Monticello to the south. Its contributions would seem to be toward firmness.

The series started impressively in 1967 and has never let down. Throughout the 1970s the winery maintained a steady gait in which the odd years slightly outshone the even ones until the end of the decade.

1975 One of the gems of them all. Held very well into 1980, then began showing its age.

1976 In the pack.

1977 Not quite the 1975, but close.

1978 Of the even-numbered years, well the most attractive through its sixth birthday.

1979 Rather hard and lacking ripe fruit flavors for a Freemark; the least of the odd-numbered years on that score, but a wine that lived well for a good eight years.

1980 An all-time favorite. Rich, ripe, yet still with its faint hint of asparagus as a counterpoint. Admirable with chicken wings in a mustard sauce, veal ragout, fettuccine with lox, *osso bucco,* salmon in sorrel, lobster, and almost everything else we love to eat. Showed signs of starting to slide late in 1986, but still a pleasure to drink.

1981 All the traditional notes—ripe fruit, asparagus, the toasty note from wood—and the typical, nappy textures. Rich enough for Trader Vic's Pâké crab, subtle enough for plain chicken.

1982 Had some harshness early, but had come around by late 1985. Probably always to run in the pack.

1983 Spot-on Freemark Abbey; perhaps the best after 1980. In mid-1986 able to stand up to a difficult pasta dressed with shrimp, Parmesan cheese, tomato, and herbs. First-rate with salmon right through its career to date.

1984 One of the best of its vintage; very close to 1983 all around.

1985 Running with the leaders of a superior vintage.

RAYMOND VINEYARD & CELLAR

Of all the Napa Valley Chardonnays, this is the one to cheer up people who like to anthropomorphize wines, because it is every bit as big and gentle as Walt Raymond, the man who makes it, and that means 240 pounds of the nicest guy you have ever met. It is a much more expansive argument for assembled Chardonnay than the Freemark Abbey. Though it started out as an estate wine, all recent vintages have come from a still-expanding string of ranches reaching all the way to Carneros.

A typical Raymond Chardonnay splits some of the differences between Trefethen and Freemark Abbey, and launches out in some directions of its own as well. It most resembles the Trefethen for silky textures, takes after the Freemark Abbey for sweetly ripe fruit, and follows a different path from either in being rather clearly marked by a toasty note from its time in barrel. This is not to say it is a woody. Not at all. But, fugitive as the note is, oak does show up as an identifying mark at more than one sip between the start and finish of a bottle.

Like most of the ripe, fleshy Californians, it is great with lobster and irreplaceable with the avocado, sprouts, sesame, roasted nuts, and fresh fruits and vegetables that define California cuisine as much as it can be defined.

The home vineyard surrounds the winery, just about dead center in the Napa Valley. The exact spot is between the state highway on the west and the Napa River on the east, on the south side of Zinfandel Lane, a crossroad not far south of St. Helena. The location is about as far north on the valley floor as Chardonnay grows to any notable end. The other contributing vineyards range south through the Big Ranch Road area and on to Carneros. As good as the estate wines were, the blended ones seem to have superior stuffings all around, perfect demonstrations of the Jack Sprat syndrome at work, with fat from the north balanced off against lean from the south.

Logic has its way in the case of Raymond Chardonnay. It ages on a longer curve than the darker, riper Freemark Abbey, but less long than the paler, firmer Trefethens, though it may be a shade early to make the latter claim.

1979 Somewhat overwhelmed by oak and other bouquets from the winemaking.

1980 Not pungently varietal in its fruit flavors, but specific nonetheless. Nice counterpoint of soft first impression with firmer finish.

1981 Perfect marriage of ripe apple and sweet oak, perfect interplay of softness and firmness in texture. We drank a bale of it through 1984; by 1986 it was beginning to show some weary qualities.

1982 Ripe and round in the house style. Not an apparent ager.

1983 A shade more wood than the 1980, but every bit as firm a structure. All polish and pleasure at the end of 1985.

1984 Much in the vein of 1980. Splendidly fresh and lively with lobster in early 1987.

1985 In the flush of youth, a short stride ahead of the 1984.

1986 Unmistakable in style, yet begins to show the migration toward cooler vineyards with leaner flavors and firmer textures.

STONY HILL VINEYARD

One fine summer's day in 1978 we trotted out a 1964 Stony Hill for two visitors, on the grounds the bottle was from the year of their marriage. We were wrong by a year or two. I felt as bad as if I had started out for the dentist's and ended up having lunch with Stephen Jay Gould instead.

The wine retaught every lesson Stony Hill had been teaching for years before. Proportion is everything. Subtlety of flavor is a virtue in a wine rigged to go for distance. Patience is its own reward. Etc., etc., etc. What I am trying to say here is that proper Stony Hills from the early 1960s through 1978 had everything: a certain tenderness of texture to cover their sturdy basic framework, altogether appealing flavors of apple, and all kinds of grace notes from one source or another.

Most Chardonnays of the first rank will do well for ten years, but one almost always looks back with nostalgia at the bottles drunk when the wine was four to seven or eight years old. Not so with old Stony Hills. The 1964s never tasted better than when they were fourteen, unless it was when they were fifteen. So it was with the 1965s, 1967s, 1968s, 1973s, and so on until, I think, the 1978s, or maybe the 1980s. The wines of later years have been a counterpoint to the vineyard's earlier history—deeper colored, fuller, more definitively marked by oak, and much quicker to start onto the downslope.

The vineyards responsible for Stony Hill's traditional durability spill down the Napa Valley's hills of the morning light from a crest of more than a thousand feet down to the winery, at about six hundred feet. Fred and Eleanor McCrea began planting Chardonnay on them in 1954. Eleanor has continued since Fred's death in 1977, and is still adding a few vines here, a few more there, as she and her crew find another pocket of earth deep enough to hold grape roots.

1975 In the grand tradition, a wine of lean, applelike flavors and lean, applelike textures. In 1987 it had rounded out some, but still had years to live.

1976 Ahead of most in a drought year. More forward than most Stony Hills, but still in good form in 1984.

1977 In the vein of 1975, but without quite so many stuffings.

1978 A curious vintage for Stony Hill. The wine started out all angles and elbows like the 1975, but quickly softened and darkened. At or just past its peak in 1986.

1979 Again, had some mature notes early compared to earlier vintages. This one appeared to have peaked by 1985.

1980 An off-vintage, very quickly over the hill.

1981 Typically lean, austere wine early. Beginning to develop some bouquets by late 1986, when it showed very well indeed, first with whitefish, then with steaks of thresher shark.

1982 New, fleshier style well established by this vintage. The wine still showed the applelike Chardonnay flavors of its vineyard in late 1987, but was softer and more definitely marked by tastes of oak than the wines of the old regime.

1983 Follows the 1982, but has more stuffings. In late 1987 it was drinking well with foods such as chicken and veal.

1984 Much in the vein of 1982, but not quite so rich in Chardonnay flavors.

SMITH-MADRONE VINEYARD

Stuart and Charles Smith ask one to wait on their Chardonnays, or maybe it is the hills of the morning light that insist on time. The Smiths' vineyard lies just upslope from the ones that have made Stony Hill legendary for long life. Whether it is the Smiths or their steep slope or both, the richest of their wines keep gaining with the years for at least seven, which is how old the oldest bottle is as these researches run into their deadlines.

The style differs emphatically from that of the Smiths' downslope neighbors. While it has some of the same firmness, a definitive toasty note runs even with fruit in the young wine and sometimes gets more pronounced after a couple of years than it is at the beginning. The 1980s got us nervous on this point, making us suspect that the vintage was over the hill when, in fact, it was just gathering itself to make the leap up to maturity. Only a couple of other wines demonstrate as well as this one how essential perfectly balanced, deeply flavored fruit is to success in the toasty style. People who try with lesser grapes make wine that rushes to senility singing a one-note song.

Using grapes only from their own vines, the Smiths have

managed to do something like a slalom on a tightrope since their debut 1980. The two ends are in the ripe, toasty style they favor for themselves. For three years in the middle of their span they went against themselves, when the clamor for "food wine" rose up before their oldest wine could speak for itself, and sent them on a wayward search for extremes of delicacy and finesse. Fortunately the brothers righted their ship in time for the useful 1984 vintage and the splendid 1985.

1979 Almost overwhelmingly rich in every aspect, but especially the toasty notes of barrel fermentation. A stunning wine again and again through 1984, and still in mid-1987.

1980 Not so mind-boggling as the 1979, but perhaps the greater wine. Forever elusive in flavor. Still, in mid-1987, definite notes of toasty oak give way more and more with each passing sip to dictionary-perfect flavors of Chardonnay. The only Chardonnay ever to put a Freemark Abbey 1980 in the shade for us (once, in the summer of 1986).

1981 Off the pace by a long distance.

1982 Agreeable, but in the pack.

1983 Running mate to the 1981.

1984 Back on form. Richly appealing fruit flavors played off against subtle ones from oak. Good balance to last for a while.

1985 Easily the best since 1980. Deeply appealing flavors of Chardonnay; welcome bouquets from wood and other work in the winery. Good balance to last for a while.

Back at the beginning of these ruminations on Napa Valley Chardonnays, I offered the notion that at least twenty wineries offer outstanding examples, and thus far I have gotten through only eight. I am not going to go much farther either, having promised at the start of the book to stick with a handful of personal favorites. But another four will serve to show how narrow these choices have to be to keep matters within some reasonable number of pages.

ROBERT MONDAVI WINERY

Mondavi, it seems, is always in the hunt. His Chardonnays have silky textures and the complex flavors that come from properly marrying fruit and oak. One of their other great virtues is consistency. Bottle in, bottle out, they give pleasure with veal, chicken, pastas in creamy or cheesy sauces, in fact with any reasonably chosen food. They come into the world all polished and harmonious and stay in top form for three, four, sometimes five years. Older, they often begin to show hints of the varnishy side of oak.

A considerable proportion of the grapes come from the two large Mondavi vineyards, Tokalon and Oak Knoll. The rest of the grapes grow from Oakville south to Carneros.

Folie à Deux Winery

Folie à Deux came out of the blocks fast with its 1981, winning a whole string of medals in major competitions and otherwise setting off critical fireworks. Young, the wines are the all-too-typical California Chardonnay: equal parts of fruit and oak running on separate though parallel tracks. What excites the imagination is their firm structure and good balance. Tasting them, one has the sense that these wines are going to age into a much greater sum than their early parts. They come from two vineyards, one just south of St. Helena, the other at Yountville.

Shafer Vineyards

Grower John Shafer and his winemaker son, Doug, strike for light, crisp textures and fruit flavors from the tarter end of the apple's range. The resulting wines are ones that have appealed to us most while they have been young—three and four years old—and when we have had lightly flavored meals to go with them. The grapes come from two family-owned vineyards, one beneath the looming brow of Stag's Leap, the other about a mile south along the Silverado Trail.

Sequoia Grove Vineyards

The label has yielded as many as three Chardonnays per vintage: one from a Cutrer property in Sonoma, one from bought-in Napa Valley grapes, and one from the winery property at Oakville, straight across from the Robert Mondavi Winery. The latter, called Allen Family Vineyard, has been a consistent demonstration of how to marry the flavors of Chardonnay with those of oak so as to have something that is neither the one nor the other, but complicated and altogether appealing anyhow. The style has enough heft and substance that the wines age well for at least five years, which is as long as we have had the patience to wait.

Carneros

More than any other district within the North Coast, Carneros keeps me uncertain. Time and again its wines, show the fleeting hint of garden-fresh asparagus that sets Chardonnay apart from other whites. In blind tasting notes from the 1987 San Francisco Fair and Exposition, the word *asparagus* crops up in the description of every single Carneros Chardonnay I tasted, and yet two or three of its vineyards yield abundantly fruity character and at least one can turn out wines that smack decidedly of pineapple. The toasty notes of barrel fermentation and on-lees aging show up readily in some of the wines from here, and little or not at all in others, and all of this in a couple of square miles of consistent southerly exposure and homogenous climate.

Ah, well, Chardonnay is a young grape variety in the neighborhood, and I am still learning.

CUVAISON WINERY

It is a deal easier to watch for well-known wineries on the way down than it is to spot the ones coming up. Leaders in a field have a track record to live up to, so their missteps magnify themselves. Not only that, people serve wines of great reputation often, giving tasters plenty of opportunity for scrutiny. Wines of no particular reputation, meanwhile, have to make one brilliant stride to free themselves from the pack, or else pull away slowly by being admirable over a long, long course.

Cuvaison has been in the quiet category for several years and could be ready to sprint for the lead. Its Chardonnays from 1980 onward have shown not only steady improvement but a sharpening focus in style; its richly scented, firmly structured 1985 alone has the quality to push the name several notches up the ladder before it is through.

The winery has suffered from an erratic history, having gone through three ownerships and at least as many winemakers since its founding in 1972. None of them agreed on style, niche, or much of anything else. However, the current Swiss owners go back to 1979, as does winemaker John Thacher. Fewer than half of Napa's wineries have that much history. More important, Cuvaison's four-hundred-acre Carneros vineyard, first planted in 1980, now contributes a long 80 percent of all the grapes. This may be the decisive factor, to judge by the two vintages dominated by it.

The Carneros vines—in the jaw formed by State Road 121 and Duhig Road, less than a mile from the Sonoma line—crest three knolls, two of them good sized. Among them they give the winery 360 degrees of exposure and a variety of shallower and deeper soils in which to hunt for balance and complexity. The evidence leans more and more in the direction of success. With the 1985 in particular, Thacher seems to have matched techniques to vineyard to produce a wine that is rich in grape flavors yet much more than merely fruity.

1980 Cleanly made, quite tart; a pleasing but comparatively simple wine.

1981 A step up in style from 1980, but still in the pack.

1982 Much in the vein of 1980, but a shade more noticeable for its taste of oak.

1983 Bigger and riper than previous vintages, it has a neatly understated touch of wood. Much the most stylish wine in the series up to its time. Holding well in 1987.

1984 Could have tasted a bit more of Chardonnay, but its distinct toasty notes did not overwhelm the fruit. With that, a balanced, firm wine.

1985 By miles the wine of the series. Rich aromas of fruit subtly touched by wood in a firm, fresh wine with all the earmarks of an excellent ager.

1986 At bottling, appeared ready to go the 1985 one better.

BUENA VISTA WINERY & VINEYARD

A lot of wineries can drive observers mildly daft by putting out three or more Chardonnays of differing stripes, but nearly all of them do so with grapes from scattered properties. Buena Vista's varied roster comes from just one place, the vineyards surrounding the cellars.

The regular bottling is not the same animal as the select one (originally called Special Selection, now labeled Private Reserve). Neither tastes exactly like the ultra-select Jeanette's Vineyard, but both can be confused for it. The salvation for fretful buyers is that all three honor their grape variety. The background is this:

The regular bottling is just that, the run of sixty acres of vines planted in 1970. Jill Davis, Buena Vista's winemaker since 1983, ferments a portion in barrel and ages all of it in oak. If there is a classical Carneros regional flavor, it is the faint suggestion of garden-fresh asparagus, and the lean, tart regular bottling has it every year. The special lot is from grapes chosen for riper aromas at the crusher. All of it ferments and ages in new barrels. The result is a richer but not fleshier wine than the regular bottling, and a set of flavors that bring pineapple to mind easily, but asparagus not at all. Jeanette's is a single clone grown in a special five-acre block. Davis puts it through the same program as the Private Reserve, but gets a wine that, somehow, wanders all around the other two. It is still too early to know how these wines will age, but I am not putting all my money on all of the special bottlings for the long haul. Some of the regulars seem to have enough stuffings to outlast the specials, and do have a greater freshness about them. All of the wines seem to want a year or two in bottle to round out.

Buena Vista's considerable plantings—sixty-five acres and more coming—straddle the Napa-Sonoma county line, all of them on a wind- and water-eroded set of slopes that face generally south, but have folds oriented more east-west then north-south. The general exposure faces straight across Ramal Road to Domaine Chandon's largest single vineyard, and beyond it toward San Francisco across the Bay.

Tasting notes reflect both regular and special bottlings.

1980 Regular bottling lean, notable for its regional touch of aspara-
gus. Riper S.S. rich with the flavors of both Chardonnay and wood; darkening by 1984, but still healthy.

1981 Both bottlings ripe and full—and more stylish than the predecessor vintage.

1982 Regular much in the vein of 1980, though more polished. The Private Reserve was almost viscous as a young wine, it was so ripe.

1983 The regular seemed a shade off the pace set earlier. The Jeanette's, meanwhile, outdid previous special lots for ripeness.

1984 Regular lot began particularly crisp, subtle, and inviting, then seemed riper, even a bit heavy by 1987. The Private Reserve began and remains rich with both ripe fruit and new wood.

1985 Lean, firm vintage for regular; fuller, fleshier one for Private Reserve; yet the two seemed closer together in both style and substance than earlier wines.

Sonoma Valley

The Sonoma Valley is where Sonoma begins to be hard to fig-
ure, partly because it overlaps Carneros. A long quarter of its five thousand acres of vineyard hold Chardonnay, this in a region with a climate that changes so quickly and continuously from its bay end northward that the variety shows a dozen different faces along its long, skinny axis.

The temptation is to think that the finest properties lie within the Carneros, or on the low-lying spots near it. Certainly the most refined wines come from those precincts. However, some more assertive styles from farther north do not brook being overlooked.

SONOMA-CUTRER LES PIERRES

Although the winery is in the Russian River Valley (and described in that section), its most notable vineyard is Les Pierres, a rocky piece of flatland near the hills west of Sonoma town.

Les Pierres yields a leaner, more reserved wine than either of Sonoma-Cutrer's Russian River Valley bottlings, and a more fascinating one for its subtleties of flavor. As a point of reference, its firm textures and understated fruit make it one step better suited to salmon than its fleshier, bolder siblings.

Bill Bonetti makes minor concessions to place, but overall the style of winemaking is exactly the same for all three, so the differences belong with the vines.

1981 Round on top, firm underneath, and saturated with fruit flavors that somehow manage to be restrained at the same time. A hint of toasty oak rounded out a house style that was born mature. Versatile with food, but outstanding with salmon and other rich fish. Still in top form in mid-1986.

1982 Much quicker to age than the 1981; already hinting at weariness in early 1986.

1983 Much the firmest and finest of the winery's 1983s. Early in its career, all elegance and complexity with a creamy mushroom dish. Seems to be splitting the difference between the 1981 and 1982 for longevity.

1984 In its earliest youth, much along the lines of the 1981. In 1987 it delivered everything one could ask with a memorably succulent chicken dish at a Sonoma restaurant called l'Esperance.

1985 *Ooh, ooh,* and *aaaah*. The 1984 all over again, only with just a hint more depth of flavor.

HACIENDA WINERY CLAIR DE LUNE

For years these wines have been small enigmas, subtle for fruit flavors and firm to outright hard for texture while they are young, then only slightly fuller of flavor and softer of texture after they have had three or four years to round out.

We would drink one or two bottles each year with somewhat puzzled enjoyment, and move on to other wines. And then the winery showed off its 1978 and 1979 at one of the seminars surrounding the Sonoma Wine Auction of 1986, and we commenced to rethink the whole question. The 1978 had the faintest hint of the tropical flavors that come to ripe, wood-aged whites in California, while the 1979 was all applelike fruit. Both put the rest in the shade, and both were poised to continue in fine health for years. Later vintages have seemed, if anything, harsher and more noticeably flavored by oak than these two ever were, but only by a jot. Whether they come around as their forerunners or not, Haciendas are Chardonnays for the patient.

The primary, sometimes only vineyard has been the one at the winery, just east of the Sonoma town plaza.

The Rest of Sonoma

Sonoma has a good deal more to its Chardonnay plantings, much of the remainder in the Alexander and Dry Creek valleys, still more in other corners. These parts of the county are harder to handicap than the Russian River Valley, Carneros, and Sonoma Valley. Vineyards of singular character come rarely, and when they do, their wines often show contradictory profiles. There is also a certain similarity to the upper Napa Valley, in the sense that some of the assembled wines based in these parts seem handsomer than those from single properties. Estate-bottled wines go first in the list, wines from specific AVAs second, and assembled wines third. There is, most emphatically, no implication of preference in the sequence.

ALEXANDER VALLEY VINEYARDS

From a climate where one might legitimately expect a ripe, fleshy Chardonnay, one gets instead a lean, light one better suited to fresh oysters and poached whitefish than to butter-soaked lobster. Equally as surprising, Alexander Valley Vineyards's owner-winemaker Hank Wetzel apprenticed at Freemark Abbey, where lobster-worthy Chardonnay is a given.

Exactly how Wetzel has gone about wringing such a light, dry wine out of vineyards that tip toward the setting sun remains a mystery. His techniques lean toward light, fresh wines, but then so do many others.

Wetzel's debut vintage, 1975, caught the attention of critics for being exactly what the label has stood for ever since. Come to think of it, there is not a freak vintage in the series to date.

1975 Early, an uncommonly light-bodied, delicately flavored, refreshing Chardonnay. In 1986 still holding to that pattern.

1976 No note.

1977 Not quite 1975, but not far off the pace either.

1978 Riper, fuller wine early, and riper, fuller wine late. A blunter wine by far than the 1975, and older in 1986.

1979 No note.

1980 So crisp, fresh, and full of appetizing but understated fruit it brought to mind thoughts of oysters during and after its youth.

1981 Kin to 1980 early. By mid-1986 had deepened and strengthened its fruit flavors, but was still impressively young and vital.

1982 A bit fuller-bodied than most in youth, but with typically delicate and appealing fruit flavors in the finish.

1983 Spot-on crisp, appley Chardonnay flavors, with a body and texture to match when released, but quickly showed fatter, riper flavors than either the 1981 or 1982. At a satisfying peak in mid-1986.

1984 On release, had the light crispness of the 1980 and 1981 and, as usual, an altogether pleasing set of fruit aromas.

1985 The usual pale hue and aromatic suggestion of apples, but harsher in youth than earlier vintages.

CLOS DU BOIS

Clos du Bois has a foot in each camp, with its Flintwood Vineyard in Dry Creek Valley and Calcaire in Alexander. The two properties differ, according to my tasting notes. Both wines catch plenty of wood for my taste, but both manage to show fruit through the oak. Flintwood manages to show a little more in blind tastings, but Calcaire, somehow, makes a silkier, subtler impression at the dinner table, particularly after it has had three or four years to mature in the bottle. They live up to two tentative generalities about where they come from. The Calcaire may show a hint of asparaguslike tones, but is more likely to smack a bit of apple; the Flintwood goes exactly in reverse.

For the sake of thinking about viticultural areas and individual properties, consecutive sets of tasting notes follow in alphabetic order by vineyard.

Calcaire

1980 Plenty of wood, but fruit showed through in the finish.

1981 Riper and fuller than the 1980 in youth. By 1985 a beautifully balanced and polished Chardonnay with enough delicacy to accompany the featheriest of soufflés.

1982 Much in the vein of 1980.

1983 Riper fruit and toastier oak than earlier vintages, but still subtle and balanced.

1984 Pretty woody, but exactly the right cooperage to marry well with ripe fruit. Again, very well balanced.

1985 Somehow manages to dance back and forth between the apple- and asparaguslike sides of Chardonnay. Well marked by oak, and well balanced, as house style dictates. Look forward to seeing this one with four or five years of age on it.

Flintwood

1980 Definite asparaguslike notes and well restrained wood. Fatter than the Calcaire of the same vintage.

1981 Fruit wins out easily over subtle oak in a wine that showed polish early. Restrained enough to match up well with Jean-Louis Palladin's Sole Watergate.

1982 Toastier and oakier than its forebears, or less full of fruit, but not far off line.

1983 Faintly riper fruit than previous vintages, and much the same toasty note as in the 1982.

1984 Some toasty oak, but fruit wins going away in the finish. Appealingly light and fresh in youth.

1985 Still young and hard in 1987, but leaning in all the right directions.

SIMI WINERY

Sometimes I wonder if the wines have changed since 1980, or if it is I who have improved. When that vintage appeared, I liked it but wished it had a bit less oak perfuming it. Not only have later vintages turned out exactly that way, so has the 1980 as it has matured.

It and every vintage since have turned out small-bottle wines, the kind that empty out before my dinner plate is bare, and that is the final measure of any wine's worth. If the food is gone and there is still wine, it does not matter how interesting the wine was. If the wine and food disappear together, the wine was a good one. But if a lot of dinner is looking at an empty glass . . .

My tasting notes regularly edge up into the gee-whiz category. Simi wines are everything—fresh, light, rich, full, fruity, bouqueted, and anything else you want to add to the list. And that, I guess, is the point. Whatever facet it is one seeks in a Chardonnay, a Simi will show it somewhere between the beginning and end of a bottle. As for versatile with food, it is that too.

Simi does not legally belong in the Sonoma section at this hour, but it is creeping up on membership quickly enough to make more sense here than anywhere else. The winery has two periods of recent history, before Zelma Long and since Zelma Long. Before Long it was all Sonoma. Since, the regular Chardonnays have waffled by origin, sometimes coming from Mendocino, sometimes from Mendocino and Sonoma. The first Reserve was also Mendocino, but all since have been pure Sonomans. The results of all this shuffling provide one of the more elegant demonstrations of the fact that, in California, the winemaker still matters as much as or more than any particular piece of ground. Long has looked only at individual properties, never AVAs or other larger boundaries. She also has set a steady, though curving, course through all the changes.

These notes dwell on the regular bottlings. The Reserves follow the same style, but up the ante all around. They have kept a little more to the toasty style than the regular bottling in recent vintages.

1980 *Mendocino* A gold hue announced a deft marriage of ripe Chardonnay with toasty oak notes in a well-balanced wine. It had charm early; it has, if anything, gotten younger. In autumn 1986 its fruit flavors dominated all. At the same hour, the Reserve maintained a toastier set of flavors.

1981 *Mendocino* Toasty oak notes dominated first impressions, but fruit always won out in the finish. In 1983 and 1986 balanced, polished, a reliable pleasure with salmon.

1982 *Mendocino-Sonoma* The usual polish and balance; from this vintage fruit seemed always to have the upper hand over toasty oak. A good bet to cellar for a few years.

1983 *Mendocino-Sonoma* A repeat of the 1982 for flavors, though possibly one shade less firm in texture.

1984 *Mendocino-Sonoma* One of the very finest of its vintage follows the pattern set in 1982 of looking more to fruit and less to toasty oak for the heart of the wine. Beautifully balanced between tart and rich in 1987, when it was just settling into stride.

MATANZAS CREEK WINERY

For several years Matanzas Creek stood as the main rival to Hanzell among Sonoma Chardonnays of heroic proportions, though it never reached quite the same size. Each year was the same story: dark gold color, powerful aromas of ripe Chardonnay, and even more powerful aromas of new oak. They could last pretty well—the 1979 stood up to turkey and all the trimmings in 1985—could intrigue one with the depth of their fruit, but they never won a fan with gentle charms. Then, the 1984 turned over a new leaf, offering well-nigh-perfect Chardonnay flavors with just a buttressing touch of wood and proportions far less huge than earlier vintages. Much the most refined wine of the series to date, it was the first vintage at Matanzas Creek for new winemaker Dave Ramey, who learned his craft as an assistant to Zelma Long at Simi.

The vineyards that turned out all the monsters could also, it seems, show a gentle side without losing the essence of Chardonnay.

1979 Big early, big late, but a fascination for the depth of its ripe fruit flavors. Still drinking very well with such as Thanksgiving turkey in 1985.

1980 Bigger than the 1979. Too much of a good thing early; failed to track it into age.

1981 Forceful toasty flavors dominated a big-to-gigantic wine in the early going.

1982 Splendid, honeyed fruit from a superior vintage kept pace with a generous dollop of oak. A pleasing large-scale wine early, and still going strong in early 1987, when it could keep perfect harmony with a fillet of salmon in spicy butter.

1983 No note.

1984 Much the most refined wine in the series to date. Adroit balancing of ripe fruit with new wood flavors; good balance, though seemed early a wine for near-term drinking rather than long keeping.

Davis Bynum Winery

Bynum's Artist Series (formerly Reserve) Chardonnays of the past several vintages have run close to the pacesetters in Sonoma Chardonnay, particularly attractive wines for catching the applelike varietal flavors of Chardonnay. While a recognizable taste of oak marks them early, favorable vintages have aged well enough for it to blend into the fruit flavors after two or three years in bottle. The base is Russian River Valley grapes, part of them from the neighborhood around the winery, part from the Chalk Hill district, but fruit from other parts of Sonoma figures in the blends. Sonoma Mountain, in particular, has been a regular contributor. The 1982 and 1985 have had particular appeal as young wines.

Mendocino

Mendocino has come even later to Chardonnay than Sonoma, and thus is, no surprise, harder to handicap. The county has fifteen hundred bearing acres and twenty-five hundred acres planted to the variety. A considerable portion of both totals is out west in Anderson Valley, but a majority lies inland, from Redwood Valley south all the way to Hopland.

The two districts yield wines as different as their disparate climates might suggest. Chardonnays from the Anderson Valley tend to be firm to outright austere in texture and understated in fruit flavors. Those from around Ukiah tend to belong to the rich, ripe school. Some admirable bottlings blend grapes from both places. For the moment, we measure the territory by the Navarros, although Fetzer and Milano come into the picture more and more.

Navarro Vineyards

Ted Bennett makes two Chardonnays each year, one identified as Mendocino, the other as an estate-bottled Private Reserve from vines flanking his Anderson Valley winery. They are distinctly different wines. The Mendocino bottling always seems to have a straightforward flavor of fruit about it, while the Reserve leans almost always in the direction of oaky bouquets, a separation that makes choosing easy for bibbers.

We have yet to test hard either wine for ability to age. The 1981 vintage first caught our eye. It was quickly surpassed by the 1982, which in turn has been outdone by the 1985s.

CENTRAL COAST

The Central Coast has done well by Chardonnay in its short history. However, its memorable wines have come from such an erratic pattern of vintages, and from vineyards so widely scattered throughout such contradictory climates and terrains, that few generalizations are tempting.

I have been a long time learning how difficult it is for winemakers in a new place to zero in on what will become, someday, the style that favors what the vineyards can give again and again. Now that I have figured that much out, sitting in judgment of the Central Coast is no fun at all. One vintage from a label appeals, and the next does not, while the neighbor proceeds the other way about. Where to put the praise, where to put the blame?

In the more crowded territories of the North Coast, possibilities lead straight to probabilities. A dozen, twenty, fifty wines say something about region and vintage together. In the Central Coast, the contributors in any one place number closer to a trio than a dozen, and history is a dozen vintages rather than thirty or forty.

And so individual wines are altogether appealing, but not altogether understandable. The notes on North Coast wines are stabs in the dark compared to regions that go back to the Romans; the ones that follow are a helluva lot less well directed than the stabs. As a gesture to orderliness, they work from north to south.

Santa Cruz Mountains

Chardonnay goes back a long way in the Santa Cruz Mountains, at least as far as the turn of the century with old Paul Masson, who planted some on steep slopes above Saratoga well before Prohibition, but a good deal remains to be learned anyhow. For one thing, the mountains are two different worlds. One set of slopes looks down into a million bedrooms of the San Francisco Peninsula, usually through a veil of warm smog. The other set looks through cool, foggy but clean air toward the Pacific. For another, the region attracts almost no one but individualists. Some would say iconoclasts. The combined effect of place and man is an encyclopedic range of styles exaggerated by variable levels of skill.

It will be a long while, if ever, before substantial acreages are planted to Chardonnay in these tumbled hills and a longer time than that before hints of consensus arrive. Every winery in the territory, meanwhile, has fiercely loyal partisans. My votes, cast at the bunker door, go to Dan Gehrs at Congress Springs and Randall Grahm at Bonny Doon.

CONGRESS SPRINGS VINEYARDS

Dan Gehrs has turned out several deft Chardonnays from little patches scattered here and there through the eastern slopes of the Santa Cruz Mountains above Saratoga. Young, his wines are light in body, lightsome in Chardonnay flavor, and less lightly touched by oak, and young is when I have come to them. California has plenty of big, honeyed Chardonnays, but not enough of this sort of delicacy.

BONNY DOON VINEYARD

Randall Grahm's impressive first vintage from his own wines, on a bench four miles inland from and eight hundred feet above the sea, was 1985, and thus is no evidence on which to build any profound conclusions. But Grahm remains the man to watch among the west-siders because he has shown a touch with almost everything he has made since 1981, including several Chardonnays from Monterey.

Monterey

Monterey is a salutary lesson in not rushing too fast to judgment. The early wines from what is now Arroyo Seco were thin, tasted curiously of something vegetative, and otherwise did little to invite themselves to stay for dinner. "Early" means late 1960s through the mid-1970s. The growers were, however, not asleep. A couple of the 1978s and a growing number of wines from later vintages have been round on the tongue, with flavors that bring to mind fresh peach. They became so distinctive that my notes from blind tastings began to be dotted with the initials MNS for Monterey New School, almost always correctly. (The flip side of the coin is that winemakers in other districts saw the charms and learned to imitate them; during the 1987 judging season I began hedging my bets with CCNS for Central Coast New School, and still came down in error for the first time. Several of my CCNSs came from Mendocino, a couple from Sonoma.)

Arroyo Seco tempts me to make one generality, and that is that Chardonnays from these precincts need youth on their side. A touch of oak does them no harm then, but they seem to live on the sweet freshness of youth.

We have hung on to a number of them for five and six years, never to a satisfying end. What seems a delicate note of oak in a young wine grows intrusive, and the soft, fleshy textures of early days turn sharp with time in bottle. A longer run of vintages may well make a liar out of me, but for now I am not tempted to hang on to wines that taste so good young and so much less so older.

The tiny AVA called Chalone could not be more different from Arroyo Seco if four hundred miles separated them, not just four. It is, at this point, a one-wine AVA for Chardonnay, and is likely to remain so, but it is not to be ignored.

VENTANA VINEYARDS

Grower Doug Meador has a considerable planting of Chardonnay in his 350-acre ranch straight west from Soledad, at the base of the west hills, and he has sold grapes to a whole troupe of other winemakers for vineyard-identified wines that have won several different sets of fans for the region. His own wines—he makes two or more differing styles a year—speak ever more eloquently for his wines, and for the rest of the Arroyo Seco AVA. The 1981s were the first to impress; the 1985s went them one better.

The history is not long. The first wine under Meador's label came from 1978.

CHALONE VINEYARDS

Chalone nestles onto a merely rolling spot in the steep to nearly vertical hills east of Soledad, right below the craggy outcrop of basalt called Pinnacles National Monument. (A stylized silhouette of the pinnacles decorates the label.) Although Chalone and Ventana are in line of sight of each other, neither the growing conditions nor the wines bears much resemblance one to the other. The Chalone vines are high above the chilling Salinas Valley fogs that visit Ventana almost daily during the growing season and are tipped toward the setting sun rather than shielded from it by nearby slopes. Dick Graff set an austere style at Chalone, based on barrel fermentation and long aging on lees in an always damp cellar. The resulting wines are understated for fruit, but powerfully marked by smoky bouquets that remind me precisely of the smell of old-fashioned wooden kitchen matches burning. The wines last for a long time in their original condition, to the enchantment of their fanciers.

Edna Valley

The small AVA of Edna Valley, just south of the cheerful small city of San Luis Obispo, won its first and thus far major fame for Chardonnays of perplexing diversity. In the early 1970s several by the since-defunct Hoffman Mountain Ranch Winery approached champagne stocks in their pale tartness. In recent years the preference seems to have been for wines in the toasty, buttery school.

EDNA VALLEY VINEYARD

The younger sister of Chalone Vineyards has been producing Chardonnays much in the latter's distinctly toasty style since the late 1970s, and no surprise. Chalone directs the winemaking. The surprise is how well Edna Valley's subtly scented fruit stands up to the test. The 1981 and 1984 come to mind as specific evocations of both style and region.

Santa Barbara

Santa Barbara, with Chardonnay as with all other varieties, remains a puzzlement, except for the prospects that the Santa Maria Valley has a lead over the rest of the county in the early going, much as it does with Pinot Noir. For my taste, two of the pioneers continue to show the way for the rest.

FIRESTONE VINEYARDS

Right from its beginnings in 1975, Firestone has put the pleasant flavors of Chardonnay grapes at the forefront of its style. That, coupled with consistent balance, has made the label one of the safest buys on any restaurant list.

The vineyards flank the winery on a tabletop mesa almost due north of the Santa Ynez Valley town of Los Olivos.

ZACA MESA WINERY

Three years later out of the blocks than Firestone, Zaca Mesa took the opposite route with Chardonnay, leaning more toward the toasty and buttery flavors that come from winemaking than the faintly peachy ones that seem to come with well-ripened local grapes, but balancing the two more adroitly than most. Of its two bottlings, regular and American reserve, the latter is the richer in both departments.

The home vineyards lie only a short distance north of Firestone's, atop the same mesa, but Zaca Mesa has also reached out to other vineyards in the Central Coast to augment its supply of fruit for the regular bottlings.

BYRON VINEYARD

The label got off the marks only with the vintage of 1984, but it belongs to Ken Brown, who developed Zaca Mesa's style from 1978 through 1983 and who is pursuing small lots with a keenly developed sense of style. His debut vintage makes him a man to watch.

GEWÜRZTRAMINER

GEWÜRZTRAMINER HAS ALWAYS SEEMED TO BE A cross we true believers have to bear. People will not give, at least so far have not given, the wine a proper day in the sun. Years' worth of old columns, old magazine pieces, and old books of mine treat of Gewürztraminer in tones somewhere between defensive and dirgelike.

One time I said trying to sell Gewürztraminer is like trying to sell a blind date. On a more optimistic occasion I allowed as how it had enjoyed a little boomlet between 1975 and 1979, but had lapsed back into limbo more lately.

This mistrust of my countrymen is, it turns out, a mite exaggerated. Production figures suggest that Gewürztraminer sales have been going up for years. From a mere 400 tons in 1960, crops increased to 1,400 tons by 1970, to 8,900 by 1980, and, magic moment, a shade more than 10,000 tons in 1983. They have waffled around the latter figure since then.

Its difficult-to-pronounce name is the most-offered explanation for public resistance to its charms, but that is only one of its burdens. In certain fussy-eater circles drinking Gewürztraminer is almost as low as eating coconut, which is pretty low indeed to hear these people tell it. Vintners shrug and say Gewürztraminer sells briskly when they pour it in their tasting rooms, but stores will not take it. The real problem, says Pollyanna, is simpler: Demand is hard to create without supply. A ten thousand-ton crop equates, roughly, to six hundred thousand cases, or not quite enough to provide San Francisco with a bottle per head per month. San Francisco does not do all it could, but, still, one imagines whole states without a single bottle within their borders.

Well, I like Gewürztraminer as much as coconut and am going to keep on trying to organize a parade for it. It will be a small parade. Without conceding anything to fussy eaters, the plain truth is, Gewürztraminer is self-limiting, like bagels or chocolate. One glass at a sitting can be enough. Even its most loyal fans will not argue to have more than a couple of bottles a month, so vivid are its flavors.

Exactly because one glass can be enough, Gewürztraminer makes a superior aperitif, one that brings guests to the table in a condition to admire the fine points of a meal. Spicy sausages, liver pâtés, mustard sauces, sauerkraut, none of these daunt it. It has such a wealth of aromas that no other wine can match it outdoors in kite-flying weather, which is as right a time for terrines and pâtés at the hors d'oeuvres hour.

Conventional wisdom has Gewürztraminer smelling spicy, based on the fact that *gewürz* translates from German as "spicy." I have smelled the whole spice rack without being reminded of Gewürztraminer. When litchi gets promoted from floral to spicy, I will take the point, because that is the definitive flavor association for me. More generally, floral perfume seems closer to right than spicy, particularly because Gewürztraminers that do not quite bring litchi to mind often recall whatever it is that perfumes Pond's cold creams. (If the latter has escaped your notice, it comes close to sweet peas.) This is a ridiculous pair of flavor associations to impose on a wine that already is having trouble gaining public confidence, particularly when Gewürztraminer does not taste like either litchi or Pond's cold cream. It just hints at one or the other while not smelling at all like apples or cherries or any ordinary fruit. In short, it goes a little past floral and not quite up to perfume, a shadowy area where it is either every man for himself or settle for litchi.

The litchi connection does not go all one way. Gewürztraminer's other counterweights, besides sausages, terrines, and pâtés, are any and all Cantonese dishes that might contain or be served with litchi.

Once, to prove a point to a notorious fence sitter in matters of Traminers, I hauled a pair of Louis M. Martinis to lunch at the Imperial Palace in San Francisco. They were the 1968 and the 1972; we were eating in 1976, if memory serves, but it might have been 1977. Before we finished, we could see a track in the carpet where our waiter had beat his way back and forth between table and kitchen in a futile hunt for the dish that would outweigh wines that had withstood *choucroute garnie.*

For a wine with so finite a number of fans, Gewürztraminer has champions among winemakers in almost every California coastal district. Their ranks are a bit thin because only the dedicated keep at a wine this hard to grow, this hard to make, this hard to sell.

John Trefethen, who grows a fine patch of Gewürztraminer in the Napa Valley but does not make the wine for his own label, says that, to pick it right, he has to stand out in the vineyard day and night from the time the fruit starts looking ripe until he smells it. The minute the varietal perfumes waft up, the harvest must start. Wait a day, Trefethen says, and the wine will go too soft. Louis P. Martini feels much the same, but believes it is better to risk too soft a wine than give up on the fruit aromas.

Along with pronounced aromas, the wine has an almost inevitable little fillip of bitter in the finish. Therein is one of the reasons so many wineries leave a bit of sweetness. Nothing covers bitter better. Nearly all of the wines that advertise themselves as dry range between 0.3 and 0.7 percent residual sugar as against a 0.5 to 1.0 percent threshold of recognition for most of us. These driest bottlings take up a much larger proportion of this section than they do store shelves. A far larger volume of California Gewürztraminer ranges between 1.0 and 3.0 percent residual. As a gross generality, the drier ones are the more likely to smell like litchi, especially if grown in a cool climate, while sweeter ones more often bring cold cream to mind, especially if they come from middling warm spots. Get down to specifics, and both sorts grow in all the same places, both are finished across the same range of sweetness. Not any too rarely, the same winery will wind up in the litchi camp one year and cold cream the next, but neither vintage nor meteorological charts holds the key to this puzzle or the fact that some cellars linger forever between the extremes.

Wherever they fall within the scale of aromas, whether dry or not so dry, the wines from favored vineyards focus their flavors more keenly after two or three years in bottle. Some that start out pale and shadowy end up powerful in their varietal aromas. The ones that start out all full of themselves do not turn shy. Now and again, a Gewürztraminer will stay fresh and lively for eight, ten, even a dozen years, but it is no goal to aim at. The same wines taste every bit as good or better at three to six. Longer waits are a mere by-product of maniacal collecting.

This is not a wine that profits from the flavors of oak, however much its varietal flavors might seem to need taming. A few winemakers pass it through barrels, but hardly ever for the express purpose of picking up a flavor of oak. The purpose is more to soften it a bit, round it out, give it a smattering of table manners.

NORTH COAST

Gewürztraminer prospers in all its guises in the North Coast counties. The Anderson and Russian River valleys most closely resemble each other; no surprise, considering the cool, foggy similarity of their climates. The warm, sunny Alexander Valley stands at the opposite pole. The rest—Napa Valley, Sonoma Valley, Carneros—refuse to be pinned down so neatly, leaning sometimes toward the Anderson extreme, sometimes toward the Alexander, but almost always falling in the middle.

As of 1986 Sonoma County handily led the league in Gewürztraminer plantings in the North Coast, with most of 1,065 acres spread about rather evenly among the Russian River Valley, Sonoma Valley, Carneros, and Alexander Valley districts. Napa had 330, the bulk of it south of Oakville and north of Carneros. Mendocino's 290 acres are primarily at or near Ukiah, but the most fascinating patches are west of Philo in the Anderson Valley.

Anderson Valley

Every now and again, in trying to sort out California's vinous geography, the fantasy strikes: The French have tunneled from their embassy into the White House basement, overpowered the National Security Council, and thus captured control of the entire government. Within weeks the decree comes down. Each district must grow only one red and one white, and no more than two districts can share any grape variety.

At this point, having been appointed commissioner of taste in spite of my weakness for coconut, I always award the first patent on Gewürztraminer to Anderson Valley. Later, doubts flood in, but the first reaction never changes, probably because

171

so many fine Gewürztraminers have come from the neighborhood, and so few poor ones.

What the valley does particularly well is move Gewürztraminer as far as it can be from a faintly minty flavor it sometimes shares with the dimly related Muscat Canelli while the litchi flavors that Muscat cannot attain come often, if not automatically. The first small hint came from a 1973 Husch Vineyards. The clinchers were a memorable set of 1977s from Husch, Edmeades, and Navarro vineyards. The Husch and Edmeades came from their own vines; the Navarro also used Edmeades grapes, its own vineyard not then in bearing. One or more of the veterans has held up the banner every vintage since, joined in recent seasons by Hans Kobler's Lazy Creek.

NAVARRO VINEYARDS

When Ted Bennett and Deborah Cahn moved to an old sheep ranch not far west of Philo in 1974, one of their avowed purposes was to make a first-rate dry Gewürztraminer from their fledgling vineyards. It was an innocent decision, based mostly on the premise that someplace cool in California must be right for the variety because Alsace and the Alto Adige do so well by it in Europe.

Theirs is one of those cases in which seat-of-the-pants research has been exactly what was wanted. Navarro has turned out an unbroken string of altogether appealing wines from twenty-eight acres of vines that tip noticeably to the west and ever so slightly to the north.

Bennett has improved upon his original conviction. Through the first three vintages, his wines measured very near 1 percent of residual sugar. The latest, 1986, has only 0.4, about as dry as the wine usually wants to be in California.

In the early years he passed his Gewürztraminer through German oak casks for a few months because that was a norm in the literature. The result was a pleasant enriching of the textures but no taste of oak, so he has kept the habit. The turn in oak is only one of several ways in which Bennett puts a bit of polish on his wine, but it remains sturdy and straightforwardly varietal even so, as proper Gewürz ought to do. This is not ruffled-shirt-and-patent-pumps wine. It needs a touch of roughhouse about it because cool-climate Gewürztraminer is not the epitome of delicate in flavor or texture.

In a world in which perfect moments are ever harder to come by, at least one is not out of reach of shop clerks or even writers, and that is to get acquainted with Navarro Gewürztraminer over a plate of Margaret Fox's Chinese chicken salad at Café Beaujolais at the inland end of Ukiah Street in Mendocino town. If every card in the deck is in place, the Navarro will have a couple of years of bottle age, for this one, more than most, keeps adding facets with time in bottle.

1976 Outstanding Gewürztraminer character shadowed by hints of oak from then-new casks.

1977 A bit drier and more tart than the 1976, and even richer in the litchi side of Gewürztraminer just after its second birthday.

1978 No note.

1979 Ripe, rich with litchi aromas by spring 1981. Fat and soft before finishing dry.

1980 No note.

1981 No note.

1982 Beautifully balanced and full of floral perfumes from the outset.

1983 Impeccable notes of litchi. This is the vintage that taught one to get to Café Beaujolais for the Chinese chicken salad when it was two and taught the lesson even better at four.

1984 Still quite rough and not typically aromatic at a year, but approaching top form by its third birthday.

1985 Precocious for aromas of litchi. Leaner than most in the early going.

1986 As precocious as the 1985, but richer feeling. First among recent candidates for aging.

HUSCH VINEYARDS

Through changes in ownership and winemakers, near-neighbor Husch Vineyards has not been as consistent with the variety as

Navarro, but, in its most impressive vintages—1977, 1980, 1982—
it has been hard to distinguish from the Navarros except for the
presence of a slightly greater sweetness. The trend in style re-
verses Navarro's, having gone from bone-dry to a typical 1 percent residual sugar since the Hugo Oswald family bought the
property from founders Tony and Gretchen Husch.

One of the virtues of poor record keeping in the cellar is the
odd lost bottle with something to say. In the spring of 1987
single bottles of Husch 1973, 1975, and 1976 surfaced from the
bottom of a stack of oddments. The 1976 was a goner, but both
of the others still looked and tasted not merely healthy but lively—
tributes to the Anderson Valley as a growing region for Gewürztraminer. The 1973, pale, crisp, and pungent with litchi,
was the wine of the lot.

Russian River Valley

The Russian River Valley, not as small or homogenous as the
Anderson Valley, shows a broader spectrum of Gewürztraminer
if it is taken whole. However, a big chunk well west of Healdsburg and north of the river turns out wines that are far easier
to confuse with their Mendocino counterparts than they are to
distinguish from them. The litchilike notes are there, and so are
the sturdy frameworks. All of the wines in this list come from
that area save one from a vineyard well to the west, but just
south of the Russian River.

Louis M. Martini

We learned California Gewürztraminer on Louis M. Martinis,
starting with the 1956s. Back then they came from two vineyards, mountaintop Monte Rosso in the Sonoma Valley, and
La Loma, down low in Napa's portion of the Carneros. During
the 1970s the Martinis shifted their plantings over to the ranch
they call Los Viñedos del Rio, well west of Healdsburg in the
Russian River Valley. As long as Louis P. made the wines, I

never could spot the differences, never would have thought to ask if they had not rewritten their back label to reflect the completion of the move. Now that Michael Martini is making them, the wines are responding to his tutelage in subtle ways, ways that pare and polish while leaving the soul of them intact.

It does not seem worth cataloging many or even any details of the vintages of the 1950s and 1960s, not even the first half of the 1970s, though we cling to a couple of ancient bottles in the vague belief that we are going to find a perfect reason to open them and the vaguer hope they will be delicious.

Thinking all the way back to the 1956 has been, however, a salutary lesson, another proof, if another one is needed, that impressive firsts shape everything that follows, particularly if consistency sets the first impressions in concrete. Those old-timer Martinis still insist on telling me what is right and what is not about a Gewürztraminer. Most of my enthusiasm for litchi comes from them, though they always showed it faintly. So does the desire for a wine maybe polished a little bit but a long way short of slick. Not least, they paid dividends for a year or two of patience, which has come to be an adamant demand in these quarters because time gives Gewürztraminer the facets that keep it interesting all the way to the last drops from the bottle.

At all events, they and their successors have washed down fearful amounts of terrines and pâtés around our place, and no small amount of everything Chinese from crab with ginger to mu shu pork. They continue to do so.

1975 The epitome of the old-style, fully flavored, sneaking-up-on-litchi, bone-dry, sturdy Martini Gewürztraminers came from a vintage that stayed in top form for the seven years it took us to get to our last bottle.

1976 From the outset, atypically dark in color, thick in texture, and ripe in flavor. A freak from a vintage that saw considerable *Botrytis cinerea* in the Martini vineyard, but a fascinating freak as late as 1986.

1977 No note.

1978 Started quietly, but blossomed swiftly. We devoted most of our supply to Cantonese dinners because it had so much litchi. Our next-to-last bottle remained in top form in 1987, when we sacrificed it to a platter of miscellaneous terrines and pâtés.

1979 Fell between floral and litchilike throughout a durable career. The balance was perfect for pâtés.

1980 A sharp turn in style toward an early delicacy of flavor and texture in the young wine. Blossomed by its third birthday. Still in peak form for pâtés in early 1987.

1981 Pallid among its peers.

1982 No note.

1983 Understated early, it blossomed with varietal aromas in mid-1985. Always in the pack.

1984 Subtle but spot-on Gewürztraminer in the early going.

1985 Follows the comparatively understated, polished style set with the 1980; a bit fuller, fleshier than most vintages.

HOP KILN WINERY

Dr. Martin Griffin makes a kite-flyer's Gewürztraminer, a trustworthy companion to fatty terrines and Cantonese food, and one that is not a bad thought around a Hunan kitchen. To put it more bluntly, it is a powerfully varietal wine.

His vineyard touches the south boundary of the Martinis' Viñedos del Rio property. Griffin, like they, has a bent for bone-dry Gewürztraminer. What he gets shows more than a trace resemblance to his neighbor's wine, but it comes even closer in character to the Navarro, much for the sheer power of its litchilike aromas, still more for its hewn-from-the-stone textures.

Griffin grows only four acres of Gewürztraminer, some on the flat, some up on a knoll, so buys a small tonnage of grapes from neighbors in the Russian River Valley to round out his annual six-hundred- to eight-hundred-case volume. He ferments his wine bone dry in stainless steel and keeps it in steel until bottling early in the spring following the vintage, intent as he is on keeping every atom of the variety's perfume.

1977 Served immediate notice that the style was dry and intensely aromatic.

1980 No note.

1981 Strongly varietal, rather tart among Gewürztraminers.

1982 Understated early, but typically firm and balanced to age well.

1983 No note.

1984 Lean and firm in texture, long and solid of Gewürztraminer aromas. Lets just a hint of bitter show through a satisfyingly dry, flavorful finish.

1985 Close echo of the 1982 for firm balance. If anything, a shade more aromatic of its variety.

DAVIS BYNUM WINERY

Davis Bynum regularly makes Gewürztraminer from a neighbor vineyard on West Side Road. The vintages from 1983 onward have been consistent and appealing. Bynum keeps close to 1 percent, residual sugar, a level that somehow exactly fits the fruit flavors he gets, which are never cold cream, never litchi, but always balanced on the narrow, meandering boundary between the two. The wine recommends itself over and over to those who like the flavors of Gewürztraminer but find the dry ones a bit much.

MARK WEST VINEYARDS

Bob Ellis grows a small patch of Gewürztraminer in among the Chardonnay and Pinot Noir, and Joan Ellis makes an unambiguous wine from her husband's grapes. At peak form, when it has had a couple of years in bottle, it has some litchi tones, but it is a bit more reserved than either Navarro or Hop Kiln, and likely to have some distinctive notes from its time in the cellar too. Ellis flavors a barely perceptible touch of sweetness—a shade less than 1 percent does the trick in a naturally tart wine. Two vintages, 1983 and 1986, stand well above the others. The 1981 was not far off their pace.

Sonoma Valley

Patches of Gewürztraminer dot the entire length of the Sonoma Valley from Kenwood south to the very margins of the bay marshes in Carneros. No small range of climate and soil produces a strikingly narrow range of wines, thereby teaching humility to those of us who tax ourselves with accounting for tiny differences of taste between this place and that.

GUNDLACH-BUNDSCHU VINEYARD CO.

When Gundlach-Bundschu turns a Gewürztraminer loose on the world, it will have a guaranteed roomful of varietal aromas in every glass. This is another one that hovers between cold cream and litchi, but is one of the few that gets to that point almost as soon as it is bottled. At the same time it has an undefinable delicacy of flavor all its own, one that gives it a distinctive, almost a signature quality. Part of the delicacy is an absolute absence of bitterness in the finish. The upshot is that we would sooner drink it sooner, and drink it for itself rather than with food, in spite of the fact that it is well below threshold sweetness, having trended from 0.7 down to 0.4 percent residual sugar during the past several vintages.

The Bundschu family vineyard yields all of it, from forty-eight acres on the flats of their Rhinefarm Vineyard just south of Sonoma town. The Bundschus and winemaker Lance Cutler aim for pure Gewürztraminer flavors, fermenting cold in stainless steel and keeping the wine in steel until they bottle it late in the winter or early in the spring following harvest.

1977 In its first outing, quickly revealed its distinctive delicacy. Wonderfully easy to drink.

1978 No note.

1979 No note.

1980 Stunning when it was released in 1981, and stayed fresh and lively through 1982. We saw no point in waiting for anything past perfection.

1981 Much akin to the 1977.

1982 Echoed the 1980.

1983 Like 1977, delicate and wonderfully easy.

1984 In the pack.

1985 Photocopied the effects of the 1980 as soon as it was released. We just polished off the last of our supply in spring 1987.

Sebastiani Vineyards Kellerschatz

The name is a bit goofy, promising the reverse of what one gets. Sebastiani's regular bottling, called just plain Gewürztraminer, is noticeably off-dry, as the Germans are wont to make theirs (and appreciable as such). The ultra-Germanic sounding Kellerschatz is the dry one. It got its name, the proprietors wryly admit, because they wanted to make a reserve wine in spite of Gewürztraminer's not having much market for one.

The Sebastianis decided to make the special lot because they had isolated several outstanding blocks within the three principal vineyards from which they draw their regular Gewürztraminer. Two are their own on low-lying ground toward the west edge of Carneros; the third is the closely affiliated Wildwood Vineyard higher up in the Sonoma Valley, on west-facing hills near the town of Glen Ellen. The Carneros vines yield wines of a delicacy that challenges Gundlach-Bundschu's without being quite identical to it; the Wildwood grapes give a little richness all around. The Sebastianis do nothing fancy, just let the vineyards speak for themselves.

They make only eight hundred to one thousand cases of Kellerschatz, and sell it only from the winery, where they can gather an audience for it. Though there have been but two, it gets notice here because the winery has done well for a decade with its widely distributed regular bottling. The first bottling, 1983, was splendidly varietal to taste, firm and crisp in texture. The 1985 surpassed it. The winery skipped a 1984.

Hacienda Winery

Hacienda is hardly ever more than half a Sonoma Valley wine—sometimes the winery takes a majority portion from a vineyard in Alexander Valley—but it nestles here to avoid a one-wine category for Sonoma County. Not many assembled wines reveal their sources as clearly as the Hacienda Gewürztraminers have. Steadier than any other wine in the Hacienda roster, their Gewürztraminers have some of the delicacy of flavor that marks Gundlach-Bundschu and Sebastiani's Kellerschatz wedded to the richer textures typical of Alexander Valley.

1978 The epitome of floral Gewürztraminer; soft and full on the palate.

1979 Regular bottling in the pack; a Reserve was outstanding early and was still gaining when we drank our last bottle in late 1983.

1980 A gentler, subtler wine than its forebears.

1981 No note.

1982 Richly scented; soft and round for texture. Just beginning to peak in 1985.

1983 Much richer than a 1982 tasted head-to-head in 1985.

1984 Early, it accented the subtle delicacy of the house style.

1985 Very ripe and softer than an already soft norm.

Napa Valley

One of the reasons I have been defensive about Gewürztraminer these last few years was the suspicion that the Napa Valley was beginning to regard Gewürztraminer as beneath its dignity. It turns out that I underestimate Napa wineries about the same way I underestimated the general public. While a couple of labels we used to watch have disappeared, and plantings have decreased by a hundred acres since 1983, the total number of producers has edged up by a couple.

The bulk of Napa's Gewürztraminer vineyards lies between Oakville and Napa city, with a few scattered ones south as far as Carneros and north at least as far as St. Helena. Several of them make a case for Napa to make a bid for the play-offs, if ever the French succeed in taking over the government and ruling producing areas down to two. Though outstanding examples are not as numerous as in the Anderson Valley and the

Russian River Valley, several of the most memorable Napans rank right at the head of my list of favorites.

RUTHERFORD HILL

Rutherford Hill is, like Navarro, Hop Kiln, and their kin, unmistakably on the dry side (but not bone) and unmistakably from the sturdy school of Gewürztraminer. In most vintages it develops the signal litchi flavor soon after it goes to bottle and holds it for years. While it never seems to show any of the cold-cream aromas that go with warmer climes, what separates it from its Anderson and Russian River valley cousins is an extra hint of warmth and sunshine on the vineyards. The idea comes mostly from its slightly fuller, richer textures rather than flavors. Whatever the signal, it is nothing gross, nothing I would like to have to make my living spotting in blind taste tests, but a haunting suspicion all the same. The longest-running example of its type from the Napa Valley, it has been around since 1976, enough years for the characterization to seem fair.

Summers in the Napa Valley are full of the kind of still, sunny days that let a body stretch out, listen to the music of small nature, soak up heat without getting out of the filtered shade of small oaks, stretch a picnic out over pretty much the whole of an afternoon, just generally drop down to slow idle. Gewürztraminer is, no doubt, the wine that caused Rutherford Hill to set up a picnic grounds designed for the purpose. We have taken plenty of coal back to Newcastle on just such days, or if not there, then someplace a good deal like it.

Almost always we reserve our Rutherford Hills for times when terrines or pâtés are to be the anchor point because it has the depth of flavor and richness of texture to meet such fare head-on, but not such powerhouse aromas as to overshadow fine points in the food. It is also hellaciously good with smoked meats, especially smoked turkey. If you ever have wondered what to have with a Reuben sandwich, here is just the ticket.

In most years it qualifies as an estate wine; in a couple of vintages it just missed. Nearly all of it has come from a vineyard owned by winery partner William Jaeger. The ranch has one corner at the intersection of Big Ranch Road and Oak Knoll Avenue, next to Monticello on one side and Trefethen on another. The patch yields a fairly steady six to seven thousand cases. The 1985 has a bit from Trefethen; the 1980 used a dollop of Winery Lake Vineyard.

Rutherford Hill sticks to straightforward winemaking: cool fermentation in stainless steel and no wood-aging at all. It differs from most of its peers for bottling its Gewürztraminers eight or nine months after the harvest rather than four or five. The wine carries 0.7 to 0.8 percent residual sugar to bottle, enough to give it a little fat, not enough for it to finish sweet.

1980 Excellent varietal; fresh and lively in texture.

1981 One of the brighter lights from its vintage, but past the peak in 1986.

1982 No note.

1983 Closed compared to other vintages as late as spring 1985. By mid-1986 it had developed nicely.

1984 Fine, lingering flavors of Gewürztraminer early; rich on the palate.

1985 Right from the beginning, at the edge of litchi aromas from first sniff to finish. Beautifully clear, clean flavors and balanced to last well.

BERINGER VINEYARDS

Sometimes collectors regret losing an old bottle in a back corner of the cellar, not because the wine has gone around the bend, but because it has not.

Such is the story of our two-bottle collection of Beringer Vineyards 1980, a wine that began life, so an old note says, not merely polite, not merely self-effacing, but invisible. The stray second bottle surfaced in time to keep company with some *chimichangas* on a soft spring Saturday in 1987, one of those midday bottles that can be dumped without a moment's regret if it does not turn out well. Dumped, hell. The wallflower had blossomed, still pale hued, still fresh and lively on the tongue, but now richly scented, a veritable paragon of that middle ground between litchi and cold cream.

If it were not for the 1985's giving every sign of being the same sort of wine, there would be more lamentations flying around here than there are. As it is, the only thing that really nags our souls is how the 1982 might have turned out.

The grapes for the whole series have grown on thirty-one acres of Beringer's sprawling Gamble Ranch, several miles north of Big Ranch Road. Myron Nightingale kept and Ed Sbragia keeps the winemaking on the straight and narrow: stainless-steel fermentation, a little time to settle down, and then to bottle in late winter or early spring following the harvest. The grapes are picked as soon as they turn color, the wine left with a touch of sweet, usually within a hair's breadth of 1 percent.

The winery does not make much noise about having a Gewürztraminer, in fact does not make much Gewürztraminer compared to its other wines, two thousand cases being typical.

EVENSEN VINEYARD

Richard Evensen makes Napa Gewürztraminer bone dry and as bold as it gets. He has never felt that the characteristic little fillip of bitter should be hidden, nor has he otherwise temporized about the basic nature of the variety. All of his nine-hundred- to one-thousand-case annual production comes from a bit fewer than ten acres surrounding his home and winery north of Oakville, almost straight across the road from Robert Mondavi.

Alexander Valley

It goes against the book, Alexander Valley does. It is warmer and drier by half than either the Anderson or Russian River valleys and a bit warmer than most of the plantings in Sonoma

183

Valley, but no matter. Some of the dry models from here are very affable for sipping. Some of the off-dry ones would melt a Scrooge. Gewürztraminers from the Alexander usually have overtones of whatever it is the Pond's people use to perfume cold cream, but just barely. "Do it right," Richard Arrowood of Chateau St. Jean has said more than once of the aroma, "and it is fine perfume. Do it wrong, and it is dime store."

MATROSE

Matrose Traminer makes an eloquent argument for delicacy, understatement, subtlety. It is not at all a kite-flier's Gewürztraminer. What it wants for company is lightly smoked turkey or grilled chicken wings marinated in soysauce and ginger.

Jamie Meves makes Traminer (he insists on calling it that, never having satisfied himself on the matter of spice) from a single blessed patch of grapes owned by Richard Hafner and family. The vineyard sits toward the southern end of the valley, right where State Route 128 makes a lunatic right-angle turn to get to Jimtown or, come to think of it, away from it.

Meves's technique is not the everyday one. He barrel-ferments a substantial portion of his Traminer and leaves some of it to age in wood. The results are not quite typical, but remain unmistakably varietal. Wood, surprisingly, plays no part in the flavors, or at least too small a part for me to notice in blind tastings. But it does give the wine just a hint of tannic spine, quite an unexpected one in contrast to the pillow-soft nature of most of its peers from the neighborhood.

1982 The first vintage. Outstanding varietal aromas and perfect balance early. Still drinking beautifully through 1986.
1983 Clearly varietal, but showed repeatedly that the subtle, soft wines of the area want delicate food flavors for company.
1984 A little softer and frailer than most vintages.
1985 Subtle, as always, but perhaps the richest and most richly flavored vintage to date. Perfect match with smoked chicken in 1987.

GRAND CRU VINEYARDS

Grand Cru Vineyards makes its Gewürztraminer much the sweetest of any noted in these pages, at a typical 2 percent residual sugar, and yet it is a drink to admire with food as much as for itself. I am always surprised to find it so, but expect to learn the fact once and for all one of these days. The first of a remarkably steady series came only from the great Gewürztraminer vintage of 1975. The 1983 and 1985 have been outstanding among recent vintages.

Bob Magnani makes the wine for its varietal character and leaves some of the sugar to help the wine age gracefully for at least two years in bottle.

J. PEDRONCELLI WINERY

J. Pedroncelli has a surprisingly long career as a Gewürztraminer producer using Alexander Valley (and some Dry Creek Valley) grapes. The Pedroncellis wait for ripe fruit, leave a healthy 1.0 to 1.5 percent residual sugar to assure a soft affability of character, and do not clutter the issue with wood aging. Not only is the wine a pleasant sipper immediately on release, it is perhaps the clearest example of what the Alexander Valley tends to grow.

Field Stone This winery grows its Gewürztraminer on winery-owned vineyards just above the Russian River, at the southern tip of the Alexander Valley. After an early tendency to pick the grapes just as they were ripening, the winery shifted toward deeper maturity. Under the later regimen, the wines have had consistent appeal as off-dry, pervasively varietal bottles for the past several years. The 1984 in particular raised the flag.

Clos du Bois A Gewürztraminer subtitled Early Harvest from affiliated vineyards in the Alexander Valley is offered by Clos

185

du Bois. Another of the 1.0 to 1.5 residual style, it is made to taste fresh and meant to be consumed early in its career. To that end it is picked just as varietal character starts to be pronounced, and moved from fermentor to bottle quickly, with no way-stops in wood. It has been consistently appealing in a gentle, almost whimsical way, best taken as a warm, drowsy-day sipper with a plate of fruit and biscuits.

CENTRAL COAST

The Central Coast plunged into Gewürztraminer with a right good will. In 1971 Monterey had 68 acres, San Benito (read: Almaden) 201, and Santa Barbara County none. In 1986 Monterey's total was 890, Santa Barbara's the same. San Benito had peaked at 265, then dropped to 60 as Almaden was decamping for Madera in its new role as a Heublein subsidiary.

I still do not know what to think, save one thing: Without exception, Gewürztraminers from every part of the Central Coast have given more pleasure as patio sippers than wines for dinner, and have shown better in their first bloom of youth than later. Almost without exception they have tended to push the cold-cream end of the flavor scale as far as it will go. Strangely, no few of them have been marked by the undercurrent of mint some Gewürztraminers share with Muscat Canelli, especially after they have bottle age. The flavor seems strange because most Central Coast Gewürztraminer is planted in cool places; the minty note occurs only in the warmest areas of the North Coast.

We have settled on Firestone Vineyards as our bellwether. It and some other Santa Barbara Gewürztraminers appear to give that county a bit of an edge over the rest of the Central Coast.

PINOT NOIR

WHEN PINOT NOIR REACHES ITS FULL POWERS, it is the wine for candlelight, ermine, and pearls, or it is their replacement. "I don't remember the girl," goes a graybeard's joke, "and the name of the restaurant slips my mind just now, but the wine was a Chambertin."

The great trick lies in finding one at its full powers. Pinot Noir gets by in all too many climates and prospers in all too few. Even where it prospers, it needs to be coaxed, wheedled, flattered, cajoled, cursed, and (or) prayed almost ounce by ounce through a series of crises that starts at the fermentors and lasts beyond bottling. Contrarily, it will rise up in the least of places every now and then to make a splendid wine by any measure, one that misleads all involved into years of misspent effort. Similarly, the odd fifty-thousand-gallon lot will make majestic progress through some cellar, causing the victimized winery to chase a melted rainbow for years to come. Cabernet soldiers through, the more the merrier; benign neglect is just the ticket. Not so Pinot Noir.

It is, thus, a wonderful wine for worriers, for grail seekers. Think to have it mastered, and it will slide away. André Tchelistcheff has pursued it all his working life, tantalized by the 1946 and 1947 he made at Beaulieu Vineyard but never came close to equaling in his own mind. At least he has the satisfaction of being a perfect role model for scores of later-comers to the quest.

Drinkers of Pinot Noir do not get off much more lightly than the producers. Taste a beauty in March, stock up in July, and wonder what went wrong at dinner in October, because the stuff ages in bottle in the kind of fits and sulks only witches can explain. One merely has to learn not to give up because the sulk probably will end, leaving twice the wine that March promised.

It is the whole point of this book that the hunt for satisfying wines needs to start with where they grow. Pinot Noir carries the idea to its furthest extreme. In all of Europe only a tiny part of France meets every one of the variety's needs. Huge expanses of California have been ruled out, leaving only a few living hopes and a few untried corners.

People hope otherwise and seize upon dim signals, ambiguous clues, even cabalistic signs for guidance. Most recently, the key to the magic kingdom has been clones. The Pommard clone, the this, the that, and the other clone is going to do what none has done before. Probably not. Karl Wente, who was a very good farmer and who made one surpassingly fine Pinot Noir, a 1963, tramped La Romanée and the rest of the Domaine Civile vine by vine and came away almost convinced that the final secret to its success, beyond being in a right place, was having a dozen clones or more mixed together. Wente was, however, cautious in advancing this as a theory because he could think of exceptions. No, the answer is going to be grounded in vineyards that yield up grapes with some haunting perfumes in them.

The hunt for signposts to California's right places for Pinot Noir never has made for dreamless sleep, does not now, will not anytime soon. A new probable location of "the place" crops up about once a decade. People go haring off after each new hope, planting more and more vineyards on faith, reaping enough rewards to keep each succeeding area well endowed with Pinot vines but not quite enough successes to keep the parade from moving along to the next promised land.

Part of the difficulty lies with how small the right places are for Pinot Noir. Big chunks of territory will do well by Cabernet Sauvignon or Chardonnay. For them the tidy maxim—find a good bottle, try its neighbor—works well. Not for Pinot Noir. A few isolated acres may be all there are for miles around.

One central problem for grail-seeking producers and drinkers alike is the long-fuzzied definition of just what the hunt is after. The pilgrims have been reduced to questing after a goal that long since has sounded like the elephant reported on by the three blind men in the fable. Some people want to imitate a Burgundy. Some want powerful fruit aromas. A few would rather have deeper color. A handful will settle for the pure taste of oak. Too few, in recent years, have been willing to settle for something pleasant to drink.

From just two labels, Louis M. Martini and Heitz Cellars, came the half dozen or so examples that defined Pinot Noir for me from the late 1950s through the mid 1960s. One was the trunk of the blind men's elephant, the other the side. The two wines had hardly anything to do with each other for flavor, texture, or anything else save longevity. Like so many Martini reds, the 1957 was all delicacy and subtlety in every department. For years it held on to delicious flavors from its grapes, whispers rather than shouts, but the sort of whispers one aches to hear again. Notes from the winemaking complicated things, but never drowned out the Pinot Noir. Long after the grace notes of bottle bouquet had joined the chorus, a taste of grapes was still the most prominent, most appealing part of the wine. The 1965 echoed 1957 for a long time before edging off in its own, slightly sterner direction. Between times, the Heitz Cellars 1959, 1960, and 1961 were quite something else, large-scale wines early, large-scale wines today, brass-band harmonies of ripe Pinot Noir and fresh-coopered French oak. With the radio-telescopic clarity of hindsight, explanation of the differences comes easily. The oakless Martinis came from cool, fog-beset Carneros, the barrel-aged Heitzes from the comparative warmth of a vineyard between Yountville and Oakville by way of Hanzell. (The vines, were, come to think of it, just down a country lane from Martha's Vineyard.) Back then, oak was just coming into play, and nobody recognized Carneros, though the Martini was the first verifiable Pinot Noir from there.

When the 1968s came along, it seemed as if the Martini 1957 had been a vision of the future all along. The Heitz and Robert Mondavi bottlings had most of the same fruit flavors as their Martini predecessor, but amplified. Beaulieu Vineyard was a shade oakier, but close on their heels. The Martini 1968, curiously, seemed a bit overshadowed at the time, but all four were wines that made people glad to have a glass under almost any circumstance. Wood flavors play a very small part in old tasting notes on the 1968s, and an even smaller part in recollections of them. It was no question of frivolous little wines though, of Californian equivalents to Beaujolais capering at the feet of a Romanée or other Olympian. Each of the four 1968s had substance enough to hold a peak for a good ten years and plenty of subtleties to admire in between the bouts of euphoria brought on by their essential flavors. They did not smell like roses or woods violets, but they smelled every bit as good. It was, according to the best guesses, mostly a matter of the year's being so cool that most of Napa was much like Carneros usually is.

And then, alack, winemakers started getting serious about Pinot Noir. The flavors of the grape just damned near disappeared from public view while grim experiments went on, designed to bring not pleasure but greatness. A vogue for hot fermentations followed one for extended aging in new barrels of heavy-toast Limousin oak, to be succeeded by a rush to dump stems back into the fermentors. Enthusiasm for ultra-ripeness in the vineyard came somewhere in the chain. Part of the problem stemmed, no doubt, from a rapidly expanded source of supply. In 1960 the state had 515 acres of the variety; in 1975 the figure was 7,800. Not every acre of that could have been in ideal ground. To judge from the long-term results, some huge proportion was not, but shortcomings in the vineyards were compounded by the more-is-better winemaking. With the exceptions of a few bottlings from old hands, one Pinot Noir of the 1970s after another was alcoholic, raisiny, tannic, and flavored mainly by wood—tolerable qualities in a port, perhaps, but no ideal profile of a wine for my dinner table. The public resisted so gallantly that their efforts show in the acreage totals. Pinot Noir peaked at 10,200 acres in 1976, then slumped back to 8,600 by 1983 and 7,700 by 1986. It would not be near that figure without the still-exploding demand for Pinot Noir grapes for champagne-method sparkling wines. On the other hand, unless appearances deceive, some plantings have gotten close to where Pinot Noir wants to be, especially the ones within smelling distance of tidewater.

With deepened attention to getting the vineyards in the right places came a simultaneous easing off in the cellars. With the 1980s have come a long dozen labels that are making me miss the 1968s less and less. Enough of this sort of thing and Pinot Noir might even start winning back some of the audience that fled to such refuges as Merlot and mineral water during the 1970s.

When it is right, by my lights, Pinot Noir is engaging for its gentle qualities. The fruit flavors are complicated beyond one-word summary, but easy to like. A faint suggestion of mint is one of the flavor associations. The faintest reflection of raisin crops up again and again in descriptions. Some young Pinots will bring berries to mind. A few call to mind the scent of roses or another handsomely perfumed flower. The most satisfying summon up all of these thoughts and more. With bottle age, ripe examples can suggest, in some elliptical way, a flavor of meats. For having fewer tannins than most reds, proper Pinot Noir has a soft, velvety, almost fleshy feel on the tongue that reinforce the idea of meaty aromas. The unifying theme of both taste and texture is soft, gentle, almost-sweet qualities, characteristics that together make Pinot Noir a matchless companion to almost any of the delicately flavored meats, but especially ones that have dried out just a bit in the cooking. Nothing puts juices back into an overdone roast of beef, turkey white meat, or pork chops any better.

Purebred Pinot Noirs do not have dark colors. The grape skins have fewer coloring compounds than most varieties, and none of the purple ones. This lack of color is, I believe, one of the reasons Pinot Noir has been made in so many misshapen ways. Aside from the aesthetics, the pale hue signals a lesser amount of tannins than darker wines have. Hot fermentations, long fermentations, stems in the fermentors, and eternities in new barrels all are meant to get every tannin they do have, and thereby construct a great wine. Such efforts are a virtual confession that the grapes did not amount to much to begin with. They almost always failed, though excellent grapes were not always ruined by exaggerated attentions.

Among drinkers, a well-crafted Pinot Noir's pale gentleness causes it to be misunderstood on the point of age-worthiness. People see the pallor and feel the softness and give up on the wine. They drink it young when what it needs most is bottle age, about three to five years for a good example, five to nine for a paragon, because bottle bouquet closes a circle, fills a gap, does whatever it is that makes this wine complete and satisfying within itself.

One searches in vain for the kind of track records that are almost common among Cabernet Sauvignons, but, as with any other sort of wine, only consistency is a valid test of a winemaker and a vineyard. The ragged history of Pinot Noir in California obliges one to drop the standards of continuity a bit, or be forever disappointed, because for all the gains of the 1980s the variety still, somehow, magnifies every little change in the weather, every small step in the cellar.

Nearly all of the paragons and a majority of the above-average examples are coming, these days, from the downstream part of the Russian River Valley, bayside Carneros, and the shore-side fringe of Santa Barbara County. A few other spots clamor for attention, not as whole regions but as particular vineyards.

NORTH COAST

Such long records as exist come from the North Coast. So do, logically, most of the wines that have set my standards for what Pinot Noirs from California ought to be. But that is about the end of logic. Today, subject to revision tomorrow, I have the Russian River Valley at the head of my list of sources, with Carneros close behind, but even these cautious assessments are based on a couple of patches in each place.

Since the beginning of, and largely because of, the boom in champagne-method sparkling wines, Sonoma County has led the North Coast in acres planted. The 1986 figure was 2,680, well down from a peak of 3,200 in 1976. Napa has been rock-steady at 2,200 to 2,400. Mendocino, running as a dark horse, had but 370 acres.

Russian River Valley

Seeing the Russian River Valley at the head of this parade comes as a bit of a surprise to me, the author of the deed. Few Pinot Noirs from it have had the early capacity to provoke the silly grins of pleasure that so clearly stamped the Martini 1957 and the several Napa 1968s. Most have something tougher about them, more reserved, even austere. This is not to say they are all one thing. If one of the valley's most appetizing Pinot Noirs is strong, dark to the point of being brooding, one of its equals for stirring appetite is pale, delicately rigged, all affability.

Tough or no, wines from this fog-cooled, shallow drainage

taste fine young and can be spectacular about six to eight years out. Even the darkest and roughest of Russian River Valley Pinot Noirs ease off right about then, with plenty of fuel left in the tank to go longer.

Dehlinger Winery

Tom Dehlinger's Pinot Noirs are the ones that caused me to write "brooding" a few paragraphs back. They are not wintry, but they are for winter, for fireplaces, for thick, dark, steaming stews, for roasts swimming in dark sauces. Not wines for the timid, these, but forces to be reckoned with in any meal. *Fruity* is never the first word that comes to mind as a descriptive. Although the specific flavor of Pinot Noir suffuses them for a long time, it comes as part of a richer broth, sort of like the sauces with which it mates so well.

Dehlinger uses every last trick in the traditionalist's book to stuff his Pinot Noirs full of all sorts of flavors, getting the grapes fully ripe, fermenting in old-fashioned wood tanks, punching down the caps by hand, aging the new wine on its lees, the works. The only place he pulls back is in using puncheons for aging rather than barrels as a means to rein in the flavors of oak.

He grows all of his own fruit on two adjoining knolls in his vineyard not far from Forestville. Seven acres yield a scant thousand cases of Pinot Noir a year, but he farms the vines and ferments the wines in six thoughtfully divided lots. In watching the crops from 1977 onward, he began to identify characteristics he wanted as coming most readily from the upper reaches of one hillock. By 1982 he was giving the laggards extra schooling, as it were, coaxing vines in lower spots to behave more like their upslope brethren.

Sturdy as the first vintages have been, they begin to pale in comparison with their ever more meticulously farmed successors. The debut 1977, from the first crop of a then-young vineyard, gave off all the signals of what Dehlinger was up to. Not it seems among the small wines in the label's history.

1979 Rich, dark hued. In youth, a tug-of-war between fruit aromas and those from the winemaking. In early 1987 a seamless marriage of the two.

1980 Richer but more austere than the 1979. Just beginning to smooth out in 1987. Fruit flavors win out in the finish.

1981 Always in the pack.

1982 All the family traits, but perhaps the most accessible vintage to date for having more fruit and a slightly less steely texture than the others.

1983 The bouquets showed stronger early than in previous vintages, but the trademark finish is all Pinot Noir again. Perhaps not quite so richly textured as 1980 and 1982.

1984 Much akin to 1979 in the early going.

DE LOACH VINEYARDS

Cecil De Loach's eight-acre Pinot Noir vineyard lies just one hillock east of Dehlinger's, separated from it by a wide, swampy spot. Their grapes share a kinship of flavor, but the two men approach the making of Pinot Noir from such opposite points of view that a taster has to work to find the parallels.

The De Loach vines offer up such powerhouse varietal aromas that the proprietor has taken to picking earlier than he did the first few years, when he already harvested at lesser sugar levels than his neighbor. He has throttled back on oak aging as well, first changing from American to French oak, then diminishing the amount of new oak used to age the developing wine. Most of the barrels come to Pinot Noir after four vintages of Chardonnay, though De Loach uses a few new barrels for his Pinot each vintage. He has even eased back on the amount of color extraction during fermentation.

The net result is a wine of appealing fruit flavors throughout an uncommonly long period of fresh youth, and who knows what eventual longevity. Only in 1987 did the debut 1979 turn a corner from young to mature wine, from vibrantly fruity to soft and perfumed of roses. Once time tames the fruit, all manner of other, hitherto hidden facets show up, causing the strides from youth to maturity to seem gigantic compared to the small steps taken by the always bouqueted Dehlingers.

From the start, De Loach Pinot Noir has had unmistakable fingerprints. My oldest surviving note on the 1979 comes from tasting it blind at the Sonoma Harvest Fair in 1981. The first phrase was "Intense, berrylike fruit," still the key clue to grasp while the wine is working its slow way to maturity. The second phrase was "In the De Loach style." Since I hardly ever miss a chance to scribble down a tasting note, and try hard not to think of who might have made a wine being judged, the previous glass must have rung a cathedral-sized bell.

Much is being made these days of clonal selection in Pinot Noir. De Loach sighs and says, "I know exactly where my vines come from. All over." The nursery he had contracted to buy from went bust just when he was ready to plant, so he scrambled to get whatever he could wherever he could. If Karl Wente was right about Romanée, De Loach might have fallen into luck in 1973.

1979 Early, the most intensely fruity Pinot Noir in memory. First major step to silky maturity in 1987, but still tart and lively in texture, with more developing to do.

1980 A bit more austere than the 1979, but still aromatic of fruit. Seems to be aging on a slower curve; still austere in spring 1987.

1981 By De Loach standards, only modestly flavored by fruit in the early going. Also a bit more noticeable for its alcohol. In the pack.

1982 Hearkens back to the 1979 in every way. Still powerfully fruity in early 1987. Has plenty of flesh and vitality to age for years yet.

1983 As nearly a mirror of the 1980 as 1982 was of 1979. A wine heaped with fruit and firmly built for the long haul.

1984 Almost as much fruit as the 1982, and the same sort of ripe, fleshy feel.

1985 In barrel, showed some signs of being the wine of the series. Intense and altogether appetizing fruit flavors couple with remarkable delicacy of texture.

Seghesio Winery

Far less powerful statements than the Two Ds (Dehlinger and De Loach), Seghesio Pinot Noirs are nonetheless—perhaps all the more—unsurpassed starting points for thinking about what flavors the Russian River Valley bestows on Pinot Noir. The Seghesios do not clutter up their gently textured Pinot Noirs with strong perfumes of new wood. Rather the wines spend their formative years in ancient, neutral redwood tanks, with only a small proportion going into American oak barrels for about four months to add a fugitive note of complication. Another extra note comes from a tiny proportion of Pinot St. George.

Nearly all of the wine comes from ten acres the Seghesios planted in 1962, just where Felta Creek meanders out of the hills to join the Russian River a long two miles west of Healdsburg. The family sets much store by the fact that their vines are right down at river level. The site almost touches the boundary line between the Russian River Valley and Dry Creek Valley, the point where morning fogs are a thin blanket. Going just a few feet up onto the benches, Ted Seghesio says, moves vines into longer hours of sunshine. Roughly 10 percent, including the dollop of Pinot St. George, comes from an older, sunnier Seghesio planting in the Alexander Valley. This vineyard is the flex point, the cushion that allows the winemaker to fatten up lean wines when the need arises.

Along with lessons in varietal character, Seghesio Pinot Noirs provide mannerly company to veal, beef, chicken, creamy pasta, and pork chops, a set of possibilities that immediately puts me in mind of Louis M. Martini Pinot Noirs, and no wonder. These are both families long in the wine business and long used to having wine on the table. The kids grow up in the cellars, learning almost by osmosis. Their attitudes are very different from those of either stockbrokers or doctors launched on second careers or freshly minted Davis graduates. What these old-line winemakers want first is wine that tastes good going in and feels good going down. What they achieve suggests strongly that there is no such thing as making great wine. The trick is to make good wine, some of which will turn out to be great.

All that aside, if Seghesio Pinot Noir is easy to like early, it lasts at least reasonably well. In 1987 the 1981 was still cruising. Though the oldest of its type under the label, it is a long way from the oldest Seghesio-made Pinot Noir. While their Russian River vineyard was maturing, they were making the wine for bulk sale, but keeping a couple of barrels each year for family drinking. The first, and still most memorable to them, was a 1971. They also recall the 1975 fondly, when it was ten years old.

1981 As soon as it appeared in the markets, it caught one's attention with true-to-type Pinot Noir aromas and flavors. Lightly rigged, with the tiniest suggestion of raisin in the finish, it seemed on the plateau in spring 1987, but was fresh enough to last a time longer.

1982 Sold in bulk, to the regret of the proprietors.

1983 The same indelible flavor of Russian River Pinot Noir as the 1981, but lightly overlaid with American oak. A little fuller, a little firmer than its forerunner; perhaps a longer ager.

1984 In spring 1987 strong resemblance to 1983 at the hour of going to bottle.

1985 Sold off in bulk, and alas.

DAVIS BYNUM WINERY

Davis Bynum has been sneaking up on the leaders for several years now with Pinot Noirs that smack stronger of the grape variety than anything else but do carry a recognizable note of oak in the nose. A shade darker and a bit leaner or harder in youth than the Seghesios, and not so dark or muscular as the Dehlingers, they come from a pair of vineyards along Westside Road, one near the winery, the other about halfway between it and Healdsburg. Bynum winemaking is traditional for Pinot Noir: open-topped fermenting tanks, thrice-daily punching down of the cap throughout a warm fermentation, then aging in a mixed lot of new and seasoned French wood. The more expensive Artist Series gets three years in wood, with a fair proportion (about a third) new; the regular lots get two years in mostly seasoned wood. Bynum makes about a thousand cases of the former, four thousand of the regular.

While the wines can be attractive young for their flavors of fruit, time in bottle does them wonders. Not only does bouquet develop, but the sharp corners round off.

Though the winery has been making Pinot Noir for fully a decade, the Reserve and/or Artist Series wines from 1982 onward seem to have raised the level several notches. The 1984 has been a step ahead of the others early, but all three vintages have given pleasurable drinking and promise more. The 1982 in particular had appeal in youth, yet enough stuffings to age into something finer.

Carneros

People could have saved a lot of time getting Carneros planted if only they had noticed how well Louis M. Martini's Pinot Noirs turned out in the late 1950s and all through the 1960s because those wines came, whole or in major part, from the winery's two ranches in the heart of the district. However, reinventing the wheel is a cumbersome, slow process and needs a goodly number of false starts to be done right. Carneros began to capture attention only after several wineries set up shop in a neighborhood with a great many more plantings of Pinot Noir in it than Martini's pair.

Still, Carneros is in here because of the Martini 1957 and 1965. They are what I want Carneros Pinot Noir to be: saturated with the flavors of the grape, only lightly touched by wood, quick to become velvety smooth, but slow to go over the hill. Nobody else has caught the brass ring yet. The Martinis have not done it for a while. But the promise is there, with Saintsbury near one Martini vineyard and Acacia a neighbor to the other, and the Martinis themselves still a part of the hunt.

The tastes of Pinot Noir in Carneros differ from its flavors in the Russian River Valley so subtly that no quick, easy description comes to mind. While Pinots from both tend to be powerfully scented of berries in their first bloom of youth, Carneros wines seem a shade less floral early and a good deal less floral later. In the place of that comes something closer to spice, or maybe mint. Whatever, it starts out in the wings and edges closer to center stage with age. Also, Carneros Pinot Noirs seem readier to show their tannins than their counterparts from farther north and west, but maybe this is only because the varietal aromas are a little less bold, more apt to let other qualities in a wine shine through. At least so I think now, on scant evidence.

SAINTSBURY

One of the ongoing dilemmas in the wine business is how to make money and at the same time hang on to wines until they are ready for the marketplace. David Graves and Richard Ward solved the problem by dividing their Pinot Noir into two lots, one subtitled Garnet, the other named Carneros Pinot Noir without another qualifier.

It works wonderfully well for them. Garnet comes out about nine months after the harvest, all soft and round and packed with berry flavors, already appealing with all of the foods Pinot traditionally accompanies, though able to improve in the bottle. Carneros Pinot Noir waits in the cellars for only three more months and still emerges less redolent of fruit, sterner stuff on that count and because it has more tannins.

In the process Graves and Ward drive form players crazy. All of the grapes for both wines come from the same vineyards, and all are fermented the same way. Somewhere between the harvest and December, some lots go affable and thus early to bottle as Garnet, while others turn stern and so stay in barrel to evolve into Carneros Pinot Noir. There is no pattern at all in the vineyards. In any one year, any one block will end up in either wine only to reverse itself in the following vintage.

Graves and Ward did not hit the road in full stride. Their first two vintages—1981 and 1982—started and, for my money, finished as modest successes at best. But the partners have been stepping up their pace each year since, having refined both their winemaking and vineyard sources in quick time.

In their first two vintages they made separate Sonoma Valley and Carneros bottlings. They launched Garnet in 1983, still with some grapes in it from a Sonoma vineyard. In 1984 they narrowed their roster of vineyards to Rancho Carneros, Lee, and St. Clair. Their own small patch was to join the roster in 1988. All four properties cluster together on a gentle, northeast-facing slope well into the Napa side of Carneros, just uphill from Louis M. Martini's La Loma Ranch.

Saintsbury only begins to test its and Carneros's capacity to produce richly flavored, age-worthy Pinot Noir with either of its bottlings. At this point, I am not even ready to decide which of the two will go the longer, because the Garnets more nearly resemble the Louis M. Martini 1957 and 1965 that lasted so well.

1981 Rancho Carneros bottling always a bit odd, and remains so. Sonoma Valley edition also had curious flavors early, but has aged to more appealing effect, seeming slightly flawed but intriguing late in 1987.

1982 Both editions—Carneros and Sonoma Valley—improved on the 1981s early, but both had passed their peaks by 1987. The Sonoma Valley, in particular, looked and tasted weary.

1983 Garnet, pleasingly fruity early, was mostly bouquets of age but not weary in 1987. Carneros always has seemed a trifle more tannic than its fruit flavors could or can support.

1984 Saintsbury hit a handsome stride with this vintage. Garnet has progressed from heaps of berrylike fruit to floral perfumes, and has the velvety textures Pinot is meant to show. Carneros, a shade more tannic and so developing more slowly along the same track, is one to watch over the next several years.

1985 From a vintage that left most producers with uncommonly wispy wines, Graves and Ward coaxed two bottlings redolent of Pinot

Noir's most appealing perfumes. Garnet is much the more developed in 1987. Carneros is a shade more delicate than its immediate forerunner, but at least as well balanced for aging.

1986 Garnet, new in the bottle in mid-1987, may be the wine of that series to date. Already it has complexities to go with a full, firm set of textures.

ACACIA WINERY

These days what we do most often with Acacia Pinot Noirs is hopeful waiting. Acacias promise to be fascinating when they are old and living on their wiles, but they refuse to grow older or wilier.

Vintages back to 1979 hang on, as fresh in color and full of varietal aroma as ever, wines that leave tasters to wonder if they ever will drop their raw vitality in favor of the silky roundness and shadowy flavors expected of a mature bottle. The 1982s in particular show no signs of coming out of puppyhood, let alone taking grave steps toward maturity.

Though nearly every one of Acacia's Pinot Noirs has been splendidly varietal coming out of the winery, it has been so only to those who can peer through veils of oak. In 1987, just when it seemed like the wines would forever taste like a tour of a lumberyard, came the first marriages between fruit and wood, especially in the 1982s. Their step forward gives hope.

There are a lot of wines to hope over, Acacia having produced as many as five separate bottlings per vintage. One is always assembled and identified as Carneros; with it come three or four single-vineyard wines from properties scattered throughout Napa's portion of the appellation. The vineyards bottled separately in vintages through 1983 were Iund, Lee, Madonna, St. Clair, and Winery Lake. With the 1984s, Madonna (directly west of the winery) and St. Clair (straight across Las Amigas Road to the south) had evolved as the mainstay individual vineyard bottlings. Iund (some distance east) continued to yield a tiny lot. Lee (also east, near Saintsbury) had become a part of the assembled bottling, and Winery Lake was out of the roster.

In all of the wines, winemaker Larry Brooks holds firm on the point that Pinot Noir does not make much of a picture without an oak frame. Partly it is a matter of complicating the flavors. More it is a need he sees for some oak tannins to build up the textures.

1979 Started in full form: plenty of new French wood perfumes set against distinctive aromas of Pinot Noir. Still hard and quite woody in 1986.
1980 Particularly strong vintage for fruit aromas, but abundant evidence of the cooperage in the early going. Still young and rough in 1986, but showing signs of rounding out.
1981 Oak perfumes first and foremost. On release, the least of the vintages to date.
1982 Excellent varietal well spiced by oak. The winery's favorite vintage through and including the 1984s. By 1987 the most impressive one for balancing fruit and oak against each other in still-youthful wine. All of the individual vineyards fared well.
1983 Least consistent of vintages to date. On release, St. Clair and Lee had balance and showed ample, appealing flavors of Pinot Noir. The others were out of sorts and tasted mostly of oak.
1984 In the early going the most appealing wines of the series for playing down the oak. The Iund stood out.

LOUIS M. MARTINI

The very first vintage-dated Martini Pinot Noir, the much-cited 1957, gave me more pleasure over a span of thirty or forty bottles and eighteen years than any other Pinot Noir before or since, though the 1965 came close, and also made it to voting age in a breeze. So I still hope for something like them whenever I pull the cork on any Pinot.

Something has been added since, and something else taken away, so far without adding a close competitor to my treasured memories. The addition is aging in oak barrels. The old-timers never saw small wood. They spent time refining their manners in redwood, or in ancient six-hundred- to fifteen-hundred-gallon oak casks or both, but they never went into cooperage that would distract from their native flavors of Pinot. Fruit still rules. Michael Martini uses barrels with so subtle a hand that it takes a fine beak to notice their aromatic contributions. The subtraction is Pinot St. George. Louis P. Martini planted a small block of it on the understanding that it was a clone of Pinot Noir. It was not, and when the vines weakened with age, out went the Pinot St. George to be replaced by purer stock. The wines that have done without it have had one layer fewer of flavors and nothing at all like the durability of their forebears. The simpleton in me wants to blame the lack of Pinot St. George; the nostalgic hopes they put it back.

Michael Martini wryly admits to stumbling with Pinot Noir in his first vintages as winemaker, which only puts him in the same box as every other enologist who works with the variety.

Individual vineyard wines from the two family-owned ranches are the ones to watch, they having supplanted the Special Selections. La Loma, the historic Stanly Ranch, sits right on the state highway between Napa and Sonoma just west of its junction with the freeway into Napa. Las Amigas, a mile or so south on the road of the same name, looks right at San Francisco across the Bay. La Loma tips slightly to the east; Las Amigas rolls more sharply and almost due south.

All of the La Loma and Las Amigas wines from 1980 through 1983 have shown some of the promise of 1957 and 1965 early, but have tended to fade quickly. The 1984s show more stuffings, signs of Michael Martini's increasing mastery of a changed style. I still want to see Pinot St. George back in the game.

BUENA VISTA WINERY & VINEYARD

Buena Vista is bidding to become a major factor in Carneros Pinot Noir. The first clear sign came with its 1981 Private Reserve, which continues to be a more impressive wine than what used to pass for pretty good, but does not come to the shoulder of winemaker Jill Davis's 1983 Private Reserve. How the latter ages will tell much of the tale of the winery's long-term prospects. (The 1984 has fine flavors, but seems a bit too tart and hard to come around.)

The vineyards are part of Buena Vista's seven-hundred-acre block on the last sharp slope above bay marshlands. The Private Reserves come from older blocks going back to 1972; the total acreage in Pinot Noir is 146.

Davis wants the wine to taste of Pinot Noir early and late. To that end she ferments it in small lots in stainless steel and ages it in French oak barrels seasoned by Chardonnay.

Sonoma Valley

There seem to be only two ways for a wine to grow old with grace: the two extremes. One is to have a lesser proportion of alcohol and a lot of acid—the cool-climate model. The other is to have a lot of alcohol and a lesser level of acid—the sunny profile.

The Sonoma Valley warms so quickly going north from Carneros and the Bay that it changes the character of Pinot Noir noticeably with each passing mile. The two grand durables of the Sonoma Valley are exactly what all of the cool-climate people are fleeing—sturdy to burly, sun bronzed stuff with a predictable lifespan of three, sometimes five decades. No other district compares.

HANZELL VINEYARDS

Hugh Johnson puzzled over the Hanzell 1965—the first one from estate-grown grapes—for a long time one autumn evening in 1978 before he finally made up his mind. "First it makes me think of Pinot Noir," he said, "then port, then Pinot Noir, and port again. May I have some more?" That has been the story in most if not all of the vintages since.

The grapes grow on a long, fairly gentle slope not far north of Sonoma town, far enough uphill to be above most of the morning fogs. A south-to-southwest exposure guarantees fruit as ripe as the winemaker wants it. Just as much, it demands a forcible style rather than a delicate one.

Winemaker Bob Sessions waits very late to pick and then uses every technique in fermation to extract from ripe, ripe grapes as much as possible of everything—color, flavor, tannin, alcohol, the works. The inevitably burly new wines go straight from small, open fermentors into a mix of new and old French oak barrels to begin a long stay. What comes out is of heroic proportions. None of the wines charm; all of them impress.

The curious upshot of the style is that it exaggerates vintage differences. When the winemaker goes for all there is, the ups and downs show much more than in wines where something is held back, leaving room for some camouflaging adjustments.

Hanzell is hard enough to come by that I do not get my hands on it every vintage. The two that stick out in memory are the 1979 (dark, ripe, heavy-bodied; blends flavors of new wood and completely ripened grapes; through 1985, very slow to change in bottle) and 1982 (a bit soft and pale, understated for a Hanzell and entirely delicious young).

Hacienda Winery

Hacienda's vineyards are less than two miles east of Hanzell's, only a few feet lower, and tipped only a few degrees more to the south, or less to the west. The environment assures that Hacienda Pinot Noirs are anything but wispy. However, Crawford Cooley and his winemakers have looked for slightly less ripe grapes, and given the wines rather less time in wood, less of it new. If a regional kinship shows right through the variations in style, the difference in ripeness and the decreased wood flavors have their modulating effects. The Haciendas show less of Pinot Noir's basic tendency to smack of raisins, more of its

berryish side. At the same time, the fruit shines through a bit
clearer without the competing perfumes of new oak.

1977 Always pale and delicate within the family of Haciendas. Soft,
supple, aging, but still showing Pinot Noir fruit in 1983.
1978 No note.
1979 Dark and surprisingly mature as early as autumn 1981. Always a
bit fiery from its alcohol.
1980 The most raisined or port-like vintage to date, but rich textures
and flavors gave it a certain heavyweight balance.
1981 Rich in minty Pinot Noir flavors early; almost meaty in both
flavor and texture by 1986. A bit hot from its alcohol.
1982 Minty again, and much the most delicate, balanced of the vintages to date on release. Still that in autumn 1986.
1983 A touch of the raisiny side of Pinot Noir, and a hint of alcohol
heat, but among the most appealing vintages early.
1984 Pale for a Hacienda. Very ripe, almost raisiny aromas and fat in
texture.

Napa Valley

The whole of the Napa Valley north of Carneros has become
suspect terrain for Pinot Noir since the blossoming of Carneros,
the Russian River, and other cooler regions. The younger the
critic, the deeper the suspicion. The youthful do not remember
the Heitz 1959, 1960, 1961, and 1962, which came from vines a
long mile north of Yountville. Still less do they recall André
Tchelistcheff's great 1946 and 1947 for Beaulieu Vineyard, two
that owed their souls to Rutherford dust.

Maybe the decisions are hasty, maybe not, but Pinot Noir is
disappearing from the mid- and upper valley. In the minds of a
solid majority of winemakers the great American test—what have
you done for me lately—has made a line touching the town of
Yountville into the practical divider between Pinot Noir country and not Pinot Noir country.

At the moment only one Pinot Noir from these parts commands our attention year after year. It is made for immediate

pleasure, not greatness, and such might be the most profitable approach in these precincts.

WHITEHALL LANE WINERY

Of all the Pinot Noirs that have come along since the sainted 1968s, the 1981 and 1984 vintages from Whitehall Lane are the only ones that have provoked the same kind of silly grins of pleasure. A more lighthearted set of fresh fruit flavors does not come to mind, and yet the wine has some extra layers, some qualities that keep a thoughtful taster sifting through the details all the way to the end of the bottle.

We drank enough of the 1981 in its early days to recognize its aromas if it went by on a upwind sailboat. Already we have done away with more of the 1984. Suddenly we have gotten interested to see what seven or eight years will do to our last two or three bottles of the latter, though we do not intend to sacrifice any more of its youthful charms than that. We had thought that these wines lacked the stuffings to age, that their charms are the whimsical kind, but a recent bottle of the 1981 says that the 1984 may still have something to say at a dinner table in 1990 or so.

The whimsicality comes as a surprise in view of the winemaking. Art Finkelstein ferments the grapes in half-ton picking bins so he can punch down the caps in the best tradition of large-scale Pinot Noirs, but large scale is not the idea. Small-lot fermentations stay cool, which keeps most of the ebullient fruit aromas that seem a trademark of Ray Mayeri's vineyard on the eastern outskirts of Yountville, from which all of every vintage to date has come. Punching down gets a maximum of color with a minimum of harsh tannins. After fermentation, the wine spends about six months in seasoned American oak, then is bottled and released staightaway.

1981 At the outset all lightness and charm. By 1987 settled in as a balanced, mature red with firm aromas of Pinot Noir still in play among its mature bouquets. Able company to rabbit then.

1982 Very soft and full of fruit early, and still holding in that pattern in 1987, when it was one shade simpler than the 1981, but much younger.

1983 Subtler, more restrained than forerunners in the early going. Quick to show maturity, but continues to drink well. As a mature wine, much the most complex interplay of Pinot Noir aromas and wine-making bouquets of any of these.

1984 Easily the most lively fruit flavors of vintages to date. Early seemed perhaps too lighthearted to age much past four years; by 1987 lengthening out to rival 1983 for complexity, but not at all mature to eye or palate. Looks more and more like the 1968s that aged well after frivolously charming youths.

1985 Closest to the 1982 for soft, delicate flavors and textures.

Anderson Valley

Several Pinot Noirs have hinted that the Anderson Valley is just as much a kin to the Russian River Valley in Pinot Noir as in Gewürztraminer. Some of the same appetizing berry flavors show up, and much of the same firm structure. Thus far, though, the wines have been like rookie left-handers—a lot of raw talent, a world of promise, but not many wins.

Ted Bennett of Navarro Vineyards has been working hard with his vineyard and the wine. In the vineyard he has adapted old vines to a more open training system that promises fuller ripening in his marginal climate. In the winery he has begun to back away from a bold, get-all-of-it style in favor of more delicacy and finesse. Thus far the wines have been hard as Pinot Noirs go. Between their slow evolution and the changes in vineyard and cellar, it remains difficult to suspect what lies ahead. At the moment, he seems one man to watch.

Other hopeful signs are coming from across Highway 128, at Husch Vineyards, where the 1985 in particular had a heaping share of Pinot Noir's loveliest aromas as it came to market. The Husch vines are among the oldest in the valley, so fair tests of its powers to grow the variety.

CENTRAL COAST

If the Central Coast can be bewildering about quick-maturing, varietally definite wines, imagine how confusing it must be where Pinot Noir is concerned, then double the estimate.

So cool is most of the region that several separate bands of grail seekers have been at work in it all at once since 1975. Their brief history is a carbon copy of all the others: Acreages shot up, the wines emerged, acreages dwindled down. Surviving vines got older, wines got older, people began backing away from hasty disappointment, and that is about where we are now.

Monterey had the biggest rush and so has the greatest decline. It still held an edge in acreage in 1986, though it had dwindled to 1,125 from a peak (in 1976) of 2,356. Santa Barbara County seems to have the new momentum. Its second round of wines has captured most of the public fancy, though its acreage stood at just 600, down from a high mark of 760 (in 1979). The Santa Cruz Mountains AVA (one hundred acres at the outside) has individual properties that bear watching. And, of course, there is Chalone.

Santa Barbara County

An evergreen quote—I forgot whose—laments about how much more fun Burgundy must have been before everyone knew that the Clos de Tart was better than its neighbors. The Clos was a walkover, a wire-to-wire winner compared to Santa Barbara's place in the race with the rest of California. As for which vineyards in the county are going to earn the loudest shouts, the prospects are that Santa Barbara's Clos de Tart is still a meadow or, at best, in spinach or garbanzos.

Santa Barbara does not have even the shaky history of Napa

and Sonoma to provide signposts. In 1987 there was not a fif-teen-year-old wine yet. All of the twelve-year-olds I have laid hands on are goners, and the ten-year-olds totter, and yet, and yet. A few patches have begun to say that the past is not even prologue.

Through a first shuffling of tasting notes from the region, it was in my mind to separate the Santa Maria Valley from the rest because of a single piece, called Sierra Madre, the identified source of several young Pinot Noirs that have made me dive deeper into my glass. Longer looks point to a different division. It begins to look more as if the main factor is proximity to the sea or, better, to the sea fog. At least two, maybe three vine-yards outside the Santa Maria Valley have produced the closest challengers to the Sierra Madres. All of them together suggest a secondary consideration—orientation. North-facing slopes—along with the sort of well-drained flats on which Sierra Madre sits—seem to do more for Pinot Noir than south-facing gra-dients in and out of the Santa Maria Valley. (Recall, these are California's only east-west running valleys.)

The tottering twelve- and ten-year-olds come, all or nearly all, from warmer inland vines. The oldest contenders from coastal and north-facing properties are 1981s. They and their successors ought not to be held to full account until they have had their chance to run the complete course. Meanwhile . . .

SANFORD

Not often in recent years has one wine been able to soar out of the pack at one of the major competitions. There are too many entries of too-near-equal quality in almost every category, Pinot Noir included. Sanford 1984 is an outright, repeated exception. Everywhere it was entered, it was so singular a demonstration of all the desirable flavors of Pinot Noir that it brought the judges to a full stop. Among other vintages of Sanford it did the same thing. It still must age velvety smooth without losing the beauty of those aromas, but the signs are promising.

While none of the other vintages in the series are its equal, they have enough enticing qualities to rivet one's attention on the label.

Richard Sanford's first vintage, as a partner in Sanford & Benedict, was 1976. The Pinot Noir from that year set him off on Santa Barbara as a home for the grape. It came from that winery's north-sloping vineyard several miles downstream along the Santa Ynez River from Buellton. Sanford still thinks highly enough of the ranch and, by extension, a long piece of that slope to have planted another patch not far east of the original, where his own winery was to be built in 1988. However, he has explored widely in the vintages from 1981 through 1986. His other choice, the source of the 1984, is an independent vineyard called Sierra Madre. It sits out on the Santa Maria floodplain less than two miles east of Santa Maria town. The 1981, 1984, 1985, and 1986 came exclusively from it. (In 1982 and 1983 he used a proportion of Edna Valley grapes, but abandoned that idea before the harvest of 1984.) He is not about to commit himself to the single source while so much remains unproven, but anything else, he says, will have to meet its standard, and nothing now in bearing and available for purchase has done so.

The winemaking is traditional for the variety: warm fermentations in open-topped tanks, punching down rather than pumping over, and maceration until the wine tastes right—usually twelve to fifteen days. Some lees go into the barrel.

1981 Dark, husky, and full of fruit early. Altogether mature, but in no way weary by spring 1987, when it still had flavors of both grape and region, but was fuller of bouquets from barrel and bottle.

1982 Lean and tart after the 1981. Has remained so, while growing markedly older than its predecessor by 1987. Fascinating regional flavors define a fully mature wine.

1983 Some engaging Pinot Noir flavors, but thin and weak among its siblings.

1984 Dark, powerfully scented of Pinot Noir. Big, richly textured in the mouth, in keeping with the flavors. The 1981 again, only much more so.

1985 Paler than any of its forebears and—rare in the region—a clear leaner toward the minty side of Pinot Noir. Delicate in texture, but not thin or weak, it seems one to watch as it ages.

BYRON VINEYARD

Owner-winemaker Ken Brown goes back a year farther than Richard Sanford with Pinot Noir in Santa Barbara County. He has had his own label only since 1984, but was Zaca Mesa's winemaker from 1975 until 1983. He, like Sanford, has zeroed in on Sierra Madre as the most fruitful source of Pinot Noir now at hand, and is free to limit his own label to grapes from it. His debut 1984 provides an intriguing comparison with Sanford's and makes him another man to watch.

ZACA MESA WINERY

Zaca Mesa Pinot Noirs before 1984 have had early charms but not much durability. Before they were eight they began developing strong vegetative flavors, and before they were ten they were wearily treading the downslope. Those wines were assembled from a variety of sources, but dominated by grapes from the warm interior of the Santa Ynez Valley. With 1984, and even more with 1985, the winery focused on a single vineyard well west, in the cooler, foggier end of Los Alamos Valley The vineyard site makes the label another one to consider in measuring the region's capacity for Pinot Noir.

Chalone

As an AVA, Chalone is all the same as Chalone Vineyard, a lonely aerie high up in the hills east of the Salinas Valley town of Soledad. There is nothing to suggest that this relentlessly sunny, almost rainless slope would be Pinot Noir country except for thousands of large quartzite crystals in well-drained soil.

That was enough of a clue for Bill Silvear to plant the property in Pinot Noir, Chardonnay, and Pinot Blanc, and for the current owners to keep the faith.

CHALONE VINEYARDS

Pinot Noir from Chalone belies every aspect of its origins. In spite of the sun and the desiccation and a nearly due-west orientation, the wines are dark among Pinot Noirs and fragrant with the variety's most delicate perfumes. The winemaking takes advantage of the fruit, adding grace notes but nothing that distracts.

Chalone Pinot Noir never shows up in competitions, and only rarely in tastings. The price is prohibitive to any writer who has not figured out what Arthur Hailey and Judith Krantz have on the one hand, and what David Halberstam and Bob Woodward have on the other. And so I come to it rarely, but always gratefully. The vineyard location's last indisputable virtue, an almost failure-free climate, has yielded one fine vintage after another.

SAUVIGNON BLANC

MY WIFE AND I HAD BEEN COMBING MENDO-
cino beaches all day in spring air with just enough mist in it to
soften the outlines of the coast, but not enough to dim its colors. Café Beaujolais was still years away—in 1966 one went to
Mendocino for sea air, not food—and so we wound up down
on the commercial fishing pier at Noyo Harbor, hungry for dinner and thirsty for wine and sitting in a restaurant designed to
give precise meaning to the word *modest*. The only ray of hope
on a five-entry wine list was Wente Bros. Sauvignon Blanc. We
asked for a bottle. The waitress looked uneasy and disappeared
for a long time. When she came back she had a half bottle in
hand, the last one in the house, she said. It was a 1954. Our
hopes having nowhere to fall, we took it, knowing from endless
reading that no California white wine was going to be drinkable
at age twelve.

It was pale, tart, fresh as the air outside, and rich with the not quite fruity, not quite herbal flavors of Sauvignon Blanc. We liked it so well in fact that we ate breaded, fried, generic whitefish with earnest appetites, and started gathering up Sauvignon Blancs on the way back to our hotel.

Sauvignon Blanc from California was not hard to keep track of then. Wente Bros. and Concannon Vineyard produced the only dry ones from their side-by-side vineyards in the Livermore Valley.[1] They were enough. Wente Bros. 1964, 1966, and 1968, and Concannon 1965 and 1968 carried us on into the beginnings of the Sauvignon Blanc boom. Considering that the list of producers numbered two and the number of districts one, those wines offered many still-useful lessons, the main ones being: Sauvignon Blanc can age at least fifteen years, but cannot be counted upon to do it; two vineyards across the road from each other can be contrary enough to ruin a vintage chart; two winemakers can do altogether different things with virtually the same fruit; and—finally—flat-out, hard-case, reeking-ripe Sauvignon Blanc does not appeal to everybody right away.

This last is part of the reason why the Sauvignon Blanc boom was slow in coming. The boom started in the early to mid-1970s, in secret. For years a grand majority thought it was a Fumé Blanc boom, because Robert Mondavi, in increasing the roster of producers to three and the number of districts to two, also added the alternate name and a whole new style with his 1967. The ensuing proliferation of names, districts, and styles added up to a cluster of boomlets before it came to a boom.

Because Sauvignon Blanc is almost unmistakable for its varietal character, it is a wonderful teacher of both regional character and winemaking style. The variety echoes its red cousin, Cabernet Sauvignon, in tasting of leaves or stalks sooner than any familiar fruit. Alone among whites it tastes so much more of herbs or grasses than berries or apples that, tasting blind, I

[1] The two Livermore wineries, Beaulieu Vineyard, The Christian Brothers, and Charles Krug had sweet models, which I was snob enough to ignore. Now I wonder what I missed.

cannot mistake it for Chardonnay, Pinot Blanc, or Semillon more often than once a week. And yet, specific as its varietal aromas are, Sauvignon Blanc tends to betray its exact origins with persistent variations on the main theme—a bit grassier here than there, an overtone of melon somewhere else—so mistaking Napa for Sonoma or Sonoma for Santa Barbara is at least as rare an event as missing the variety.

In spite of overlaps in regional overtones, all California Sauvignon Blancs separate themselves into four main camps, useful when it comes time to think of them with food.

At one end of the scale, a fruity note plays against the subtlest of the herbaceous or grassy varietal character. Melon is as close as we can come to a flavor association for the tone of fruit. The most reliable source of melon-tinged Sauvignon Blancs has been the upper Napa Valley and its eastern satellites, Chiles and Pope valleys; Beaulieu Vineyard, Flora Springs Wine Co., and St. Clement Vineyards have been the textbook examples. The melon note also will show up in Sonoma (Iron Horse Vineyards) and Mendocino's Ukiah Valley (Husch Vineyards). As a flavor, it echoes chicken or whitefish in creamy sauces, and contrasts neatly with chicken or whitefish basted in herbs or dressed in herb sauces. The most delicate of them keep polite company with pale-flavored whitefish grilled plain. The sturdier ones will meet a lightly to moderately curried soup or stew about as well as any wine can.

Not very different is a set of flavors we have come to call sweet-grassy because they remind me of those long, jointed, sweet grasses I learned to chew by studying Norman Rockwell paintings on the covers of *The Saturday Evening Post*. It is almost as much a matter of texture in the wine as taste, a sort of juicy feel. The cooler southern parts of the Napa Valley deliver this sort of wine, as Monticello Cellars, Robert Mondavi Winery, and Silverado vineyards will demonstrate year after year. Livermore Valley Sauvignon Blancs at their peak have much the same identifying mark. The 1954 Wente Bros. that got us started had it in spades, and so did the 1966. Paso Robles (Martin Brothers

Winery) can do it, though it does not often. The sweet-grassy Sauvignon Blancs make versatile company at the table. They are fine with chicken in creamy sauces, chicken basted with herbs, mulligatawney stews, vegetable and/or mushroom quiches, crepes, or soufflés. They are among California's finest fish wines, the subtler ones with lean, delicate types such as sole and white bait, the richer ones with red rockfish, angler, monkfish, and the like. Sweet-grassy Sauvignon Blancs are indispensable with Mexican-style fish dishes, *enchiladas suisses,* anything with cumin, and low-BTU *chiles rellenos.*

Third in our quadripartite cosmology are the grass-grassy or lawn-grassy Sauvignon Blancs, the kind Sonoma seems to produce effortlessly in almost every one of its many corners. Again, it may be more a matter of texture than taste because these wines almost always feel lean, light, even sharp on the tongue rather than juicy. Dry Creek Vineyard, Preston Vineyards, Glen Ellen Winery & Vineyards, and Kenwood Vineyards provide unambiguous demonstrations. At their most flavorful, these are rewarding with the same fish as the sweet-grassy Sauvignons, particularly if the fish comes with an herb butter. Full-flavored examples also will stand in for reds with stuffed, baked pork chops, pork roasts, even a boneless leg of lamb braised in white wine with vegetables and garlic, and, not least, pasta with a garlicky sauce. Ah, garlic. We measure these Sauvignon Blancs by how well they stand up to garlic. In *The New James Beard* (Alfred A. Knopf, 1981) James E. Beard published a favorite old recipe for chicken 40 cloves of garlic, a dish that wards off colds and curses, gets one a seat on the bus, collapses any subtle wine, and does considerable damage to fairly stout ones. First-quality grass-grassy and sweet-grassy wines will go the full 40 cloves. Down to 30 cloves a wine may be very good. Below that, and they go all the way down to 4 or 5, they trail off in uninteresting ways.

Our flavor association for the last division is—call it grass or call it vegetable—outright asparagus, fresh in its mildest forms, cooked or canned at its most intense. Monterey can grow it anytime, Santa Barbara most times. Zaca Mesa Winery and Ballard Canyon Winery Sauvignon Blancs have been two to use as test models right through the 1980s.

Full-power Sauvignon Blanc, to get back to the general point, is not for everybody. For years the University of California advised winemakers to blend the variety with a more neutral grape if they wished to make wine for mortal citizens. Winemakers looking to throttle back have found other ways to do it. The four primary ones are: blending other grape varieties as the school suggests, blending Sauvignons from both highly aromatic and lightly aromatic vineyards, fermenting in wood, and aging in wood.

Blending with a proportion of the similar but subtler Semillon has been the orthodox solution among winemakers who want richer textures and subtler flavors than typical Sauvignon Blanc provides on its own, and has been since Robert Mondavi Winery's earliest Fumé Blancs. Chenin Blanc is a rarer choice as a blend grape.

The prevailing choice is to blend vineyards, or to move away from ones with more pungent aromas than the winemaker wants.

Fermenting a portion of Sauvignon Blanc in barrel ranks with either sort of blending as a way of toning down an aggressive Sauvignon. If the wine is left on its lees, particularly, it gains some of the weight Semillon might otherwise provide. Fermenting a Sauvignon in stainless steel and aging it in barrels produces other effects. Sometimes the result is the added flavor of oak just the way it comes at the lumberyard. Sometimes time in barrel gives, somehow, a faint impression of tropical fruit, especially pineapple. At least I think it is the oak, because the same flavor has shown up in Chardonnay, Chenin Blanc, and other whites aged in wood. The prejudice here is that at the best of times barrel aging adds a faint, unidentifiable extra to a wine that still tastes particularly of its grape.

The university was not thinking about me when it counseled mitigation. I am thinking 40 cloves and I am thinking age-worthy whenever we go hunting Sauvignon Blanc, even though we buy mostly 25- to 30-clove editions for the sake of the fish, and we do not age many bottles, even the 40-clove ones.

LIVERMORE VALLEY

The place of honor goes to the Livermore Valley more for what it has done than for what it is doing now. Only Wente Bros. and Concannon Vineyard have long track records with Livermore Sauvignon Blanc, and both of them have been of changeable minds these past few years. However, so long as there are Sauvignon Blanc vines pushing roots down through Livermore rocks, the potential for something splendid is here. The combination of considerable summer heat and an old arroyo full of small boulders and no soil at all seems to be exactly what the variety wants, for it yields powerfully focused flavors in wines balanced to age. Yet, for all the focus, those flavors remain strikingly subtle. The notion of grassy never comes to mind; neither does any other simple, readily recognizable flavor association. They have something of herbs about them, first-rate Livermore Sauvignon Blancs do, but you will never catch one tasting just like dill or sage or any other kitchen familiar.

It comes pretty close to a criminal offense that only 125 of Livermore's 1,500 acres were in Sauvignon Blanc in 1986, and only another 185 in Semillon, but how can we put the whole populace in jail for failing to recognize how great the old Wentes and Concannons were? God knows, the wineries tried to get the word around all through the 1960s and into the 1970s. Their only mistake was trying when the country was not ready.

The down times seem to be ending, if, in fact, they have not already ended. Sergio Traverso has restored emphasis to the variety at Concannon, and the Wentes have done the same on the other side of Tesla Road.

Traverso's approach involves both a proportion of Semillon and a readily noticeable taste of oak from aging in new barrels.

The 1984 Livermore Estate bottling is, he feels, a model of what he is after. (A second bottling with a California appellation is more straightforward.)

The Wente family is sticking with pure Sauvignon Blanc and a stainless-steel aging regimen, one that leaves plenty of varietal character. After drifting away from a Livermore-appellation wine for several seasons during the 1970s, they have returned to the ancestral vineyards for the past several vintages and restored a boldness of flavor that went missing for a time.

NORTH COAST

Against Livermore's 125 acres in 1986, the Napa Valley had 3,750, Sonoma 2,000, Mendocino 740, and Lake 560. Against Livermore's 3 or 4 producers, the North Coast has close to 150 of them. For a time during the 1970s a quarter as many seekers after a distinctive style using half that expanse of grapes almost overwhelmed Sauvignon Blanc admirers with new choices. During 1980s the trend has seemed more toward consolidation. It is not time to talk about a mainstream yet, but at least the river is down to a comparative handful of channels, most of them aimed in one degree or another at preserving Sauvignon Blanc's broad character, but with civilizing touches.

Napa Valley

Right now, for my money, the Napa Valley has an edge over the rest of the field for purebred and blended Sauvignon Blancs alike for several reasons, the main one being an extra depth or structure that allows the richest of them to age in predictable, profitable ways. Both the melonlike examples from the warmer parts of the valley and the sweetly grassy ones from cooler places have shown these sorts of stuffings with consistency. Vintages may be worth noticing, but in all of Napa north of Carneros the grape ripens so steadily that it is no great worry to see the end of one and the coming of the next. In addition to that advantage, individual labels have become reliable in style.

An impressive concentration of first-rate sweet-grassy vineyards occupies the valley floor between the town of Napa and Rutherford, and between State Route 29 and the Silverado Trail. The ones that yield more melonlike aromas in their grapes come from more scattered sources. Some are on the valley floor. A greater number are up in the east hills, all the way from Napa north to the top of Pope Valley.

Exactly where the dividing line between melon-warm and sweet grass–cool runs on the valley floor, nobody knows, or at least tells. Possibly it drifts—northward in cool vintages, to the south in warm ones. Maybe it depends more on whether the soil tips toward gravelly or loamy. Probably it is more mysterious than that. As best my tasting notes say anything about it, the line runs somewhere between Yountville at the south and Rutherford at the north, probably somewhere between Robert Pepi's vineyard and Jack Cakebread's.

ROBERT MONDAVI WINERY

When Robert Mondavi brought Fumé Blanc into the market, he opened a whole new path for the variety. Against the traditionally lean, austere, varietal Sauvignons of Livermore, he offered a fat, rich, wood-aged model that almost begged to be called poor man's Chardonnay, which it quickly was. The wine has slimmed down noticeably in the few most recent vintages, edged a few steps closer to straightforwardly varietal, but all of the changes in its making have left more family resemblances than differences among the individual vintages.

In that sense, it is not only satisfying wine but a convincing demonstration that there is more than one path to a goal. From the beginning the Mondavis have sought to temper but not extinguish Sauvignon Blanc's grassy flavors, to give the wine more body, more flesh than it usually has, and to hone the inherently sharp finish smooth. Since their vineyards run from Oakville south, where Sauvignon is at its sweet-grassiest, they face the whole challenge. The main sources are the Mondavi-owned Oak Knoll vineyard, which faces straight across the Silverado Trail toward Stag's Leap Wine Cellars, and two other leased vineyards close by. Several blocks in the Tokalon Vineyard at the winery also contribute substantially.

In the earliest years barrel aging and a proportion of Semillon moderated the grassiness, and the Semillon also put weight on Sauvignon's lean frame. In later seasons the Mondavis all but replaced the Semillon with uncommonly ripe Sauvignon and barrel fermentation. The current practice uses less barrel fermentation, less ripe grapes, and more aging on the lees. Wines made in the latter two ways have kept the extra flesh while growing truer to Sauvignon, occasionally pungent of it. In most years the Mondavis offer a reserve bottling along with the regular one. The style is the same as the regular one, just more so.

Among many lessons, their twenty-year record teaches that the grape ripens early enough in Napa to give a satisfactory wine vintage after vintage. Between Mondavi and Beaulieu, there is room to suspect that warm vintages give the finest wines in the southern valley, cool seasons the finest ones to the north.

What Mondavi Fumé Blancs do in our cellar these days is bridge the gap between Chardonnay and other Sauvignon Blancs. Anytime whitefish or chicken get into cream sauce, a young Mondavi Fumé Blanc is the first candidate. With bottle age—when they are three or four—they come out for plain baked salmon as well. Another curious lesson they have taught is that curry intensifies the grassy flavors of Sauvignon, sometimes resurrects it from the depths of Semillon and oak.

1977 Definite Sauvignon, but still well freighted with oak and Semillon.

1978 The definitive poor man's Chardonnay remained remarkably fresh in 1985; the richest and most durable Sauvignon of its decade.

1979 Much like the 1978 early, but without quite so many stuffings.

1980 Spot-on Mondavi mixture of fruit and wood flavors, and strong of both. The ultra-ripe, heady Reserve remained remarkably youthful early in 1986.

1981 Crisper, lighter young wine than its forerunners. Rich on the palate by 1985.

1982 Forthrightly sweet-grassy in flavor early; more so (and still lively) by 1986.

1983 Pleasing Sauvignon flavors early, but not so lively or fresh in its youth as the previous two vintages.

1984 No note.

1985 Appealing Sauvignon flavors in a crisp, fresh, lively wine barely touched by oak.

1986 Firm Sauvignon flavors in an uncommonly tart wine; altogether appealing with fish dishes.

MONTICELLO CELLARS

In every vintage since the debut 1981, Monticello Cellars has gotten the sweetly grassy form of Sauvignon Blanc subtle enough to make the wine engaging with mild fish, yet with all the power it takes to be right for fat fish with strong doses of coriander, cumin, and other Mexican seasonings. Not only that, it hangs in against garlicky chicken.

All of it comes from winery owner Jay Corley's own vineyards just at the north edge of Napa town, and not far south of the main Mondavi plantings in their Oak Knoll Vineyard. It is one of a scarce few estate-bottled Sauvignons in the valley. Corley planted in 1972, but did not make wine for his own label until his vines were mature in 1981. Winemaker Alan Phillips blends as much as 15 percent of Semillon to temper the flavors and fatten the textures. The wine takes a brief turn in oak to smooth out the roughness of youth, but does most of its aging in stainless steel so both varietal and local character can go intact into the bottle, usually around June following the harvest. Monticello also makes a reverse blend under the name Chevrier Blanc. It is noted in the Other White Wines chapter.

1981 The debut wine had the richest Norman Rockwell, sweet-grass flavors of any vintage to date; still a young wine in early 1986. The most impressive single Sauvignon for me since the old Wentes.

1982 Similar flavors to 1981, but a shade less forceful. However, aging well in 1987.

1983 Full of the grassy flavors, and tinted by some that remind me of cooked asparagus—a typical cool-season Sauvignon from a region about as cool as the grape seems to want. Sharp early, then rounded out by mid-1985.

1984 Middling in the series; rather like the 1982, except a bit headier.

1985 Excellent balance and slightly understated flavors, in the vein of 1982.

SILVERADO VINEYARDS

Silverado Vineyards Sauvignons usually strike me as gentler echoes of both the Robert Mondavis and the Monticellos. They have the sweet-grass character of their southern Napa neighbors, but in a less forceful form than either.

The restraint is winemaker John Stuart's choice. The estate vineyard, from which all of the grapes come, lies less than a mile north of Mondavi's Oak Knoll property, stretching west from the winery to the southern edge of Yountville.

The real hallmark and the particular virtue of the Silverados, though, is not their understatement but rather their silky polish. A subtle but identifiable touch of oak complicates the flavors and smooths the textures just enough to make vintages to date fit better with mild, unsauced fish than with garlicky or Mexican dishes. We have drunk unconscionable amounts of it with the airy fried onion rings at Mustard's Grill, which is just a couple of miles north of the Silverado vineyards.

1982 All sweet grass to smell. Oak showed up primarily as part of a lush, ripe feel on the palate.

1983 Almost wispy sweet-grass aromas and a shade more of oak than the inaugural vintage. Aging very well in late 1986.

1984 Ripest flavors to date, but still understated; impeccable polish and balance from the beginning.

1985 From the finest vintage to date, wonderfully perfumey of both grape variety and place of origin directly after bottling. By early 1987 developing the polish and elegance that is the house style.

BEAULIEU VINEYARD

Whenever we want a delicate evocation of a melony Sauvignon Blanc, Beaulieu is whither we go. Its flavors are specific, but underplayed enough to let mild-flavored whitefish shine through. Most of it comes from vineyards right around Rutherford, the rest from ranches farther north.

Alone of all these Napa Sauvignon Blancs, the Beaulieu sees no wood at all, fermenting then aging in stainless steel to keep its fruit flavors foremost. The debut 1976 had a tiny proportion of Chenin Blanc; that idea was history by 1980.

Though the wine is reliably right with sand dabs and sole, it has stood up successfully to *salade niçoise* and blackened redfish (not the fiery original from Paul Prudhomme's K-Paul's Louisiana Kitchen, but a tamer echo from a quieter quarter of New Orleans).

1976 Pleasant. Not strong for varietal. Faintest hint sweet.

1977 Virtual twin of 1976.

1978 The first truly melony example. Crisper, fresher than previous vintages.

1979 No note.

1980 Somehow unimpressive early, but held together well. Remained fresh and lively in 1986.

1981 Started well as an understated, crisply refreshing, almost austere wine. Still every bit of that in 1986.

1982 Particularly aromatic of melon early, and continued to be so as late as 1985. One of the very best for flavor and balance.

1983 Seemed rather softer and less refreshing than preceding three vintages. Not so specific of Sauvignon in its aromas.

1984 Steady, but only in the pack with the 1980 and 1981.

1985 Equal or superior to the 1982, and much in its vein.

FLORA SPRINGS WINE CO.

A light touch of oak does no more harm to the delicately melony sort of Sauvignons than it does to the delicately sweet-grassy ones. Flora Springs Sauvignon Blancs have had much the same melonlike flavor as the Beaulieu, but with a persistent fillip from barrel aging to complicate them at no cost to their subtletly of flavor or polished textures. The hint of oak and their silky polish makes them as closely kindred to the Silverados as to the Beaulieus. The sum of their parts recommends them with most of the same dishes—the onion rings at Mustard's Grill, the whitebait salad from Jean-Louis at The Watergate, and other such feather-light dishes. On the reverse of the coin, they are quickly overmatched by coriander, peppers, garlic, and all such. On the Beard scale, they are in the neighborhood of 10-clove wines. Delicate flavors have not meant swift decline. Every vintage to date has lasted at least four years in top form.

The grapes for the vintages through 1986 all came from a winery-owned vineyard on the valley floor east of Oakville. The wines ferment in steel, then go to a mixed bag of French and American barrels and French casks until bottling, usually in May following the vintage. The owning Komes family and winemaker Ken Deis set great store by the contribution of American oak to their Sauvignon.

1980 Subtle in flavor. Crisp, refreshing after a harsh first few months.
1981 Exact echo of 1980.
1982 Beautiful example of the melon flavors barely tinted by oak.
1983 Subtly melony; crisp early, then fuller and rounder by early 1986. The hint of oak continues
1984 Much in the vein of 1983.
1985 Fuller of fruit than any previous vintage; simultaneously crisper and livelier in texture.

CAKEBREAD CELLARS

For Sauvignon Blanc bibbers after bold, sometimes outright startling flavors, this is the one. First Jack and now Bruce Cakebread have managed to pack their Sauvignon with more of the melonlike side of the variety than anybody else, no qualifications.

To match its flavors, the wine is built sturdy, not rough. It has a vitality about it that goes on, I suppose, for six, seven, eight years. I do not know this for a fact because, in its head-strong youth, this is a prime choice for dishes we eat often—chili- and cumin-spiced Mexican stews, monkfish, black cod and other fatty fish, hearty vegetable soups—so we never have any left to test in age. It also does well by a bale of garlic, more so than any of the other melon-tinged candidates in the field, though this is not its highest calling.

The backbone vineyard is twenty-plus acres at the winery, about a mile north of Oakville and flanking the state highway. It is supplemented by the grapes from two independent growers, one nearby, the other a few miles north at St. Helena, to bring the volume to a shade fewer than seven thousand cases a year. Bruce Cakebread ferments the wine in steel, then gives it a carefully measured brush with barrel aging, just enough to soften the wine, not enough to flavor it with oak.

1978 A bit rough-hewn, but full of Sauvignon flavors.

1979 More polished than the 1978, but still very sturdy and far fuller of melonlike Sauvignon. The balance said it would last for years.

1980 Continued the movement toward more polish at no expense to fruit flavors or firmness of texture.

1981 A bit stronger in the perfumes of new French oak than its predecessors, it could wear out its welcome against a plain dish such as roasted chicken.

1982 Much in the vein of the 1981.

1983 Back to the style of the 1980, and balanced much like it.

1984 One of the tartest and most cleansing of the wines to date, and still rich in ripe Sauvignon flavors. With the 1980, a superior vintage.

1985 Stunning concentration of ripe, melonlike Sauvignon in a wine of imperishably sturdy textures. Perfect company to an Italianate chicken dish brimming with olives, herbs, and other pungent ingredients.

ST. CLEMENT VINEYARDS

The St. Clements offer another opportunity to those who want their Sauvignon Blancs bold, ready to take on Mexican seasonings, spicy sauces, even well-herbed pork or lamb. They have some of the intensity of flavor of the Cakebreads, and some of the stuffings. They differ in being less aromatic of melon, more firmly marked by their time in wood.

Winemaker Dennis Johns draws grapes for an annual three thousand cases of Sauvignon from independent growers in Chiles Valley and near St. Helena. Johns ferments slow and cool to keep all the fruit flavors, and gives the wines a three- to four-month tour in French barrels, not unusually long, but enough to produce a specific taste of oak, sweet at first, faintly varnishy after five or six years. The resulting wines have power young and stuffings enough to age well, though they have not seemed to hold a peak quite as long as some of their peers.

For us, these have been just what is wanted for veal, even rabbit and pork, but not our first choice when fish or shellfish have been on the table. The more delicate the seafood, the more this has been true.

1980 More of the sweet-grassy flavors than melon ones; definitely tinted by wood. By 1986 just past its best days, but still a pleasure.

1981 Early, richer in melon than its forerunner.

1982 A little grassier than typical, and not so well balanced as other vintages. By 1986 it was aging faster than its older mates.

1983 Richest in melon flavors of the vintages to date, and also the wine most marked by its time in oak. A mere hint soft, a stronger hint heady.

1984 Rich fruit flavors and near-perfect balance put it first on our list. It had enough vitality to go well with scallops, a notoriously difficult test for wine, and a particular surprise for a St. Clement Sauvignon.

1985 In the early going, not quite the equal of either of the preceding two vintages for intensity of fruit, but it had a pleasing delicacy of flavor and texture.

BERINGER VINEYARDS

Beringer's Napa Valley Fumé Blancs have always had a leanness about them and a highly developed Sauvignon aroma. After years of trying to fatten them up through ripeness and ample time in barrel, in 1985 the winery switched gears and went after the lean-ness, leaving to its quick-maturing Sonoma Fumé Blancs the market for weighty poor man's Chardonnay. The new plan uses a dollop of Semillon to temper the Sauvignon and, at the same time, put a hint of flesh on the bones. Wood is a smaller part of the whole than in earlier seasons. A superior vintage in 1985 got the new plan off to an impressive start.

Most of the grapes came from Beringer's Gamble Ranch east of Oakville; the remainder come from two other winery-owned ranches within a mile of Gamble's south boundary.

1981 Unmistakable sweet-grassy Sauvignon aromas and a lean, firm structure made for an attractive wine, especially with poultry in creamy sauces. Showed the first faint signs of fading late in 1984.

1982 If anything, a shade lighter and leaner than the 1981.

1983 A bit heavy, and always in the pack.

1984 The wine of the series on release. Still drinking well late in 1987.

1985 Nicely understated for Sauvignon flavors. Crisper and more cleansing on the palate than any of its forerunners.

In the Hunt

Napa's strengths with Sauvignon Blanc reach a deal farther than this list. In truth, we come to nights when we would just as soon have one of the following wines as any on the main list. These five are here to remind us that dozens if not scores of wines have been left out of this book by the thinnest of margins.

Clos du Val   Bordeaux-born and trained, Bernard Portet makes a Sauvignon Blanc that is sometimes understated in every way, sometimes striking for how much flavor it packs into such a light body. It is, thus, a considerable fish wine.

Inglenook Vineyards   The winery seems to have turned a corner with its 1983 Reserve, and kept the corner turned in the vintages since. Winemaker John Richburg has drawn on several vineyards from Yountville south to make deft understatements of Sauvignon's sweet-grassy side. Oak is a barely perceptible hint of a flavor. The feel of the wines is light and crisp.

Robert Pepi Winery Sauvignon Blanc is the specialty of this small winery with its own vineyards alongside the state highway between Yountville and Oakville. Here, if there is a boundary between sweet grass and melon, is the northernmost of the consistently sweet-grassy territory. The wines have gained steadily since the premier vintage, 1981.

Raymond Vineyard & Cellar For several years Walter Raymond made a ripe, fleshy wine well marked by aging in oak and called it Fumé Blanc. With the 1985, he shifted toward a crisper, less woody style, and signaled the change by renaming the wine Sauvignon Blanc. The vintage gave him a head start, but the new notion seems to show off his grapes to fuller advantage than the old, which did not do badly.

Stratford Since 1981 Tony Cartlidge and company have made a consistently pleasing, melony Sauvignon based in grapes from Pope Valley, but heavily supplemented by others from the hills east of St. Helena, the valley floor at Rutherford, and the Big Ranch Road area just north of Napa. The wines fit neatly between Beaulieu and Flora Springs in style and substance.

Sonoma County

To settle for the single, simple heading Sonoma County rather admits defeat. Sonoma grows the grape very well in every one of its subdistricts. The trouble in pinpointing any identifying marks arises because so few wineries draw all of their grapes from a single AVA, and the few that do tend to spread themselves out, one per region. There is some validity in blending from different sources. Sonoma has more than a few pockets that turn out Sauvignon Blancs of such overpowering character that people's eyes roll up like Little Orphan Annie's at the first sniff of them. Tame one of these powerhouses with help from some understated vineyards, and a winemaker can control varietal character within an atom of what he or she looks for. Such got to be the habit early, and it persists.

The general, all-purpose descriptive term for Sonoma Sauvignon Blanc is *grassy*. Not the tall, jointed kind that the cooler parts of Napa will evoke, but blade grass, good old lawn grass. The flavor is not the same, but the comparison is as close as my nose knows. In blind tastings, when I jot "Sonoma" in the notes, it is when that aroma comes to mind. The guess is right more often than for any other region. Wines thus fingered have come from every part of the county. Dry Creek Valley and Alexander Valley seem readiest to yield the flavor, with Sonoma Valley not far behind, but it is not money in the bank either way. These places will turn out a melonlike model just often enough to keep me from being sure that it is a signpost for Napa, and other districts will yield one of the grassy sort. To keep a body completely unsure, any one of the regions can turn up a wine with enough asparagus to fool me into thinking Central Coast. And so, no separating the players by AVAs.

A surer marker than aroma for Sonoma Sauvignon Blancs from whichever corner, or corners, is a certain lightness or delicacy of texture. One after another they sit lightly on the tongue, great refreshers on a warm evening. On texture, you mainly get fooled by Lake County counterparts, and there are not many of those.

Hardly any sense of order reigns in this list of favorites, because, in my estimation, they all sit at a round table. The pioneer comes first out of respect, the AVA-identifiables follow, and the assembled wines bring up the rear, but only to have a sequence.

DRY CREEK VINEYARD

David Stare is the father of Sonoma Sauvignon Blanc, the first serious producer starting with 1972. The wine has been startlingly consistent through all the vintages since, particularly in view of the ever-changing roster of vineyards that contribute to it.

Young, it ever has been and still is the very model of Sonoma grassy, a perfect wine with which to track down that flavor association. Old, it is a complete original, but of that more in a moment. The first three vintages came from a single vineyard toward the western edge of the Russian River Valley. The next few came primarily from Stare's own vineyard at the winery and the Preston Vineyard just upstream in Dry Creek Valley, but included bits from several others. Currently, the mix is about half Alexander Valley, a quarter Russian River Valley, and a quarter from the winery property. The sources sound more far flung than they are; all three AVAs coverage at Healdsburg, and all three vineyards do too. The volume in the beginnings was a couple of thousand cases; in the mid-1980s it is running at a shade more than twenty thousand cases.

In spite of all the changes, not only has the basic varietal aroma remained constant but so has the light, gentle, polished texture of the wine. Oh, there has been a small shift. The first wines could handle 40 cloves if they had the wind in their faces. Later ones have lightened up enough that 35 is about all they handle, at least while they are young.

Old is another story. Old they want garlic. For some reason, as Dry Creek Sauvignon Blancs develop bottle bouquet, they begin to smell a bit like an Italian deli. With a lot of bottle bouquet, they smell a lot like an Italian deli, the whole thing— pickling spices, smoked provolone, sausages, herbs, you name it. The image is Stare's own. He loves the wine when it gets to that point. So do most of his familiars. It does shock novices.

The grapes, always 100 percent Sauvignon Blanc, hold no clue.

233

Nothing in the vineyards explains the change; the roster has migrated too much, and other buyers from the same sources do not get the same results. Nothing in the winemaking explains it either, at least not readily, because it is conventional all the way: cool fermentation in stainless steel, then a five-month turn in well-seasoned French oak barrels to soften the edges just a bit before bottling, and release in the spring following the harvest. It is just one of the more appealing, mysterious tricks that wine does to keep us happy. The general pattern is to drink a Dry Creek by its third birthday for the Sonoma grass character, most profitably with whitefish, or to save it until it is past four for the Italian-deli tastes.

1974 Strong Sonoma grass early, but delicate in texture. Still lively in autumn 1982, but full-fledged deli bouquets by then.
1975 A curiously weak vintage. Went over the hill early.
1976 Perfectly balanced, full of flavor. As of 1982 still in top, grassy form.
1977 Followed exactly the path of the 1974. Hinted of Italian deli beginning in 1982, shouted it by 1984.
1978 Not quite the riches of the 1977 or 1974.
1979 Richly scented of Sonoma grass and as full-bodied as any Dry Creek. Just getting into stride in 1982; still on top of form in 1985.
1980 One of the gentle ones early. Well on the way to Italian deli by spring 1983.
1981 Abundant Sonoma grass in the early going, but still polished and delicate for texture. First vintage in which oak seemed an identifiable note.
1982 Followed 1981 closely.
1983 A bit of an oddity for having less Sonoma grass, more melon than any in memory, but all appealing.
1984 Echo of 1980.
1985 Spot-on Dry Creek, much in the vein of 1981.
1986 Right with 1985.

PRESTON VINEYARDS

Lou Preston makes the real thing, a Sonoma grassy Sauvignon Blanc with the sturdy textures and other stuffings so dear to the hearts of chicken 40 cloves of garlic people.

It is an estate wine from grapes Preston grows on gravelly bottomlands not far down Dry Creek Valley from Warm Springs Dam. One is forced to assume it is typical of Dry Creek Valley Sauvignon Blanc for lack of other evidence, though it ought to have inspired several imitators by now for being a flawless evocation of Sonoma grassy.

Preston keeps his Fumé Blanc 100 percent of the variety, touches it lightly with oak, and bottles it in the spring following the harvest. For contrast he offers a proprietary Cuvée de Fumé, which is 85 percent Sauvignon Blanc and 15 percent Chenin Blanc.

1977 Impressive opening shot. A definitive Dry Creek grassy; rich and balanced enough for chicken 40 cloves.

1978 If anything, more tart and tougher than the 1977.

1979 Twin of 1978.

1980 A tiny step back, but continued the style and substance.

1981 Had us looking for bigger chickens to use more than 40 cloves.

1982 Close kin to the 1980, but a little gentler and more polished.

1983 Weak by the standards of the house, but still plenty of wine for almost anybody.

1984 Hearkens back to the 1982 for gentleness and polish. First vintage in which French oak showed through.

1985 Rich in both flavor and texture; one of the finest.

Alderbrook Winery

Alderbrook Sauvignon Blancs might be mistaken for an argument against the Prestons being typical of Dry Creek Valley, but they should not, as the winemaking takes the other fork every time the road splits.

Preston is all Sauvignon Blanc, Alderbrook fattened with a bit of Semillon; Preston advertises the presence of oak, Alderbrook does not, and so on. Predictably, the Alderbrooks are full-bodied, polished smooth, and well tempered in matters of regional grassy flavors—wines for chicken in creamy sauces sooner than chicken laden with garlic.

Though none has had a real chance to go gray at the temples, not one of the five vintages to date shows any signs of doing so. The inaugural 1982 remains almost as fresh as it was when it went to bottle. Another point in their favor is a remarkable consistency through a skein of wildly differing growing seasons.

John Grace gets most of the grapes for his annual fifty-five hundred cases from a neighbor vineyard within the legal confines of Dry Creek Valley, but he does not use its name on the label. That the AVA boundary separating Dry Creek Valley from the Russian River Valley is about a three-wood shot south of the last row of vines may be reason enough not to do it. The principal vineyard sits straight across US Highway 101 from downtown Healdsburg, and straight across Westside Road from a gravel quarry, which is to say it is about as far downstream from Dry Creek Vineyard as Preston Vineyards is up. The second vineyard is a mile west, in the Russian River Valley.

1982 A deft balancing act between herbaceous and melonlike, with melon winning at the wire. Feels rich on the palate.
1983 Similar balancing act to 1982, but this time herbs win at the finish. Same rich, firm, structured feel.
1984 Photocopy of 1982, except oak a more noticeable note. Perfect mate to a perfect vichysoisse.
1985 Powerfully varietal; full and firm on the palate.

GLEN ELLEN WINERY & VINEYARDS

If ever a label made a Hollywood entrance into the society of Sonoma Sauvignon Blancs, Glen Ellen did, winning the best-of-show award at the Sonoma Harvest Fair wine competition within weeks of releasing its first vintage, the 1981. Bruno Benziger's winery has kept its Sauvignon Blanc banner flying since, with a repeat performance as sweepstakes champion in 1985, and four silvers and a bronze in the off years.

The wine does what most Sonomans seem to do effortlessly: concentrates the herbaceous aromas of Sauvignon in a wine of almost airy lightness of body. Rather, the *wines* do. The Benzigers make at least two each year. The ones to watch are the Estate Sauvignon Blanc and a Sonoma Valley Fumé Blanc from purchased grapes. The latter further separates itself from the Estate Sauvignon for spending more time in newer French oak barrels.

The estate vineyard clings to a steep, east-facing slope above the town of Glen Ellen, but well downhill from Jack London's old ranch. It gets a little more sun and thus a little more growing-season heat than the valley vineyards the Benzigers draw upon for their Fumé, hence the wine is a tiny fraction fuller or richer than its running mates, but this is a distinction I would hate to have to find in blind triangular tastings. The extra smack of oak in the Fumé is easier to spot, but not much. Definite as their flavors are, the light, crisp feel makes both wines versatile at table. As part of the rigorously disciplined research for these comments, we took a bottle with a quenelle of salmon and seabass at a Sonoma restaurant called Les Arcades, and another with cumin-basted chicken at home. It got high marks all around, while reinforcing the notion that the wines will age, but letting them do it is foolish. A year in bottle gives every gift one could want.

1981 Plenty of Sauvignon plus a definite hint of wood. Fat and rich on the tongue among typically light Sonomans.
1982 More delicate all around; set the style that has continued.
1983 Not quite the crisp delicacy of the 1982, but a charmer all the same. Showed best against sole and other delicate fish.
1984 Early it showed the rich flavors of the 1981 and delicate textures of the 1982. The vintage of the series until . . .
1985 Everything the 1984 had and more. Richer flavors, crisper, more cleansing textures. Great with vegetable quiches, salmon quenelles, miscellaneous whitefish.

IRON HORSE VINEYARDS

Iron Horse is one of our sure-bet snapper Veracruz (in a sauce of vegetables and Mexican seasonings), shark in cumin butter, and/or *chiles rellenos* Sauvignon Blancs. It will perfume a room almost as fast as one from Napa's Cakebread Cellars and is almost as firm on the palate. What is more, during its young days it has enough of the melonlike side of the variety about it for me to confound it with the Napans sooner than other Sonoma Sauvignons.

Why all of this is so remains a mystery, pending the appearance of some rivals in its own neighborhood, which is the east side of the Alexander Valley in hills above a crossroads called Jimtown. As usual with AVA-entitled Sauvignon Blancs in Sonoma County, a comparison is hard or impossible to come by. The lone source is a seven-acre patch belonging to Iron Horse partner-winemaker Forrest Tancer and his family. No other estate Sauvignon Blanc comes from these west-facing hills; not another Sauvignon in the style is to be found for miles around.

Tancer uses no blend grapes, ferments the wine in a combination of stainless steel and large and small wood, then ages it for only two months in oak.

1981 Enough melon and enough oak to summon up the image of a poor man's Chardonnay early. By 1985 it was a rich, complicated Sauvignon and perfect company to snapper Veracruz.

1982 A bit overweight for texture and underweight for fruit flavors compared to its siblings.

1983 Fine melon flavors and much livelier on the tongue than either of its forerunners. A shadowy hint of oak complicated it in youth. Delicate enough for salmon mousse, sturdy enough for chicken with Mexican seasonings.

1984 Early the most herbaceous vintage to date. By mid-1986 a bit overweight and not so pronounced in flavors.

1985 Powerful melon. Great balance. In the early going the vintage of the series to date.

KENWOOD VINEYARDS

At the start it was another perfect evocation of Sonoma grassy, an altogether reliable wine for chicken 40 cloves of garlic. More recently it has turned down the volume just a touch, to 33 or 34 cloves, but the Kenwood still epitomizes the assembled Sonoma Sauvignon Blanc.

The family Lee draws upon a dozen to fifteen grape growers, who are scattered the length and breadth of a long, broad county. The Lees took a careful look before they plunged, waiting until 1980 to produce their first vintage of the varietal. The style they hit on has moved their Sauvignon from a tiny initial offering to something on the order of 40 percent of their total production in its first six years.

The Lees use no Semillon and very little oak, preferring to drive after varietal character. The range of vineyards provides most of the complexity as well as reliable balance. Generally, the most pungent lots are the ones that see wood; the lighter ones stay in stainless steel from fermenting until all are blended for bottling about six months after the harvest.

1980 Abundant grassy varietal. Very firm in texture. Outweighed delicate fish, but splendid with spicy or herb-sauced dishes.

1981 As richly flavored and sturdily built as its predecessor. Still fresh and lively in mid-1985.

1982 One shade lighter and crisper than either of the two previous vintages.

1983 Split the difference between 1981 and 1982. Calibrated at exactly 40 cloves during its youth.

1984 A bit less bright and lively than typical, and a hint fiery at the finish, but still agreeable.

1985 Rather more polished up and polite than the early vintages, the first one to weigh in at a few less than 40 cloves of garlic.

1986 A shade more refined than the 1985, and a bit more refreshing.

DOMAINE LAURIER

The Domaine Laurier Sauvignons live partly on subtle varietal character and partly on bouquets that cannot be described but must be admired.

Though the label makes no mention, this is a Russian River

Valley wine. Proprietor Jacob Shilo grows some of the grapes on a narrow little strip of bottomland at the winery and buys the rest from hilltop vineyards in the immediate neighborhood around Forestville. The division is intentional. Shilo's home vineyard yields a definite Sonoma-grassy set of flavors; the hilltop neighbors provide both fruit and subtlety to the mix.

Winemaker Steven Test adds the indescribables and an admirable polish, partly through fermenting a portion of the wine in barrel, partly through keeping some two thirds of the four thousand-case annual production in wood for several months, and partly with blue smoke and mirrors. Test has a particular knack for getting the wine mature just as it goes to bottle, no small virtue when dinner is tonight and the cellar is empty. Complete as they are early, the vintages to date have aged fairly well. At all stages they have been notably versatile with food, but we seem to gravitate toward chicken and turkey with herbed stuffings or gravies when we have a bottle to try.

1981 No note.
1982 Almost sweet-grassy. Beautifully balanced, polished from the outset.
1983 More of the fruity side of Sauvignon than the 1982, but just as supple and balanced.
1984 Showed more of the bouquets of barrel fermentation than its predecessors, but had the characteristic balance.
1985 Leans just a shade toward grassy; nicely marked by bouquets of barrel fermentation. Beautifully balanced, polished. The wine of the series to date.

SIMI WINERY

In spite of Zelma Long's towering reputation for Chardonnay, if it were to come down to just one white wine from Simi, I might well plead for this one because California offers so many fine Chardonnays and Cabernets, and so few completely rewarding Sauvignon Blancs. Simi's Sauvignon plays grass down and fruit up without borrowing anything from any other region, has extra touches that come from the winemaking but are so discreet they seem to come from some loftier source than mere technical steps, and lays lighter than a veil on the tongue. It is, in short, perfectly proportioned. The pale color promises delicacy of aroma, which in turn promises delicacy of texture. The wine has delivered on all counts in every vintage from the debut 1982 onward. It is a short history, not even five years, but the winemaker is a proven hand.

Every wine Long makes betrays her years of rigorous training at Robert Mondavi at the same time that it demonstrates how individual and distinctive is her own stylistic bent. Nowhere does this show more fully than in the contrasts between his Fumé Blanc and her Sauvignon Blanc. Rather, it shows in the contrasts between his Fumé Blancs and her Sauvignon Blancs, plural, because one of his legacies is the ongoing willingness to modify in small steps on the way to a goal.

Long has already used (1982, 1983, 1984) and not used (1985) Semillon as a blend grape, as vintages and vineyard sources have dictated. She has used and not used barrel fermentation, and so on through the winemaker's range of options. Not only are these factors imperceptible, but they have hidden the steady shift in vineyards in a wine of admirable consistency. The winery started with a roster of ten ranches and has shaved it to four major ones, two in the Chalk Hill district, two in Alexander Valley. One of the Chalk Hill properties yielded about half of the 1985 and is on the list for its ability to deliver pungent Sonoma-grass aromas. The rest made the cut because they help tame the tiger and otherwise keep matters in balance.

1982 Ever-shifting balance of fruit and other flavors. Surprisingly sturdy with such as spicy lentil soup. Still fresh and lively in late 1986.

1983 Outperformed a generally fragile vintage. In its early days subtle enough for a poached fish, sturdy enough for one of John Ash & Company's rillettes of duck. Continued to improve through 1986.

1984 A bit stolid early, but only in comparison to the 1983. Still gaining in mid-1987.

1985 Very much like the 1982. If anything, even richer.

MATANZAS CREEK WINERY

Merry Edwards established a bold winemaking style at Mount Eden Vineyards, and stayed true to form during her incumbency at Matanzas Creek. Dave Ramey settled on a subtler approach while he was assistant to Zelma Long at Simi, and brought his ideas with him when he succeeded Edwards at Matanzas Creek in 1984. Put it as bald as that, and one would expect a sea change in the wines. However, no such thing happened.

The Sonoma Mountain vineyard Edwards had tracked down for the mainstay for Matanzas Creek Sauvignons suits Ramey just as well. He has shuffled the supporting cast a bit in favor of a ranch in the Chalk Hill AVA and retuned some of the winemaking details until the sum of the changes weighs a bit lighter on the tongue, but the constants are as numerous as the variables in a wine that has been fine company to dishes with some authority to them, and still is.

1980 Forceful notes of both Sauvignon and oak in a slightly overweight poor man's Chardonnay sort of wine.
1981 Similar flavors to 1980, but more deftly balanced.
1982 Another ripe, fat Sauvignon with noticeable bouquets of wood early, but perfectly balanced as such. In 1987 still in peak form.
1983 No note.
1984 Very much in the vein of 1982.
1985 For admirers of subtle flavors and refreshing textures, the wine of the series. Compared to earlier vintages, plays up Sauvignon and plays down wood.

Mendocino and Lake

Neither Mendocino nor Lake counties has a winery with a long, steady track record in Sauvignon Blanc, but both counties have shown considerable and differing promise.

Lake County, inland and upland, has turned out several Sauvignon Blancs that have some of the lightness and delicacy of texture of Sonoma paired with some of the sweet-grassy to melonlike flavors of Napa. The county served striking notice that the combination has appeal when wines from there took five of the first seven places in an international all-comers tasting in 1987, all from vineyards close by the town of Kelseyville, on Clear Lake's western shore.

Konocti Winery These Sauvignons have been models of what the Clear Lake AVA seems to do naturally: faintly rather than forcibly grassy and delicately rigged. The style has been dry, with little or no oak aging from the beginning, 1981. Buena Vista began making a Lake County Sauvignon Blanc with the vintage of 1985, and achieved almost an exotic perfume of fruit in the early going (an old tasting note says it went past melon, almost to peach). The 1986 comes closer to a typical Konocti, and no wonder. Buena Vista's assistant winemaker, David Rosenthal, grew up in a family with Lake County vineyards and worked at Konocti before joining Buena Vista.

Mendocino, with most of its Sauvignon Blanc grapes ringed around hot, dry Ukiah, seems to lean more in the direction of the full-bodied, melonlike Sauvignon Blancs typical of Pope Valley in eastern Napa County, but does produce at least one notable exception to the generality.

Husch Vineyards A steady string of well-rounded, melon-tinged Mendocino Sauvignon Blancs has been turned out by the owning Hugo Oswald family's La Ribera Ranch, a long, skinny strip that runs east from the Russian River between Hopland and Talmage.

Obester Winery Obester has made the exceptions, a string of light, crisp, sweet-grassy Mendocino Sauvignon Blancs that goes back to the late 1970s without a disappointment. All have come from a vineyard toward the north end of Potter Valley, the upland district almost on Mendocino County's shared boundary with Lake County. Logic has an innings in this wine, which, like its vineyard, is halfway between the fatter, more melony Husches and the leaner, grassier Konoctis. Paul and Sandy Obester's small winery is, incidentally, in the distant and improbable neighborhood of Half Moon Bay, a grapeless fishing and farming village some miles downcoast from San Francisco.

CENTRAL COAST

The long-term reputation of Sauvignon Blanc in the Central Coast beyond Livermore has rested in relatively few hands to this point. Not quite a dozen wineries in Monterey, San Luis Obispo, and Santa Barbara counties have made it from local grapes for more than five years running. Given these sparse numbers and the expanse of territory, Sauvignon Blanc has established itself as a leading variety with surprising speed.

Its whole preformance is a surprise. Here, more than anywhere else in California, are the places to test the notion that Sauvignon Blanc's flavors resemble herbs and grasses more than fruits. Cool climate is what seems to provoke the flavor, just as it provokes the taste of bell peppers in Cabernet Sauvignon, and cool is what the Central Coast has plenty of. Remove ultra-warm Paso Robles from the equation and nothing in nature seems to make a large difference in the Central Coast flavor. Remove the warmer parts of the Santa Ynez Valley from consideration, and it begins to be hard to find any regional differences at all. From Monterey south to the last row of vines in Santa Barbara County, this pervasive regional characteristic approaches very near canned asparagus when it comes at full strength.

For me, the full-fledged regional aroma is impossible to enjoy. I don't know why canned asparagus was so cheap during the Depression, or so plentiful during World War II, but my childhood was full of the gray, limp, slick, quickly cold stuff, which had become a penance well before I could ride a bicycle. People who escaped it, on the other hand, admire the same wines that cause me to turn away.

Winemaking can temper this regional contribution to the varietal aromas almost to extinction if the grapes have just a bit of heat to push them through the growing season. The bottles on the following short list come from one warm and one hot spot.

Santa Ynez Valley

The warm, inland end of the Santa Ynez got out of the blocks fast with Sauvignon Blanc, primarily because C. Frederic Brander brought a deep interest in the variety to Santa Ynez Valley Winery in 1977, and then to his own in 1979. Brander has done something interesting and appetizing with Sauvignon in each vintage since, always within a sharply defined style. He remains the only consistent voice on the subject in the territory, although others show strong signs. Rich Longoria began well at J. Carey Vineyard and appears to be on track at his more recent post, The Gainey Vineyard. Ken Brown made several intriguing examples at Zaca Mesa, and has started in a similar vein under his own Bryon Vineyards label. If they are names to watch, Brander is still the one to trust.

THE BRANDER VINEYARD

Fred Brander had a touch with Sauvignon Blanc going in; it has not deserted him. His intent, from vineyard to bottle, is to temper almost to extinction the Santa Ynez Valley's tendency to make Sauvignon Blanc taste like asparagus, canned or otherwise. Brander harvests fairly early, before the aromas come into full bloom. A substantial portion of the wine ferments in new French barrels. The proprietor blends Semillon (typically 20 percent, a top of 35, a low of 18) to give extra body, and also induces malolactic fermentation to mitigate the tartness. Then the wine ages in a mixture of new and old wood until just before its first birthday.

The largest single adjustment of style came with the vintage of 1985, when Brander cut back barrel fermentation by half and otherwise diminished the use of any technique that might mask the flavor of the grapes.

Before and after 1985 the results have not been stern, but not far from it either. Herbaceous flavors of Sauvignon, real tartness, and perceptible textures from oak do not lend themselves to thoughtless sipping. No, this is a basic Beardian 40 cloves wine, one that stands up to cilantro and chiles as well. We have come to prefer the Branders when they are three and four years old. They last longer in top form as far as texture and balance go, but the regional flavors start sneaking back in with more time.

This is, emphatically, an estate wine. Brander is almost adamant on the point that every vineyard worth a name should have its own winery. All of the grapes for every vintage have come from the family's forty-acre vineyard, 120 cases in 1979 (when most of the crop went to Santa Ynez Valley Winery), about 6,000 cases now. The property tips very gently to the south on a long slope next to the town of Los Olivos.

1979 The debut vintage had no Semillon, so was intensely varietal, leaner, and more austere than its successors.

1980 Set the style to perfection. Impeccable balance and intricate interweaving of Sauvignon, Semillon, and winemaking flavors early.

1981 Very lean and tart at heart, but fattened by Semillon and wood. By spring 1984 began to show previously masked regional asparagus flavors, but remains a wine of many facets.

1982 Typical mix of delicate flavor and sturdy texture; excellent balance.

1983 In flavors, the most revealing of barrel fermentation and related winemaking techniques of any vintage to date, but only in direct comparison.

1984 In line with 1982.

1985 As tart as its forebears, but emphatically fruitier.

Paso Robles

Paso Robles would seem to be about the upper limit of Sauvignon Blanc's tolerance of heat. If the well-ripened Sauvignon Blancs from the region automatically avoid smelling like canned asparagus, most of them have a way of exhausting the frail to weary charms of their youth within a few months after bottling, then sliding downhill quickly. Of several winemakers working the territory, Domenic Martin has found what strikes me as the most appealing as well as the most effective answer to that problem.

MARTIN BROTHERS WINERY

Domenic Martin picks early, ferments cold, passes the wine quickly through barrels, and bottles it early, all for the same reason: to keep all there is of some underplayed varietal aromas. The first thing one notices is how tart, almost lemony the wine feels in the mouth. Right after that comes a delicate but ringingly clear set of grassy Sauvignon flavors, the gustatory equivalent of a familiar voice carried a long distance through still air on a freezing night.

In spite of their coming from a district in which typical Sauvignon Blancs weary before they are three, the Martins endure in peak form for at least five years. We save them for red rockfish, snapper, cod, all of the fatty but delicately flavored fishes. The wines pair well with such fish plain or—surprise—when it is swimming in the vegetables and Mexican seasonings that go into Veracruz sauce.

The first vintage came exclusively from a vineyard called Tierra Rejada, some miles east of Paso Robles; the whole ton, the entire yield, twenty-four cases. Tierra Rejada has continued to be the backbone. In 1984 Martin's own vineyard next to the winery added its first four tons to Tierra Rejada's ten. The yield was 290 cases, a step back from the record 625 cases of 1983.

1980 Showed signs of what was to come, but pale against its successors.

1981 Also very delicate in flavor, but not so self-effacing as the debut vintage. Tart and fresh in youth.

1982 Noticeably underripe flavors; tartness softened by a faint suggestion of sweet. Great with fish early; greater yet in late 1985.

1983 Clear-as-a-bell sweet-grassy flavors complicated by a barely perceptible note from oak. Sturdy enough to weigh in against spicy lentil soup. Finest balance in vintages to date. As fresh as new wine in mid-1986.

1984 Same sweet-grassy flavors as earlier; same tartness, but fuller, richer on the tongue than its predecessors.

ZINFANDEL

IF ALL THE PEOPLE WHO HAVE ANSWERS ABOUT
Zinfandel got together with all the ones who have questions,
the wine would be in more trouble than it already is because
the people with the answers are always thinking about a different Zinfandel than the people with the questions.

Back when I was a boy and California had only 125 or so
wineries, people used to talk about the grape variety producing
America's Beaujolais, a claret, a port type, or a rosé. It was never
quite Beaujolais (too forceful for that), was never even close to
claret (Zinfandel is outright chewy), but was a whole cast of
characters all by itself even so. Now, with six hundred wineries,
no small few of them wildly experimental, Zinfandel is everything it used to be and White Zinfandel and Late Harvest Zinfandel as well.

Zinfandel's excessive versatility owes in part to its lack of pedigree. The most scholars will say is that it may be a descendant of the same parent as Italy's Primitivo. Whether it is that or something else, the story is the same: no illustrious forebears, no inhibitions.

A more immediate reason for its rampant case of multiple personalities lies in the vineyards, where the grapes misbehave themselves in all sorts of ways, streaking from ripe to overripe during one warm day, collapsing at the threat of rain, or—absent the mildest of threats—ripening in notoriously uneven patterns. In the best of seasons an average cluster has raisined berries on the shoulders, green ones inside, shot berries here and there, and the rest more or less ripe, which is to say that, in a single bunch, a winemaker is looking at appropriate makings for White Zinfandel or rosé, light red, dark red, and a port type. The overall balance changes by the year, the row, even the vine, sometimes toward White Zinfandel, sometimes toward port, and this may be as true in outstanding red-wine vineyards as the rest. Nothing else, not even Pinot Noir, amplifies the variations in California vintages half so much as Zinfandel from some one— any one—place. No other wine makes scrap of vintage charts faster or more completely.

Still and all, several people—if not always the same ones— make proper Zinfandel every year, and it is one thing to me: a bright, tart red wine persistently scented of fresh berries, dry, barely chewy, just tannic enough to help keep it refreshing, with very close to 13 percent alcohol. A little dash of oak fits well, but is not required. In some years a dollop of some blending grape can make the wine more like itself than it would be without the help, as Gamay and Petite Sirah have done from opposite directions more than once.

Over the span of thirty years, maybe six wines have hit the mark exactly, while several score have come close, leaning sometimes toward fuller body and less fresh berries, sometimes toward paler, friskier textures and tastes. It is sort of like hearing somebody other than Duke Ellington play "Take the 'A' Train"— close can be pretty good too.

Twenty years or so ago Louis P. Martini said that the time to drink proper Zinfandels is when they are about four years old, still full of fruit but rounded out just a little by time in bottle. Zinfandel will age, eventually to the point that it can be mistaken for an old Cabernet Sauvignon, but where is the virtue in that in a wine charming principally because it tastes so much like fresh berries?

If there is any reason to have Zinfandel, with Cabernet Sauvignon and Pinot Noir already on the track, it is to have a wine that does something the others cannot. Leave it to herbaceous Cabernet to cut through fat with its abundant tannins. Leave it to Pinot Noir to keep gently stimulating company with gentle dishes. But give to Zinfandel's vibrantly fruity flavors and chewy texture the chance to dance with rabbit stews, game meats, and, above all, *cacciatori, cioppini,* and all other dishes swimming in spicy tomato sauces. With these a proper Zinfandel knows no peers, especially when it is still a young wine.

I know, I know. A school of drinkers wants its Zinfandel inky dark, astringent enough to tan hides, and freighted with 14 or 15 percent alcohol, the sort of wine sometimes labeled Late Harvest. Nothing, the anointed say, digs in and battles hot sauces and gamy meats on such even terms. Maybe the claim is true for linebackers and their spiritual kin, but I have fallen asleep too many times in my bear-knuckle stew to take pleasure from such stuff. Oh, people ought to be allowed to make it, but those who do should be required to sell it under an advisory name. Cardinal Zin sounds more penitential than Late Harvest, but that may not be cautionary enough either.

It does not seem an accident to me that Zinfandel began to be a tough sell four or five years after the high-extract, high-alcohol, hair-shirt style became a small vogue. The climate for Zinfandel became so glum that even a great vintage would be a Pyrrhic victory. Cassayre-Forni closed up shop on the heels of a memorable 1982. Simi and Balverne made outstanding 1982s and gave up on the variety. Buena Vista reduced it to a tasting room-only entry on its list with its 1982, and Louis J. Foppiano pushed Zinfandel down to its second label, Riverside Farm. Dehlinger toughed it out through 1983, then stopped. And so on and so forth, as Kurt Vonnegut used to say in the face of bewildering facts.

It also seems no accident to me that Zinfandel's fortunes are on the way back up among cellars that take a gentler approach to the variety.

Admirers of Zinfandel have been lucky and not lucky during the long slide of Zinfandel. Plantings of the variety had just begun to suffer from the diminishing market when Bob Trinchero of Sutter Home re-invented White Zinfandel as a *saftig* sipping wine. The rest of that story is history. One of the lucky side-effects is that White Zinfandel has saved a lot of old Zinfandel vineyards, and caused some new ones to be planted. The unlucky aspect is that White Zinfandel is soaking up not only the low-profile grapes that ought to be going into it, but also some of the deeply flavored ones that ought to be making tart, berrylike reds to go with tomato sauces.

Even back when people were buying Zinfandel, the wine, the grape variety had to compete for space head-to-head with Cabernet Sauvignon throughout several of the most favorable parts of its climate range. With Cabernet Sauvignon selling more quickly at ten dollars a bottle than Zinfandel did at six dollars, and with Cabernet grapes easier to farm in the first place, all too many growers and almost as many winemakers already had decided not to fool around with Zinfandel before it stopped selling at six dollars.

One of the truisms about Zinfandel is that most of its finest red wines come from old vines, the kind that yield two tons an acre and down. Another great economic incentive to the grower: get half to a quarter as many grapes as Cabernet vines will bear, and get half the price per ton.

Withal, a few people will not yield to the bottom line in any line of business, so red Zinfandel remains with us. The way to hunt for it nowadays is the same as for Pinot Noir: Hunt for the names of the winemakers first. The rest will fall into place.

NORTH COAST

Sonoma County is, incomparably, the place for Zinfandel. The grape variety does not grow easily there, but it yields splendid wines of several sorts between the poles of dark and tart on the one hand, pale and silky on the other. Though it has the steadiest and broadest base of vines, and the longest history of growing Zinfandel well, Sonoma is not the only place. Mendocino and Napa counties can raise a challenger anytime.

Sonoma's plantings exceeded forty-one hundred acres in 1986. The major portion of them is in the Russian River watershed, in the Dry Creek and Alexander valleys. Sonoma Valley has smaller plantings, but for my taste they show the way to the rest. Mendocino, with fourteen hundred acres, has its principal plantings along the Russian River too, from Hopland north into Redwood Valley. To the west, Anderson Valley's acreage of Zinfandel is tiny, but to be treasured. Napa has its Zinfandel—1,625 acres of it—here, there, and everywhere, but mainly on the valley floor north of St. Helena and in the east hills. Lake County, in the throes of re-establishing Zinfandel in its vineyards, had but 330 acres bearing in 1986.

As much as the North Coast is home to a majority of the most prestigious plantings of Zinfandel in the state, it has very few properties that can rightly be called famous for the variety. Zinfandel is not often an estate wine anywhere in the territory. When it is, the public does not ooh and aah the way it does over Martha's Vineyard or Robert Young Vineyards. Indeed, some of the wineries best known for it draw on two or more vineyards as a hedge against the vagaries of vintages, leaning in one direction in cool years, the other when the growing season has been warm and dry. Some divide their attentions between two AVAs for the same reasons.

Sonoma Valley

Revisionist historians have been at Colonel Agoston Haraszthy for some years now, stripping away one after another of his claims to the paternity of California wine, but one of his accomplishments is beyond challenge. He started growing Zinfandel where it most belongs, in the Sonoma Valley, and trumpeted its successes to the world.

There is much dispute these days about where he got his Zinfandel, and some doubt that he was first in the state to have a planting of the variety when he set out his first vines at Buena Vista in 1857. But there is not much arguing that this is where the wine took shape, and where it began to claim critical notice. Thomas Hardy, the founder of a still-famous Australian label, was more impressed by Sonoma Valley Zinfandels than any other wines when he passed through California in 1883. Between 1980 and 1982, Zelma Long turned away from the Alexander Valley and to Sonoma Valley as the source for Simi Zinfandel, only to have her winery pull out of the race on the centenary of Hardy's visit. Hardy and Long are far from alone in recognizing Zinfandel's qualities in the valley, but the Long story is more common than the Hardy.

The virtues of the Sonoma Valley for Zinfandel are soils just heavy enough and a climate that stays warm and dry all summer yet cools enough at harvest time to keep Zinfandel grapes plump and juicy and ripening at a seemly pace.

KENWOOD VINEYARDS

If one winery epitomizes Zinfandel's ups and downs in recent years, Kenwood is it. As new owners, the Martin Lee family started out with a balanced, easy-to-drink 1972 that remained a wine to want with dinner in mid-1987. In succeeding years Kenwood plunged after critical acclaim with the kind of inky, tannic monsters that so afflicted my palate during the mid- and late 1970s, and watched their sales dwindle, then plummet. With 1980, however, the winery came back to the lively sort of wine with which it started, and forthwith reversed the decline.

If the 1972 is a harbinger of what will become of the 1981 and succeeding vintages, and I believe it is, the news is good. Young, the Kenwoods are heaped with the sweet-tart flavors of wild blackberries. Older, they lose the wildness without losing all of the flavors of fruit. The textures soften in tune with the flavors, leaving a wine with a bit more depth and a few more facets. At fifteen the 1972 still has some spring left in it to play off against a whole tapestry of the flavors of age.

In youth the Kenwood style goes as well as any of its peers with pasta and tomato sauces. With just a bit of time in bottle, two years or so, it outshines most Zinfandels and many middling Cabernet Sauvignons as company to rack of lamb, tenderloin of pork, and other dishes for a fancy table.

The vintages from 1981 through 1985 have been a successful exercise in fine tuning, a remarkably steady sequence of wines. The most noticeable of the fine tunings came with the 1983 and 1984, the years in which winemaker Mike Lee and the rest of the family stopped using two vineyards in the east hills and started using two on the westerly slopes, both of the latter within the Sonoma Mountain subappellation. With the new vineyards came a new intensity of the familiar varietal and regional flavors, as if the morning sun had just a bit more to give than the setting one. Jack London Ranch, uphill from the village of Glen Ellen, provides the backbone and the depth. A smaller planting at Ivy Glen adds the grace notes.

1981 Fine fruit early in a wine of lighter body than following vintages. Note of oak more noticeable by 1987, but still balanced and drinking well. (A Reserve lot aged in French oak was aging less successfully, wood being the dominant perfume.)
1982 One of the best from an outstanding vintage. Fuller and fleshier than the 1981, and more intensely fruity. Still a young wine in 1987.
1983 A subtly flavored, tart wine among its siblings. In 1987 exactly

the sort of Zinfandel that matches perfectly with spicy tomato sauces and pasta, but balanced to age into something softer, rounder, and subtler.

1984 Ripe and packed full of berryish Zinfandel, it has plenty of body to carry the flavors. One of the finest from a difficult vintage.

1985 Easily the wine of the series for its rich flavors and a firm balance much like that of 1982.

Haywood Winery

The hard way to make Zinfandel is from a single steep slope with varying sun exposure and erratic soils. Nothing else abets the grape so much in its habit of uneven ripening. Nothing gives a winemaker more fits than a mixed bag of green berries and raisins.

Not too far downslope from Louis M. Martini's famous Monte Rosso Vineyard, and not too far uphill from Sonoma's town plaza, Peter Haywood grows one patch of Zinfandel in red soil on a tall, steep, curving, south- and southeast-facing slope that hangs small crops out for the sun to warm all day long.

Not surprisingly, Haywood Zinfandels are not merely sensitive to vintages, but a bit quirky on the point. The surprise is how uniformly Haywood has grown the grapes and how level winemaker Charles Tolbert has kept the wines through the seesaw weathers of the past few seasons. Tolbert homes in on the tart, wild-berry flavors that mark Zinfandel in the Sonoma Valley, matching them with sturdier, perhaps slightly rougher textures than, say, the Kenwoods. Any flavors from wood are at or below the threshold of consciousness. What we have here, in short, is a Zinfandel perfectly attuned to tomato sauces with some spice in them. Most Zinfandels do well against tomato flavors, but this one comes right toward the head of my list. In view of that, we tend to drink up our supplies when the wine is three or four.

1981 A shade, tart, as many 1981 Zinfandels were, but full of fruit early. By 1987 it had excellent bottle bouquet, and still had fruit to live on.

1982 This one got away. Heady, and tastes that way.

1983 Caught the wild-berry flavors of Zinfandel perfectly. Has some flesh to go with all the fruit.

1984 A huge wine in every respect, but balanced, even harmonious as such.

1985 Handily the wine of the series when it appeared. It evokes wild berries to perfection, and has the balance and body to age well.

1986 Forthwith outdid the 1985 for Zinfandel flavors, balance, and finesse. It, more than any other, shows off an engaging spicy note that seems to come from the vineyard.

Dry Creek Valley

Fanciers of the heavyweight, heady Zinfandels have turned particularly to Dry Creek Valley for grapes, because it will turn out raisiny-ripe ones without extra effort by anyone. The curious aspect of the region is that it also can turn out the mildest sort of stuff. My quirky insistence on wines of gentle harmonies and modest scale puts me at odds with both extremes. This valley will ripen crops balanced more in line with the kind that come from Sonoma Valley, and full of the same tart, intense flavors of wild berry, but only if one looks on its benchlands.

First-rate Zinfandel comes from soils heavy enough to keep plant roots in touch with moisture, but not so heavy as to keep them wet. The benches on either side of a short, narrow valley fit the bill exactly, especially in years of late-spring rains and cool summers. (Hot, dry years are the ones for fanciers of heady heavyweights; the more light and quick draining the soil, the more this is so.) Benches on both sides have well-suited exposures because the valley runs at an odd, oblique angle, from southeast to northwest.

Zinfandel has been growing on Dry Creek benchlands at least since the 1880s. Some of the vines there now went into the ground before Prohibition. If tiring Zinfandel vines on marginal soils are no source of wealth, they do produce superior wines for growers who will nurse them along.

Dry Creek Valley Zinfandels have cheered my dinners from half a dozen different directions. Duxoup, Marietta, J. Pedroncelli, and Preston all have had their moments, but the two that have captured my undivided attention—in altogether different ways—are Nalle and A. Rafanelli.

NALLE

The rule behind this book is that two Zinfandels do not a track record make, nor do three, but three are as many as Doug Nalle has put into the world, and in his case three are enough for me. He has the touch, or all three would not be as pleasing as they are, and his other two tries would not have disappeared into the bulk market. Still less would he be in a one-wine winery devoted to Zinfandel, which his is.

Nalle made Zinfandel at Balverne from 1981 through 1983, though only the 1982 ever saw the light of day under that label. He began making wine under his own name with 1984. Nalle's record will build up faster over the next years because he will have two cracks a vintage at the variety, having signed on as consulting winemaker to Quivira Vineyards in time for the 1987 harvest.

Like nearly all of the others noted in this chapter, Nalle Zinfandels sustain the berrylike flavors of the grape to perfection and otherwise have a gentle, balanced character—enough tannin to stay healthy but not enough to bite, enough alcohol to carry the grape flavors but not enough to be a flavor itself, and only the faintest echo of oak. Without being so refined that they do not seem like Zinfandel, they have table manners enough to keep company with tenderloin of pork in a reduction sauce of raspberry the way John Ash cooks it in his quietly elegant restaurant, John Ash & Company, a few miles down the road.

The grapes come from three properties, two devoted to Zinfandel, a tiny third one to Petite Sirah. The Zinfandels are both bench properties, one at his winery right next door to a small airport on Lytton Springs Road, the other not far away on

Canyon Road. The Petite Sirah piece flanks Nalle's house, a couple of miles southeast of the winery, on Dry Creek Road.

A great vintage in 1982 made his debut Zinfandel at Balverne Winery & Vineyards the newest among my group of six perfect demonstrations of what the wine is all about. It made me want to jump up and down and shout the first time I came to it, and has cemented its standing a dozen times since. Almost as impressive is the fact that Nalle and Balverne's owner, Bill Bird, looked at their 1981 and 1983, shrugged, and put them into the bulk market as not up to snuff. (It is as fair to measure a Zinfandel producer by what he or she does not do as by what gets done.)

A. RAFANELLI WINERY

Old-fashioned, hands-on, low-tech winemaking lies at the heart of this pure throwback to the kind of rich, dark, pungently flavored Zinfandel that old-line Sonoma growers know and love best.

People who complain about California wines being clinically clean and correct have not tasted this one. It betrays warm fermentation in open tanks and other givens of country winemaking, and it is the kind of wine that will comfort you when cold rain is beating against the back of your neck, though it will taste better in front of an open fire with game meats, hearty stews, or, best of all, some of Ig Vella's Bear Flag brand Dry Sonoma Jack cheese.

It is poetic justice, then, that the founder of the label was an old Sonoma grower who knew something about cold rain, good stews, and Dry Sonoma Jack. Americo Rafanelli founded the winery in 1974 as a defense against retirement and ran it until his death early in 1987. His son, Dave, took up the reins then.

The wine comes from vines Americo planted right at the intersection of Lambert Bridge and West Dry Creek roads. The 1975, 1979, and 1982 are the ones that linger in memory, but all of them had America's stamp on them, and so were guaranteed protection against cold rains.

Russian River Valley

There are tougher places than the Russian River Valley to grow Zinfandel, but not many. It is not so much the cool climate as it is the fog that makes it cool, Zinfandel being notoriously subject to any and all molds because of its thin skin and tight clusters. But in those odd spots where it does grow—usually toward the top of westerly slopes of well-drained knolls—it will yield the tart, wild-berry–flavored quintessence of Zinfandel as red wine.

DE LOACH VINEYARDS

Castaways never have enough time to think about what they would put into their desert island cellars. If they did, De Loach is one of the wines that would drive them crazy before they left. The series has not been homogenous.

Had the 1979 been in the market when I was about to take up life as the forewarned victim of shipwreck, that is probably what I would have opted to take along. It is another of the half dozen Zinfandels that make my list of paragons, and the very top of the list as company for pastas and tomato sauces, which would have been my other staples. If it had been the 1981, on the other hand, I would have looked elsewhere.

1979 Perfection: intense wild berry flavors of Zinfandel backed by an underplayed touch of oak in a wine that at once managed to be tart and richly textured. Still drinking well in 1987.
1980 A tall wine to stand so deep in its sibling's shadow.
1981 Inky, tannic, heady.
1982 Photocopy of 1981.
1983 More of the mortal dimensions of 1980; a bit of an enigma for flavors in the early going.

1984 Not quite as full of flavors as the 1979, but close, and neatly balanced.

Anderson Valley

First of all, the heading is a lie. Three out of four of the vineyards under discussion in this section fall just outside of the Anderson Valley's western boundary. However, they have no other club to join, and the number of place-names is great enough without another one.

If there were more than twenty-two acres of Zinfandel on Greenwood Ridge, or even the prospects of more, the area would rate right up there with Sonoma Valley in my copybook. Only five vineyards dot the long, high, forested ridge that separates the Anderson Valley from Mendocino County's Pacific shore. Four of them are planted to Zinfandel. Of those, three survive from the nineteenth century, when local loggers had Bunyan-esque-enough thirsts to support four hundred acres of vines on these heights.

Greenwood Ridge is not easy country for Zinfandel. The ridge is exposed to a good deal of moody weather when other parts of the grape variety's typical range are enjoying reliable sunshine. However, the top is high enough to stay out of the incessant mists of lower elevations, and so keep thin-skinned, mold-prone Zinfandel healthy and ripening on a slow curve.

The plantings are not likely to expand soon, but I will grieve if they shrink a foot while I am still around and in need of a bottle of proper Zinfandel.

Kendall-Jackson Vineyards & Winery

This is not a story of Kendall-Jackson, but rather the current chapter in the saga of Jedediah Tecumseh Steele.

Steele tracked down the three nineteenth-century patches of Zinfandel vines on Greenwood Ridge early in his stint as the winemaker at Edmeades Vineyards, and began making wines from them in the vintage of 1975. Anderson Valley was hardly recognizable as a name then; Ciapusci, DuPratt, (now DuPratt-DePatie), and Zeni were outright mysteries, and the notion of growing Zinfandel in so cool a place was not part of the conventional wisdom.

Anderson Valley has gone on, with help from Steele, to win broadening recognition for Chardonnay, Pinot Noir, and Gewürztraminer. Zinfandel nuts, meanwhile, had already pegged him as one of their own. Anybody who could even find those vineyards, they reasoned, had to be motivated beyond the norm.

When he moved across the Lake county line to Kendall-Jackson, Steele brought his sense of style in Zinfandel, and the rights to the three original ridgetop vineyards, plus a fourth—a recently planted patch now called Mariah in tribute to tree-bending local winds.

The recent wines have been rich grounds for debate between Jed Steele and me on two principal counts: vintages and style. He sees great continuity from vintage to vintage, and I see differences. I suspect it is only the way our positions make us look at wine. His task is to hew to a line, to stay within recognizable limits, and so he works to minimize change, and is tempted to see the similarities. What I long to see are the variations that tell me wine is still a natural thing, to be tamed only so much by man, and so I snuffle and root to find the smallest signs that this year is not last.

Without conceding an inch in the debate, I have to admit that powerful resemblances mark the family. On the surface, it seems odd that the vintages are so equable, given the prospects for late rains in spring and early rains in autumn on Greenwood Ridge. But, says Steele, Zinfandel fits between the wet seasons as if it had been put there for the purpose. More to the point, the grapes do not raisin in the cool climate and so can be left to ripen to the exact point.

As for style, he favors new French oak, and I do not. It takes a power of Zinfandel perfume to hold its own against French oak because the two are so opposite. Zinfandel smacks of tart, wild berry. French oak smells sweet with vanillin. It takes very little of the latter to subdue the former, especially if the wine is going to wait around in a cellar for three or four years. The smells of French oak even seem to fatten up the wine, to give it fuller body. Were I commissar of taste, I would make Steele drop or at least downplay new wood, but, in the same breath, I have to confess that no other Zinfandel grapes in my experience come close to playing off as well against it, and that a very sparse handful of Zinfandels of any stripe please me more than his, especially when a roast loin of pork comes into the equation.

The vineyards impose their own variations on Steele's themes. Ciapusci (locally corrupted from Chee-ah-poos-chee to Kapootchy) clings to steep, south-facing slopes, and so ripens most fully. Zeni, tipped slightly to the north, is the steadiest and slowest to mature its crops. Mariah, with young vines at twenty-four hundred-feet elevation, and DuPratt-DePatie with old ones at fourteen hundred, sit level atop Greenwood Ridge and ripen between the extremes. Not all are made as separate vineyard wines every year; sometimes they go together into a Mendocino bottling.

1983 Beautiful fruit flavors in the Zeni—ripe, but without a trace of raisin. Excellent balance promised good staying power. A second bottling from the other vineyards under the Chateau du Lac label was less concentrated, but deftly buttressed by French oak.

1984 In its debut vintage, the Mariah stole the show early with a well-nigh perfect concentration of the flavors of wild berry tinged lightly with new French oak. The balance is as good as the rest. It was and still is one of the six that hit my center stripe spot-on. The Zeni was a bit thicker and chewier, but still able to compete with the Mariah.

1985 In the Mariah the same taste of wild berry as in 1984, but embodied in a slightly fleshier wine. The Zeni was deeply marked by its stay in French oak.

Incidentally, as of 1987 some of the old Edmeades bottlings continue in good form, the 1979 in particular. A 1982 Ciapusci had almost as much depth of flavor then, and the advantages of youth.

Ukiah

The Ukiah district and Dry Creek Valley together always come to mind when Zinfandel is in question. Both are narrow valleys. Both grow the variety on benchlands. Both will overripen it without putting a grower to any extra effort, but will ripen it to perfection if the winemaker is willful enough and his grower is watchful.

The Russian River runs almost a true north-south course through Mendocino County from Ukiah down to Hopland. Most of the outstanding patches of Zinfandel are on the river's east side, but not leaned too sharply toward the setting sun. Probably it is the early onset of autumnal weather in this northerly district that saves the day. If the harvest were as hot as the rest of summer, Zinfandel's tendency to raisin might well become uncontrollable. In some years, in fact, it does.

Zinfandel has been in the vineyards hereabouts for as long as grapes have grown in and around Ukiah. The first labeled varietal from it came in 1944, from the Parducci Wine Cellars, still a reliable source all these years later.

Whaler Vineyards

Russ and Annie Nyborg own a rolling patch of Zinfandel that looks down across East Side Road to the Russian River about five miles south of Talmage. For years their grapes disappeared, anonymous, into a blend, until, wearied of low prices, the Nyborgs launched their own Whaler label with the vintage of 1981. (The nearest whale is a long way away, but Russ was a deep-water captain and now is a San Francisco Bay harbor pilot.)

Their first wine had everything Zinfandel should—color, texture, mighty perfumes from the grape and only faint ones from its time in oak. Its successors have kept to that original line, none of them more faithfully than the 1985.

The Nyborgs do not make much red Zinfandel from their twenty-three acres, and most of what they do sells close to home.

Napa Valley

Napa Valley Zinfandels, as a breed, do not have quite the critical luster of the rest of the North Coast districts. There is no knowing why. The grapes ripen well from Oakville northward along the main valley floor at least as far as St. Helena—another chance to compete with Cabernet in one of the latter's strongholds. They also do well in the east hills, especially in the uplands between the main valley and Chiles Valley, from Lake Hennessy north beyond Angwin.

Nowhere in Napa do Zinfandels seem to develop the bright, almost wild-berry flavors that come easily in Sonoma and Mendocino. Rather, the aromas are of softer, tamer berries, and the wines a shade thicker or fuller in texture.

Acreage devoted to Zinfandel never has been large, but it gained from 870 acres in 1970 to 2,000 in 1978, and has held steady since. However, not many wineries in Napa make a Zinfandel, relatively speaking. Quite a few that once did have dropped out, and not all of those that continue use Napa grapes.

Clos du Val is the steadiest bright spot. It is, in fact, the only Napa Zinfandel I am willing to buy sight unseen. Burgess Cellars and Caymus Vineyards have helped to keep the lamp lighted in one vintage or another since the mid-1970s. Frog's Leap Winery and Joseph Phelps Vineyards have been impressive during the 1980s.

CLOS DU VAL WINE CO.

Most times the new kid on the block changes things around a little. In the case of Clos du Val and Cabernet Sauvignon, Ber-

nard Portet did just that. In the case of Clos du Val and Zinfandel, Portet took a look around and did pretty much what
had been done before he arrived.

He looked partly to the valley floor and partly to the eastern
uplands for vineyards. He walked until the grapes were good
and ripe before starting to pick. And he fermented and aged the
wine to capture all of the stuffings inherent in points one and
two. Since 1978 Portet has used only grapes from the Stag's
Leap area, and eased back on ripeness. Still, in one era as much
as the other, his wines stand apart just a bit. He is not so completely enchanted with pure varietal flavors as California old-
timers, and he manages to give proportion to big wines so they
have some grace about them. The differences are not so noticeable at the first glass, or even the second. It is when a bottle
nears empty and still holds interest that drinkers begin to wonder just what has been done.

There seems little point in digging back through the vintages
of the early 1970s, except to note that they had a consistency
about them not often found among Zinfandels. Every one of
them was dark, sturdy with tannin and alcohol, thoroughly perfumed with the aromas of Napa Zinfandel, and very lightly
scented by oak. If I had to choose two vintages, they would be
the 1972 and 1975, and I would skip heady 1978.

1979 Big, sturdy, a shade more tannic than most. Still aging very well
as a sturdier, plainer wine than later vintages.

1980 Not one of the big vintages, but mouth-wateringly tart and rich
in flavors, yet subtle enough for a pizza from Berkeley's Chez Pan-
isse to outweigh it in 1987. One of the finest in the series.

1981 Continued the gentler style begun in 1980, and from a lighter
year to begin. Still in good form in 1987.

1982 Only middling for Zinfandel flavors, but comparatively firm and
tannic against others from the decade.

1983 One of the most richly varietal of the vintages to date, and also
one of the most polished and stylish. Competes most favorably with
the outstanding 1980.

1984 One of the lightest, palest wines of the series. All smooth polish
as early as 1987.

1985 In the early going, a serious competitor to 1980 and 1983; heaped with berryish Zinfandel, and lively on the tongue.

JOSEPH PHELPS VINEYARDS

After years of turning out ink-dark, tannic, heady heavyweights from Alexander Valley grapes, Joseph Phelps turned the other cheek in 1982 with a wine patently meant to remind its drinkers of the reason Zinfandel was once known as America's Beaujolais. Succeeding vintages have leaned ever more in that direction. The Napa Zinfandels go to market little more than six months after the vintage, just a bit rough, yet balanced and packed with enough fruit to age into something still fresh, but smoother and rounder.

The fruit flavors are Napa's tamer berries rather than wild ones, but otherwise the wine has almost uncanny similarities to the recent Haywoods from Sonoma Valley.

Phelp's estate Zinfandel comes from seventeen acres in several small patches, all facing west from considerable slopes just on either side of the winery building.

1982 A wine of such immediate appeal that none of our supply lasted two years.

1983 No note.

1984 Early, an echo of the 1982. By the time it was three the vintage showed excellent Zinfandel flavors balanced against intriguing ones from the winemaking in a smooth, polished wine.

1985 A lighter, livelier wine than either the 1982 or 1983. In 1987 it remained all youthful charm.

1986 In early 1987 light of body but saturated with flavors of the whole blackberry plant, stalks as much as leaves. Still rough in late 1987, but balanced to last until it settles into the path carved out by 1982 and 1984.

BURGESS CELLARS

Tom Burgess takes almost all of his Zinfandel from vineyards in the easterly uplands of Napa, starting with the crop from his own property at the winery, and reaching north above Angwin and south as far as Lake Hennessy for the rest.

With all of the wine coming from hillside fruit, Burgess has a head start on a thick, dark, tannic wine. After some ponderous wines in the 1970s, the house style began moving in 1981 in subtler directions. Burgess still means to capitalize on the regional chance for wines of size, and usually does. Wines from some seasons still go a bit past my taste in those directions, but the lighter vintages are much what I hope to find in Napa Zinfandel.

The 1984 ranks at the head of my list by a considerable margin because it had livelier textures than any of its forebears, with no loss of Zinfandel flavor. The 1981 and 1983 come close to its pace.

CAYMUS VINEYARDS

Old-hand Charley Wagner looks in much the same territory as Burgess for Zinfandel grapes. The varietal and regional flavors betray that similarity of sources, but the Wagners make sterner wine out of them. Not only is Caymus Zinfandel lean and even hard in texture, but it also tends to smack firmly of new oak. Some vintages round out, some do not. The 1984 is one of the round ones, the 1985 one of the freshest and liveliest in the series.

FROG'S LEAP WINERY

One of the measures of adept Zinfandel makers is their patience in the face of adversity, their willingness to sit out a round or two when the makings are not there. In 1981 John Williams and Larry Turley coaxed an all-world Zinfandel out of Mary Novak's Spottswoode Vineyard, which nestles right up against the town of St. Helena on its west side. The next year, Spottswoode grafted Zinfandel out of the vineyard in favor of Sauvignon Blanc. Williams and Turley hunted for a replacement patch without satisfaction until 1985, when they make another all-world Zinfandel from two vineyards near their winery, one on a knoll just north of it, the other in gravel straight toward the Napa River. The anticipation is that these will be the long-term backbone (supplemented, for a time, by grapes from a Rutherford vineyard bought by Williams in 1987; the 1985 has a touch of Cabernet Sauvignon from that source.)

North Coast

And so back to square one, to pick up the only winery with two entries in my circle of six perfect Zinfandels. We speak, of course, of Louis M. Martini. Martini's Cabernet Sauvignon opened that chapter to point out the virtues of assembled wines in California. His Zinfandel comes as close as it can to the end of this section to drive home the same point.

LOUIS M. MARTINI

Monte Rosso, almost at the top of the mountains above the Sonoma Valley, delivers Zinfandel grapes of memorable flavors year in and year out. It delivers wines of perfect balance less often, its lean, well-drained soils leaving Zinfandel vines a shade too prone to stress and, thus, the high sugars that come with dehydration. Potential alcohols of 15 percent are easy to come by, and so the vineyard is almost never a sole source of Martini Zinfandel. However, it is always the backbone, the source of memorably intense flavors of wild berry. In recent vintages three small ranches between St. Helena and Zinfandel Lane in the Napa Valley have provided leavening, distractions, obbligatos, whatever it is that brings balance at no cost in richness of flavors.

These flavors the Martinis guard with all the skills they have learned in three generations of working with the main property and many of its supplementary sources. Oak figures in the program little or not at all. By preference the proprietors keep the wine in large redwood tanks until it has softened enough to be bottled. After that they put it in well-seasoned oak ovals to slow its maturing, if bottling has to wait. Barrels are anathema to the Martinis, new barrels worse than the plague, new French barrels an unspeakable insult to the wine.

The vintages with the richest varietal flavors—which is to say the ones from cool, slow-paced harvests—put delicious lie to the notion that red wine cannot go with fish. Not many wines of any hue go better with salmon or with a seafood that swims in tomato sauce. *Cioppino* is the prime example, but bouillabaisse does not lag far off the pace. But this is a wine for all seasons, the best lesson I can think of that the whole business of matching wines and foods is being taken too seriously nowadays. There are suggestions in all of the chapters of this book, all of them offered only as probabilities for showing the wine to best advantage. In looking back through old tasting notes, I find that we have drunk Martini Zinfandel with enough dishes to fill another *Joy of Cooking* and enjoyed it every time.

I still do not know, probably never will know, whether it was the Martinis who hit a curious, loping rhythm of outstanding vintages or whether it was only a matter of my buying so much of a few favored years that we never needed to check out all of the others. In any case, the ones that flood our memories are 1958, 1964, 1968, 1974, and 1978, especially the 1958 and 1968. Those are the ones that tasted powerfully of fresh berries and little or none of raisins in youth; those are the ones that paid the greatest dividends for an extra bit of patience. An extra bit of patience means two or three years in the cellar to let the rough edges of youth hone themselves smooth, and the first touches of bottle bouquet add their mysteries to the more explicable flavors of grapes.

Nowhere does this chapter have the long chains of tasting notes that mark Cabernet Sauvignon and Pinot Noir because Zinfandel ought to be used up while it is between its fourth and seventh birthdays. Of all the Zinfandels that might argue otherwise, the Martinis head the lists. Some of them have been graceful, polished, freshly flavorful wines at twelve and fifteen years. The 1968, to take the most rewarding example from the bottles we have sacrificed on the altar of research, held its own quite well into 1986, but was not half the wine then that it had been in 1976, while the similar 1964 had faded too far at twenty-two to give any pleasure at dinner. And so, even here, the list of notes sticks to the most recent seven vintages.

1978 Good but not outstanding varietal character, but strikingly well balanced. Just enough flesh to help dry meats turn succulent again.

1979 One short step off the pace of the similar 1978.

1980 No note.

1981 Close to perfect berryish Zin flavors with intriguing overtones from the winemaking. A bit soft for texture; at its peak as a near-termer.

1982 In the pack among Martinis.

1983 Echoed the 1981 in the early going.

1984 Well, the fours and the eights have all of history going for them, and the fours repeat here. Much the finest since 1978, probably since 1968. We are going to drink ours early for the joys of the fresh fruit flavors.

SIERRA FOOTHILLS

The Sierra Foothills, most especially the shallow bowl called Shenandoah Valley, are Sonoma's first rival for ancient Zinfandel vines. The Gold Rushers had decided on Zinfandel by the 1860s, and it has been there ever since.

Against this advantage, wine nearly disappeared from the Sierras during the 1950s and early 1960s. The region was down to a single cellar, though almost eight hundred acres of Zinfandel survived in small patches scattered throughout Amador and El Dorado counties. And then, mystery of mysteries, people outside the region began to make wine with its grapes. The list was long, but indisputably headed by Ridge Vineyards. Ridge's influence spread wider than its own wines: Many of the young Turks who streamed into the Foothills between 1966 and 1976 to make wine got their starts at Ridge's doorstep.

Eschen and Esola were already household names among the fanciers of large-scale Zinfandels when the new age opened, they being the two properties Ridge had uncovered to its own benefit and the benefit of several other wineries. Oddly, their names are not much seen in the mid-1980s; neither have any others supplanted them. The owners of Eschen and Esola spread their fruit among so many wineries that few make enough to sell separately.

However many vineyards might underlie a Foothills Zinfandel, the one sure bet is that it will be a wine of considerable scale. One of the curious sidelights of Sierra Foothills winemaking is how many of the winemakers are dropouts from advanced-technology industries in the San Francisco Bay area, and how many of them seem to have turned toward rustic approaches to their wines. This is not to say crude, just basic, back-to-nature styles. Given the long, warm growing season of a district that looks almost straight at the setting sun, rustic means big, fleshy, often heady wines.

It is no easy trick to find a harmony of scale among the deeply ripe aromas of Zinfandel, the bouquets of wood and time, and the textures of tannin, fruit acid, and alcohol. The winemakers in these parts juggle bowling balls, soup kettles, and anchors, not tennis balls, teacups, and spoons.

Time after time in tastings of a broad range of Sierra Foothills Zinfandels, two—Karly and Baldinelli—have stood apart from the rest for having a certain extra polish or finesse. These two are the compromises between me and the Cardinal Zin people.

KARLY WINES

A. E. (Buck) Cobb is one of the ex–Bay area technocrats, but one who has kept his admiration for controlling fine points.

Cobb juggles bowling balls, soup kettles, and anchors just like all the others. He only makes it look like he juggles tennis balls, teacups, etc. Behind the proportions and the polish, his Karly Zinfandels are heady, full of stuffings, anything but wines for the timid.

The basic strength comes from shy-bearing old vines in three turn-of-the-century vineyards Cobb has winnowed out of a larger field. One of the mainstays is Eschen. A proportion of Petite Sirah from Cobb's own vineyard adds a measure of complication to the fruit flavors and, one suspects, a lightening touch to both flavor and texture. His first couple of vintages aged in more American than French oak; the last couple have spent their formative time in French wood almost exclusively, on the grounds that it is the less harsh of the two. Most of the barrels are well seasoned to keep the wine true to the grapes rather than the coopers, but Cobb likes the faint hint of perfume that comes with replacing a handful of old barrels with new ones for each vintage.

There are the mechanics of it, which are strikingly like the mechanics of a lot of other, rougher Zinfandels. Every wine is a product of proportion as much as procedure, and timing as much as proportion. Every maker of admirable wines has an inner voice that says when to take a step and how big it should be. In few regional comparisons is that inner voice as much on display as between Karly and the typical run of Sierra Foothills Zinfandels.

Polished as they are, the wines show most appealingly with red meats and spicy sauces. Not Mexican hot sauces, not even the roughest of Italianate tomato sauces, but sauces with some authority of flavor. It has gotten to be a habit to drink the Karlys when they are four and five years old, still full of the ripe fruit tastes the Sierra develops so well.

1981 Definite bouquets from wood matched Zinfandel aromas even up in a nicely polished young wine. It was little changed and running on a level field in 1985.

1982 Has the earmarks of its region—a hint of raisining behind powerful berry perfumes and a touch of fire in the finish—but the result is all harmony and balance on a large scale.

1983 Very much kin to the 1981.

1984 The wine of the series to date has more layers of flavor and finer balance than any of its running mates under the label.

1985 Powerfully scented with Zinfandel, and only lightly touched by oak, but a wine that got away. It is too heady for any but the hardiest.

BALDINELLI VINEYARDS

Ed Baldinelli has been running a close race with Karly's Buck Cobb in the balancing of powerful Sierra Foothills Zinfandel flavors and textures with finessey winemaking, or so a couple of vintages say.

Baldinelli's is one of a handful of Estate Zinfandels from the district. He has seventy acres of Zinfandel vines planted in 1923 by somebody who had to be one of the great optimists of his time. The vine rows crown a low, gentle rise not far east of the town of Plymouth, and not far south of Buck Cobb's patch of Petite Sirah.

The wines differ from the Karlys in some tiny but discernible ways. From his debut vintage, 1979, Baldinelli has struck for a balance much like that of his neighbors, and aged the wines in a similar mixture of French and American oak barrels more for their softening effect than any wood flavors. However, somewhere along the line those tiny differences creep into the finished product. The main one seems to be slightly riper fruit flavors. Of the vintages to date, the 1980 has made the greatest impression, not only in the early going but as recently as late 1986.

CENTRAL COAST

As Zinfandel country, the Central Coast comes down almost to Paso Robles. Monterey has had young vines, and so has Santa

Barbara County, but so far, the wines to watch have come—no surprise—from Paso Robles.

Paso Robles

Paso Robles bears many climatic and social resemblances to the Gold Country of the Sierra Foothills. Its Zinfandels carry the similarities a step further for coming from old vines, having intense flavors that mix berry and black pepper, and being heady but pretty well balanced on a large scale.

In one way at least Paso Robles is the reverse of the Sierra Foothills. Nearly all of the district's Zinfandel grows on east-facing slopes from Paso Robles south to Atascadero, with the greatest concentration west of a small town called Templeton. York Mountain Winery was founded well up in the west hills in 1882 and soon won a name for Zinfandel. Ignace Paderewski won his greatest fame on the world stage as a pianist and president of Poland, but his local reputation owes to a patch of Zinfandel he grew between 1900 and Prohibition. His place, part of it still in grapes, is not far downhill from York Mountain.

Nowadays the first names I look for in seeing what the district has grown are Mastantuono and Ridge, the latter reaching in from outside the region for grapes.

OTHER RED WINES

THE THREE MAJOR REDS—CABERNET SAUVI-
gnon, Pinot Noir, and Zinfandel—do not exhaust the roster of
varietals and proprietary types by half, but sometimes it seems
like it.

At least the number of other varietal reds of particular interest to us does not take up much room in our cellar. Barbera
and Charbono, Gamay, Grignolino, Merlot, and Petite Sirah
and Syrah are the lot, and there are not many of them in the
racks. This is so, I suspect, because reds resemble each other
more closely than whites to the degree they are a great deal
more difficult to separate in blind tests. Sweet is not a welcome
diversion in reds, so the range of style narrows too. The upshot
is that the three major varietal types do not, in their diversity,
leave many jobs open for the rest of the field.

Proprietaries are wines that, for ever loftier reasons, evade the legal minimum percentage for varietals. In the 1960s proprietaries tended to be mere commercial conveniences, those being days of far fewer acres of fine grapes but also more generous labeling regulations. After fine grapes became abundant, the varietal regulation could stiffen from 51 to 75 percent and did, just as many California winemakers were beginning to explore blending Cabernet Sauvignon with several of its more gifted cousins, and a few were looking into medleys of grapes commonly blended together in the Rhône. In direct consequence, proprietaries as a class are now offered with greater pride and higher price tags than counterpart varietals.

The list of pricey proprietaries is even getting long. Opus One is both the costliest and the most widely recognized of the lot in the late 1980s. The joint venture of Robert Mondavi and the Baron Philippe de Rothschild, Opus was preceded by Insignia and has been joined by Dominus, Rubicon (Niebaum-Coppola Estate), Trilogy (Flora Springs Wine Co.), Meilleur du Chai (Rombauer Vineyards), and Estate Five (Cain Cellars) as higher expressions of the family of Cabernets. Bonny Doon's Randall Grahm, marching to his own polyrhythms, has invented Le Cigare Volant to show off the virtues of Grenache, Syrah, and Mourvedre in concert.

Proprietaries

The tough part of establishing a proprietary is that it has to do something a varietal cannot, has to have a personality with inimitable facets. Otherwise it is just one more point of confusion for us sainted bibbers. For my taste, only Opus has begun to do that among the Cabernet-based blends.

OPUS ONE

Opus is not yet what it is meant to be, an estate bottling styled to be neither traditional Napa Valley Cabernet Sauvignon nor

278

traditional Medoc, but some hitherto unachieved bridge between the two. The estate part of the formula has yet to contribute. The rest of the progress is impressive.

Since 1978 Opus has advanced by cautious, consistent steps
from an appealing but relatively typical Napa style toward the
announced goal. Taste any two consecutive vintages, and no
differences leap out. Taste the 1978 against the 1983, and the
direction is plain to see. The wine begins to have more of the
textures of Bordeaux than Napa, and more of the flavors of
Napa than Bordeaux. In short, it begins to be distinctive.

Much remains to be done, according to the co-proprietors,
most particularly the shift from vineyards the Mondavis planted
some years back in the traditional wide spacing of California to
an estate property with vine spacing modeled on but not a copy
of the Bordeaux system. The Opus vineyard has been planted
in the corner formed by State Route 29 and Oakville Cross Road,
almost straight across the highway from the front door of the
Robert Mondavi Winery. It was to yield its first grapes in 1987.

Bonny Doon Vineyard Le Cigare Volant

Some babies who look like Winston Churchill grow up to look
like Winston Churchill. Le Cigare Volant, unlike the Cabernet-
based proprietaries, appears to be such a baby. Though a short
history does not meet my five year qualification period, in just
two seasons Le Cigare has become an easily recognizable and
altogether substantial wine.

Randall Grahm's approach is not timid. His wine is heady,
dark, almost chewy, tart, and packed full of raspberry flavors
that start out almost fresh but quickly settle into a more vinous
stride for the long haul. Very little oak gets in the way of the
fruit. Le Cigare takes to fatty, spicy, and smoked meats including venison, and does nearly as well with cheeses.

Grahm validates the notion that neither estate-grown nor pure
varietal is the only road to the truth. Grahm's blend hovers around
75 percent Granache, 20 percent Syrah, and 5 percent Mour-

vedre. The Grenache comes from Gilroy in Santa Clara County, the Syrah from Paso Robles in San Luis Obispo County, and the Mourvedre from Oakley, in the San Joaquin River delta. All of this comes together in the Santa Cruz Mountains, where Grahm is growing still other varieties with ancestral ties to the Rhône River valley.

The first vintage, 1984, seemed intensely flavorful only until the 1985 came along. The one question that still needs answering is whether to drink them young or hang on for a few years. We are going to hedge our bets on the first few.

Barbera and Charbono

If there is any difference between pure Barbera and pure Charbono, a finer sensor than mine will have to dig it out. Both varieties (if there are two) yield soft wines of understated, even indistinct fruit flavors. As young wines they are merely agreeable. It is age that gives them a depth of character worth walking a while to get.

The whole description fits the Inglenook Charbono. The Martini Barbera is something else.

INGLENOOK VINEYARDS NAPA VALLEY CHARBONO

For years Charbono has been the only grape variety in California with a fan club, and Inglenook's Charbonos are the reason for its existence. In fact, for years Inglenook had a virtual patent on the varietal wine. (Though several other producers have come along during the 1980s, the entire state has but eighty-four acres, seventy-four of them in the Napa Valley, and most of that in Inglenook's grasp.)

People who only know the wine young wonder why the fuss. For its first few years in bottle it is merely agreeable red wine. Only after age makes the wine live by its wits does it show all of its virtues. Then it goes velvety for texture and so complicated in flavors that people wind up heaping too many adjectives on it for any of them to make sense.

Old Inglenook Charbonos show to perfection that saturating a wine with tannins is no way to have a beautiful old-timer. They are remarkably modest when it comes to tannin, and still live thirty and forty years without breaking stride.

LOUIS M. MARTINI CALIFORNIA BARBERA

Very few, in fact practically none of California's red wines can stand in comfortably for a fine Tuscan red. Martini Barbera is the exception. As soon as it gets out of the winery it has a whole galaxy of flavors to recommend it—subtle hints of fresh fruit, fainter hints of sun-dried fruit, echoes of the smell of well-seasoned, wine-soaked wood the way it drifts around in a winery, and several other notes harder to pin down. All of this is embodied in a wine of middling color and middling body. And the whole works is immutable for years.

From 1974 until 1985 my wife and I settled on Martini Barbera 1966 whenever we went to the real Trader Vic's, the one in Cosmo Alley in San Francisco. The vintage stayed on the wine list at ten or twelve dollars all that time, getting better by tiny degrees until 1983, when it leveled off. At home, meanwhile, we dwelled on the same vintage for a while, then shifted over to the 1974, which we have just about polished off. The 1981 will replace it, more as a matter of happenstance than design. Martini is reliable from vintage to vintage. The 1974 and 1981 just happened to be the wines on hand when we needed to restock.

This Barbera is not a wine we save for this dish or that. It is a wine we thirst after about once a month, on average, and drink with whatever meal happens to be at hand.

The Martinis have made it the same way since the 1930s: Blend some Petite Sirah in with the Barbera in the fermentors, ferment the wine dry, then age it in old redwoods or old oak ovals or both for two or three years, and bottle it.

Gamay

Now and again the lighthearted flavors of fresh fruit are exactly what is wanted in a wine, and so is some of the heft of red, but not much of its tannic bite. Barbecue on a warm night, charcoal-grilled steak on a warm night, hamburgers on a warm night, any of the above on a not-so-warm night; these are the spots where Gamay comes in.

Though it is the red counterpart to Chenin Blanc, not a wine to drone on about, the grape needs some explanation. The Gamay in question is just Gamay, or alternatively, Napa Gamay. It is not Gamay Beaujolais. The grape long known as Gamay Beaujolais in California was finally identified as a frail clone of Pinot Noir, one that made few if any admirable wines and now is weeding itself out of vineyards everywhere.

The Gamay in question may be the Gamay common in the Beaujolais district in France *(Gamay noir au jus blanc)*, or may not. Ampelographers are locked in debate, years from a clear decision. However the variety is finally identified, it produces fairly dark, pleasantly fruity, admirably soft wines in most of the coastal counties. That it sometimes is known as Napa Gamay restores some of the confusion lost with the imminent elimination of Gamay Beaujolais, especially if it is Napa Gamay from Sonoma County or some other county not Napa.

Whatever pedigree it finally earns, the state does not have vast amounts of it, with most of 2,280 acres scattered throughout the coast counties.

CHARLES F. SHAW VINEYARD & WINERY NAPA VALLEY GAMAY

Charles F. Shaw, the man, transplanted himself from Texas to the Napa Valley with the express intent of making a first-rate Gamay. That he has done.

Shaw's is not one of those tutti-frutti carbonic-maceration types that had a vogue during the 1970s, but rather is a proper, vinous red that just happens to have almost whimsical fruit flavors about it. Indeed, it is well balanced enough to age for several years, but doing that only costs it its greatest virtue, a rich taste of fresh fruit.

The wine has not been sensitive to vintages, or else the Napa Valley just north of St. Helena has had a helluva run of years for Gamay. Shaw's vines grow on a gentle slope between a state highway and the river, at Big Tree Road.

Duxoup Dry Creek Valley Napa Gamay

Deborah and Andy Cutter grow their Napa Gamay toward the upper end of Sonoma's Dry Creek Valley, and make the wine in all the conventional ways. It retains altogether appealing flavors of the grape, and still tastes and feels vinous. It fits into almost the same niche as the Shaw, yet has the stuffings to replace Zinfandel.

The neighborhood seems particularly well adapted to the grape. Preston Vineyards, J. Pedroncelli, A. Rafanelli, and others have had almost equal luck with it.

J. Lohr Monterey Gamay

Monterey's Salinas Valley is the source of the grapes for the Lohr, which leans as far in the direction of fresh fruit as red wine can. In the earliest bloom of its youth it seems thick, almost jammy in comparison with the Shaw and Duxoup editions. It streamlines itself within a few months, but always remains fleshier than the others and right at the edge of overwhelming in fruit flavors.

For all of that, it is the hot-weather line of the lot because it takes to the ice bucket the best of the lot. Like the Shaw, it is not a wine to think of in terms of vintages. The current one is the one to drink.

283

Grignolino

Years ago an idiosyncratic Frenchman named Leon Brendel ran a tiny Napa Valley winery under the name of Only One, an oblique reference to the fact that he made only one wine, Grignolino. Heitz Cellars bought the place as its first winery, and quickly set about expanding the roster with famous results. But Heitz still makes Grignolino, and for all practical purposes it is the only one.

HEITZ CELLARS

In 1987 Angelo Gaja bought a case of Heitz Grignolino out of curiosity, took it home to Italy, and forthwith wired Heitz for eighty more. If Gaja's championing it does not put the wine over the top, it is no doubt doomed to maunder along in the marketplace forever, as it has done so far.

This wine is unique. The fruit flavors set the mind to skipping and darting in every direction. Sometimes it evokes one of the orange liqueurs. At other moments it brings to mind some faint note of black pepper. Once in a great while it suggests a kinship with one of the black-skinned Muscats, though much less directly than Gewürztraminer announces its ties to the family. These odd bedfellows of aroma gather themselves together in a decidedly tart, refreshing wine of surprising intensity.

Grignolino's other odd quality is its infinite youth. As best we know from having lost a couple of bottles in the cellar for more than fifteen years, it will not show signs of aging. Kareem Abdul-Jabbar is not clinging to his salad days any better.

Its unvanquishable youth, tartness, and intensity of flavor tell all about its role with food: soups and stews with fatty meats, pizza, anything with spicy Neapolitan tomato sauces, or anything with non-Neapolitan spicy tomato sauces.

Merlot

Madeleine Kamman, the great teacher of chefs, threw up her hands at a cooking class one day and said, "Merlot doesn't go with anything." It is a hard point to argue.

To this point, at least, a great deal of Merlot has been shapeless stuff, blurred in flavor and uncomfortably soft in texture. If not that, it has been a shaky imitation of Cabernet. In both regards it has been an object lesson in how difficult it is to find a role for one more varietal in a crowded field.

The grape came into vogue during the 1970s as a way to blend extra complexity into Cabernet Sauvignons and to blend some of their tannic austerity out. It succeeded, especially at the latter, which led straight to its career as an affable counterpart to Cabernet. When it turned out to be not merely affable but outright compliant, several winemakers started stiffening its spine with a dollop of Cabernet. Most of them succeeded too well, ending with a tannic wine of only modest flavor interest. And thus Madeleine's lament.

The times they are a changing. Quite a few winemakers have begun to get a handle on the variety, to find a balance that gives it intriguing flavors and a texture between shapeless and austerely tannic. Lakespring Winery, Pine Ridge Winery, Rutherford Hill Winery, Newton Vineyard, Sterling Vineyards, and Buena Vista Winery & Vineyard have all been admirable more often than not during the 1980s, but for us just two—Clos du Val and Louis M. Martini—are showing the way to the rest.

The list of successes comes, nearly all of it, from the Napa Valley. Napa's 755 acres lead all counties by a wide margin. Of the rest of a state total of 2,025, Sonoma's 465 acres appear next-best placed, though many Merlots from there have been more tannic than the rest of the wine has been able to support.

285

CLOS DU VAL WINE CO.

Bernard Portet grows the Merlot for Clos du Val on the same property that yields the Cabernet Sauvignon, blends a part of the crop into the Cabernet, and makes from the rest a wine that is to a haunting degree a sibling of that Cabernet. Even the vintages run in close parallel. Much of the similarity seems to come from Portet's sense of style, but some of it must come from the vineyard. The kinship is that close.

The Merlots are just a touch more straightforward all around, easier wines to come to a decision about, easier wines to drink early, not because they are lesser but because everything comes together in them sooner. The 1983 has been the absolute stand-out in the series to this point.

Portet's Merlots are versatile at the dinner table, but never show better than with roast chicken in an herbed sauce.

LOUIS M. MARTINI

Something of the same family feels that mark the Clos du Vals can be found in the Martinis, but the resemblance is not quite so close. Unlike the Clos du Vals, the Martini Cabernets and Merlots come from entirely different locations.

The Merlot vineyard is Los Viñedos del Rio, well west of Healdsburg in the Russian River Valley and otherwise memo-rable for its Gewürztraminers. The family-owned property has been turning out lean, tart, intensely flavored wines vintage after vintage since the 1968–1970 lot that was California's first com-mercial Merlot since Prohibition.

The weather at Los Viñedos is not so steady as it is below the rocky outcrops of Stag's Leap. A few of the wines—the 1982 comes especially to mind—have been right at the edge of lemon-tart. But the majority balance only slightly in that direction, and it is their tartness that seems to recommend them with a whole range of meats from chicken to steak, and almost any saucy pasta.

At one point we took it on faith that the four- to six-year aging curve of Zinfandel would be just the ticket for Martini Merlots. It may still be, but they have the house capacity to age for far longer than seems to be the case at first glance.

On a bleak afternoon late in 1986 a roomful of us gathered to think deep thoughts about Merlots ranging back from 1984 to the 1968–1970 and the 1969 Martinis. The 1968–1970 had done all it would do, but still foreshadowed the series in all ways— pleasing flavors from the fruit and a cleansing tartness set themselves against definite bouquets of age. The richer, darker 1969, meanwhile, seemed just to be reaching its prime, had indeed gained every advantage of maturity without suffering one of the indignities. When we all finished with our intellectual debates, it was the bottle I hoarded to have with my rabbit.

Of recent vintages, the 1983, 1980, and 1978 have seemed one cut above the field.

Petite Sirah and Syrah

Petite Sirah, the grape variety, is California's old standby for blending in red wines. It has enough color and tannic backbone to be the solid core in a jug red otherwise confected out of scraps, and so has more than enough solids to firm up rain-weakened Cabernet Sauvignons, Zinfandels, Gamays, Merlots, whatever, but not so much flavor that it drowns the originals. Such have been the principal roles of a substantial and widely spread acreage since Prohibition ended. Petite Sirah was around in the nineteenth century as well, though to less clear ends.

In the 1960s it began to make a modestly successful varietal wine. While Petite Sirah naturally has the kind of tannin wine-makers have to strain to get in Cabernet Sauvignon, it does not have the same depth of flavor. The fullest flavored ones have agreeable but indistinct fruit flavors, an advantage in blending but not a way to get headlines. The truest to type may set themselves apart from other varieties by a hint of something close to freshly ground black pepper.

Given the givens, the alternatives are three:

· Drink the wine young out of a fondness for rough, tough reds.

· Wait several years for age to work its subtle magic.

· Blend it with something of less forcible textures, a possibility that keeps being mooted. The blends in which Petite Sirah is a majority report all seem to come and go, however good they might be. We particularly mourn a Stag's Leap Wine Cellars 1978 with a softening spot of Pinot Noir in it. It was and is a treasure, but Warren Winiarski gave up the variety directly after he made the one try.

Both drink-now and wait-it-out bibbers go looking for the same unblended wines, which, when they hit the mark, can be memorable. For admirers of the full-tilt style, Hop Kiln, Ridge, and Stag's Leap Winery set the pace. At least a dozen wineries do well with mortally proportioned examples of the variety more often than not, Concannon Vineyard, Inglenook Vineyards, Fetzer Vineyards, and Guenoc Winery prominent among them. The two most consistent sources of recent years have been L. Foppiano and Parducci, both of whom pronounce the name "Petty Sarah" in the best California tradition. That may even be the secret to the search. The people who call it Petty Sarah are the ones to trust first.

L. FOPPIANO WINERY

When he first started making Petite Sirah as a varietal, Louis J. Foppiano had the good sense to let it have its head, be itself, escape the travails of new oak barrels. What his winery has gotten out of its straight-ahead approach is a wine with appealing fruit flavors and a pleasing balance, though one that does not lack for tannin. It drinks well young, and better older. I can still recall with some vividness a bottle of the 1969 that I had in 1978 in a small restaurant on Geary Boulevard in San Francisco. I bring this up because of the wry line that starts off the discussion of Pinot Noir; I cannot for the life of me remember the name of the restaurant. (I do remember the girl. I had better, she being my wife.)

As they have from the start, the Foppianos grow their own Petite Sirah in a gravelly vineyard flanking their winery at the south side of Healdsburg, and they still make the wine to taste of its grape variety. The program has lead to a string of successes in 1978, 1979, 1980, and especially 1981, the most recent vintage on the market at the hour of writing.

PARDUCCI WINE CELLARS

John Parducci's Petite Sirahs from the Ukiah district in Mendocino County echo the Foppianos in style and substance. They are plenty tannic, but have enough of the grape variety's black pepperlike aromas to make a complicated wine.

The district does well by Petite Sirah in most vintages, but some years do stand out in memory, most particularly the 1978.

For years Californians cruised along, assuming that Petite Sirah was one of the heavyweight varieties of the Rhône. When close examination revealed it to be mere Duriff, one of the lesser lights there, some status-conscious winery owners began cultivating the true Syrah. In 1986 California had but ninety bearing acres of it, all except a few tiny plots spread fairly equably among San Luis Obispo, Napa, and Mendocino counties. To this point, Syrah has demonstrated only more forcefully what Merlot has— that developing a suitable wine style for an unfamiliar grape variety is long, difficult work.

At this point, Preston Vineyards Sirah-Syrah, a blend of Petite Sirah and Syrah, has done the greatest credit to the true Syrah, which again brings us back to the virtues of blending.

OTHER WHITE WINES

IT GRIEVES ME TO SHOVE EVERY WHITE WINE other than Chardonnay, Gewürztraminer, and Sauvignon Blanc into a category called Other, not only because I rail against a narrow choice of chocolate, vanilla, and strawberry in anything, but because some of my oldest and dearest loves are relegated to such a grab bag. However, there is no making long stories out of short lists, and so the deed is done.

Within this section are gathered, in alphabetical order, a quartet of varietal types, plus variations on one of their themes.

Chenin Blanc

Chenin Blanc is going to come and go fast. It is a serviceable wine of modest character, not one for deep reflection or much of any reflection at all, whether it is a dry stand-in for Chardonnay or Sauvignon Blanc or an off-dry alternative to Riesling.

It is planted in substantial volumes everywhere in the state, is in fact the most-planted white-wine variety of California. If Chenin has a natural home, it must be the San Joaquin River delta, directly to the east of San Francisco Bay. In the Clarksburg AVA there, deep, well-moistened soils and a reliable growing season give the vines what they need to develop a distinctive set of aromas in their fruit. The regional note is curiously musky, bringing to mind Crenshaw, musk, and some of the other more flavorful melons.

The odd superior specimen will come out of Napa or Sonoma, and one comes regularly from Paso Robles. In all of these places the flavors are milder than the delta's, faintly reminiscent of pears if of any specific fruit. The delta wines have been welcome at picnics; the others have been saving graces at restaurants that price their Chardonnays for the benefit of oil explorers and drug dealers.

These as much as every other Chenin Blanc are more profitably drunk during their first year in bottle than later.

HACIENDA WINERY

One of the first producers to turn to the delta for grapes, Hacienda has been rock-steady as a producer of barely off-dry Chenins. They have just enough of the melonlike regional character to stand in well for Sauvignon Blancs, especially for people who look dimly upon the more pungent flavors of the latter.

A reliable climate leads to one equable vintage after another.

KENWOOD VINEYARDS

The story is almost identical to Hacienda's, the wine at least the equal of its down-valley neighbor.

GRAND CRU VINEYARDS

Grand Cru is the third member of a triumvirate of Sonoma Valley wineries that has found its Chenin Blanc in the delta AVA called Clarksburg. The style is as similar as the source.

CHAPPELLET VINEYARD

The Napa Valley's longtime contribution to dry, oak-aged Chenin Blanc comes from estate-grown grapes from high hills east of Rutherford. The fruit flavors are altogether understated in a consistently balanced wine that has been another useful refuge in restaurants where wine prices run high.

DRY CREEK VINEYARD

For a long time Dry Creek Vineyard proprietor David Stare stuck with Sonoma grapes, but beginning with 1986 he added some fruit from Yolo County. The wine feels a shade firmer on the palate than such as Hacienda, and the fruit flavors lean more in the direction of pears than melons. Though the wine has a typical 0.6 percent of residual sugar, it finishes dry enough to fit at the table as well as or better than a sipper.

MARTIN BROTHERS WINERY

Domenic Martin makes Chenin Blanc dry, lean, and tart, much along the lines of the Chappellet for fruit flavors and body, but not so clearly marked by wood. It gets along with fish, but fits better with poultry. I cannot think of a Chenin Blanc that is first-rate fish wine.

SIMI WINERY

Of all the sipping-style Chenins, Simi's has the magic balance. The fruit flavors are seductive. No other word describes them.

No other Chenin's perfumes are quite as refined. No flavor association comes to mind for the wine, though the tastes are about as intense as a juicy pear's, hinting not at all at tart. Quite the contrary, Zelma Long leaves just enough sweetness to avoid any suggestion of that.

Mendocino County is the source of Simi's Chenin Blanc. Specifically, the wine comes from a vineyard at the village of Talmage, just downstream from Ukiah.

Pinot Blanc

Pinot Blanc is not going to make any headway against Chardonnay anytime soon, and alas. Its fruit flavors are compatible with Chardonnay's, but quite as rich and not as easy to taste as complex. With that, its textures are leaner and firmer than Chardonnay's. The wine, then, is exactly what people who do not care for big Chardonnays demand: understated enough to be versatile, tart enough to be cleansing, but still of a character that lets it match the same foods as Chardonnay either as a young wine or after it has acquired bottle bouquet.

Superior examples will age. In January 1987 Drs. Bernard Rhodes and Robert Adamson plumbed their cellars for wines to test the limits of California wines to age. Three Heitz Cellars Pinot Blancs from the McCrea vineyard at Stony Hill were all in fine fettle. The vintages were 1965, 1967, and 1969.

After dwindling in acreage all through the 1970s, the variety has rebounded a bit in recent seasons, to two thousand, because the grape has proven useful in champagne blends. A mere handful of producers make it as a varietal, and no wonder. No matter how impressive, the wines fetch lesser prices than Chardonnay under the same label, sometimes less than half.

And so, in spite of its rarity, it is a wine for bargain hunters to squirrel away in the cellar for a couple of years for as long as a stubborn few will keep making it.

Among the regions that offer varietal bottlings, vineyards are too scattered to attempt any sort of guesses about where to press the case for Pinot Blanc, but the Santa Cruz Mountains, Mendocino's Redwood Valley, and Chalone are the sources of the memorable current editions. In spite of the old Heitz Cellars successes and several others, and in spite of a healthy two hundred acres of vines, only one Napa winery at the moment seems to be bottling Pinot Blanc as a varietal.

As if the variety did not have enough old troubles, now experts have begun to question its true identity. Some ampelographers believe what California knows as Pinot Blanc is, in fact, Melon. What the hell. The wine is just as good as ever, and maybe would sell better as Melon. Pinot Blanc has not been an advantageous name.

CONGRESS SPRINGS VINEYARDS

Dan Gehrs of Congress Springs makes the quintessential Pinot Blanc from vineyards in the Santa Cruz Mountains above Saratoga and Los Gatos. The first several came from his own and other properties. Recent vintages have come entirely from winery-farmed grapes. Gehrs's Pinot Blanc are so crisp and light they almost dance on the palate, yet have haunting depths of flavor from grapes on the one hand and barrel fermentation on the other. The 1984 was just settling into full stride in late 1987, which makes it a typical vintage.

CHALONE VINEYARDS

Monterey County has the largest share of California's Pinot Blanc, but Chalone's twenty acres or so differ markedly from all the plantings down at the foot of the hills. I am not the only soul around who thinks Pinot Blanc is, by more than walking distance, Chalone's finest white. It is for people who like their wines tart and firm, almost sculpted feeling on the palate. It has the variety's usual understated aromas, but they are indelible, the gustatory equivalent of the commanding whisper, and the winemaking leaves them to make their point.

FETZER VINEYARDS

The sleeper in the crowd, Fetzer Pinot Blanc is richer than most of its running mates and shows signs of being one of the most durable ones. Early in 1987 Fetzer showed off its 1979 and 1980 vintages as appetizers for a rainy-day lunch at the winery. The 1980 was impressive, and completely overshadowed by the 1979, the latter the sort of wine that demanded a second glass even though another nine enticing wines were already in full view on the table. As lunch went along, both Pinot Blancs put some pretty good Chardonnays in the shade. In fact, they put most Chardonnays in the shade with their depths of flavor and richness of texture.

"Depth of flavor" always looks dumb after I write it, but no other shorthand conveys as well the notion of flavors revealing themselves not all at once, but in layers, or waves, with succeeding sips from the glass, then succeeding glasses.

Several Fetzers and winemaker Paul Dolan looked pleasantly surprised by what they found in their glasses of 1979, but said the 1980 was merely typical. It comes from Redwood Valley Vineyards, close by the winery. Dolan ferments in steel and ages in wood, taking care not to let the latter cloud the rich, ripe flavors of the grapes.

Riesling (also White Riesling, Johannisberg Riesling)

It still strikes me as passing strange to find Riesling relegated to a list of other wines. Back when I was getting started with California it was one of the Big Four with Cabernet Sauvignon, Chardonnay, and Pinot Noir, a kind of D'Artagnan to the Three Musketeers.

What seems even stranger is that it has come to be the ultimate test of my notion that age-worthy wines are the ones to hunt for every time.

In January 1987 I got to do a little time travel. At the same dinner at which the old Heitz Pinot Blancs came out, the first wine of the evening was a 1968 Souverain Napa Valley Johannisberg Riesling. It riveted me in the moment, and it took me back.

Souverain was the wine that got us going on Riesling when it and we were a lot newer. Its light, crisp textures played off against almost wild-berrylike flavors that seemed sometimes sweet, sometimes tart, always entrancing. The pounds of crab and the loaves of sourdough French bread we went through testing the charms of that wine mounted up to indecent totals before we were through. In 1970 and 1971 alone we sacrificed a few more than fifty Dungeness crabs to its beauties with never a pang of guilt.

One of the ways I know I am getting to be an old fogy is counting the number of times I have raved on about this wine, but until the recent evening of time travel my ravings had begun to have a dated quality. Now I can brush them up. At nineteen, the wine still had most, perhaps all, of its original powers to charm. Nobody thought of risking cold cracked crab on a nineteen-year-old Riesling, but they could have. And if one wine can last like that, it is not asking too much for others to linger in top form for five or six years. That I do. Some exceptional bottlings have passed the test.

Most California Rieslings are evanescent at the very best. A few months of fragile charm and they slip into Victorian declines fit for the heroines of costume novels. Appealing scents of berry descend first to cardamom, then to fernlike, and finally to outright petrolish. Ultra-ripe, the fragile young are reminiscent of apricot, but these too follow the rest of the evolution to petrollike fumes. Either way, textures slip from lilting to plodding. A lot of winemakers know it; a lot of them have quietly dropped the wine from their lists; a good many more should.

But the exceptions! The exceptions make not only the price

of fresh, cold, cracked Dungeness crab worth paying, they make lake crawdads worth the hunt, turn steamed clams into royal feasts, and save the price of Champagne to go with the strawberries and cream.

The exceptions do not start out tasting like fresh berry. They start out tasting like something perfumed by a concentrate from raspberries—not jam exactly, more like a raspberry *sirop* portioned out by a sensitive hand. They balance on the thin lines between dry and sweet, luscious and tart. It ain't an easy act.

These exceptions come down to a precious few, from a precious few places. The places are Napa's hills of the morning light (from whence the famous Souverain 1968), the long ridge above Greenwood town in Mendocino County's Anderson Valley, and, I think, from less certain evidence, Arroyo Seco in Monterey County. The few are Stony Hill, Smith-Madrone, and Greenwood Ridge year in and year out, and several others not quite so regularly, but almost.

STONY HILL VINEYARDS

The Napa Valley's longest running success story with Riesling stretches back to the early 1960s. In the earliest years the wine was dry. Slowly it picked up a suggestion of sweetness that has leveled off somewhere close to 1 percent residual sugar. The addition brought the wine from good to much-better-than-good company for fresh cracked crab and steamed clams. The touch of sweet also seems to help the wine keep longer. We have no qualms about losing a bottle in the cellar for four to six years.

Stony Hill's vines grow at very close to the same elevation as the ones that yielded the Souverain 1968 and 1969, and little more than two miles north of them. They are made in much the same way. I do not know whether it is the winemaking, the vineyard, or both, but they give a similar feeling of structure in the mouth. Some white wines are thin, some are fat. A very few are neither, giving rather a feeling of having shape on the palate. There is no pinning down what shape, but the feeling will not go away. The Stony Hills are one such.

They are very hard to come by. Nearly the entire annual production goes to mailing-list customers who pass their memberships along from generation to generation like fifty-yard-line seats.

SMITH-MADRONE VINEYARDS

Separating wines one from another by their qualities is risky business. My wife and I, familiar with each other's palates from thousands of shared bottles, can sit face-to-face and disagree as to which of two wines is the fuller-bodied, or tarter, or hotter. These distinctions get so subtle that they depend on how agreeable one's day has been. When the wines come from virtually neighboring vineyards and are made in much the same style, the effort can be outright foolish.

Such is the case here. Charles and Stuart Smith's vineyards are straight up Spring Mountain from Stony Hill. Their wine has very nearly the same degree of sweet in the finish as the neighbor, and very nearly the same perfumes of Riesling. But it is not the same wine to me. It is fatter, less geometric as it sits on my tongue, and that is what makes me favor it with a bucket of steamers sooner than a cold cracked crab. Feel free to argue.

The first vintage, 1977, continues in fine fettle, another bit of evidence that these particular slopes give their Rieslings an uncommon longevity. Vintage differences, incidentally, are altogether negligible.

TREFETHEN VINEYARDS

Of all these Rieslings, Trefethen White Riesling is the light, crisp one, and the most subtly flavored. (Wines can be curious in their balances. None tastes more specifically of Riesling than the Trefethen, and none more restrainedly of it.) Part of the delicacy owes to its being drier—half a percent of residual sugar against 1.0 to 1.5 percent for the others—but some may owe to the valley-floor vineyards. At least a part of the crispness owes to the wine's seeing no wood.

In any case, it is a universal charmer with shellfish and not out of place with chicken or summer salads or any other meal with a light heart. Trefethen White Riesling will age comfortably for two or three years in bottle, but I have never seen a point in it beyond one trial to make sure of the stuffings in a wine that can fool one into thinking it is fragile rather than delicate.

STAG'S LEAP WINE CELLARS

Of all the current Rieslings, Warren Winiarski's come closest to the ageless Souverain 1968, and for good reason. Winiarski did a major part of his apprenticeship in the Souverain Cellars of Lee Stewart, the man who made the marvel. For years the Stag's Leaps came from the Birkmyer Vineyard in hills east of the town of Napa. More recently they have been assembled from Napa and Sonoma vineyards. If anything, the shift in sources has gotten Winiarski closer to Stewart's model.

It does not do to explain too much the minute differences among these wines. Suffice it say that these are as juicy in the mouth as Riesling gets, and the aromas of berry as rich.

CHATEAU ST. JEAN

Richard Arrowood, longtime winemaker at Chateau St. Jean, has a favorable reputation for almost every wine he makes, but Johannisberg Riesling in all its forms from dry to resoundingly sweet is his longest suit for my taste. He has found the vineyards that please him in Robert Young and Belle Terre, in Sonoma's Alexander Valley, and he coaxes well-nigh-perfect flavors out of the grapes and into his wines. The ones that are making my mouth water here are styled as Cabinets, at 1.5 percent residual sugar or thereabouts. They are supple, silky things, suited to fresh fruit and pound cakes much more than shellfish. I have never been able to figure out exactly why this is so, but it is.

As with all of the others, we have kept a few bottles back to see that the flavors stay true to berries and do not wander too soon toward petrol. They do hold well, but they give their greatest performances in the first flush of youth.

GREENWOOD RIDGE VINEYARDS

Of all the wines that benefit from precise control over sweetness, Riesling leads the league, but only if the winemaker finds and keeps a balance point that seems to vary with every vineyard. Allan Green has caught that balance from the grapes he grows on his rolling property near the top of Greenwood Ridge, in far-western Mendocino County, at the seaward boundary of Anderson Valley. Technically, the balance point is right around 1.5 percent residual sugar, but numbers are not the test. Half the trick is to suspend Riesling between sweet and tart. The other, harder half is to make it taste exactly as rich as it smells. Few wines disappoint more than a Riesling that smells ripe and fat, then feels and tastes thin and sharp. The challengers are Rieslings that promise delicacy everywhere, then plod across the tongue as thick and heavy as oil.

Greenwood Ridge Rieslings promise and deliver refinement everywhere.

NAVARRO VINEYARDS

Down the Anderson Valley floor, several hundred feet lower than Greenwood ridge, Ted Bennett makes a perfect case for the irrelevancy of numbers. His Johannisberg Riesling, like Allan Green's, weighs in at 1.5 percent residual sugar. Yet, somehow, the wine has bolder varietal perfumes and feels fuller. Not heavy, just fuller. The two together provide a perfect lesson on the subject, especially if they can be set off against a picnic of cold cracked crab and sourdough bread with sweet butter. The correct backdrop is blue seawater and a wind-washed sky.

JEKEL VINEYARD

One wine has tipped me toward Arroyo Seco as a home for durable Rieslings, it being a Wente Bros. 1973 lightly touched by *Botrytis cinerea*. The wine was still in good form in January 1987, at the same dinner graced by the Souverain Cellars 1968. There have been few like it, but the promise is always at hand in the driest of the two or three Johannisberg Rieslings released each year by Jekel.

The flavors of Riesling are impeccable, not infrequently concentrated just a bit by *Botrytis,* alias the Noble Mold. Now and again the wines become overweight (1976 is the outstanding example, 1986 a less dramatic one), but most find harmonies of flavor and weight. The Jekel Vineyard, to dote on sugar once more, delivers such balance with residual sugars very close to 1 percent if *Botrytis* does not play much of a role, a bit more if it does.

The fair test of them, as usual, is cold cracked crab.

Semillon (also Chevrier, plus Semillon-Sauvignon blends)

It is an article of faith with Louis P. Martini that the United States has a fixed gene pool of Semillon fans. When one is born, one dies, and that is that. Martini bases the opinion on the inflexible sales of Semillon under his family label. For years the Martinis made and sold exactly *x* cases of Semillon. Other varieties would wax and wane in the marketplace, but Semillon stood still. They finally turned their share of the gene pool over to others. I believe Alderbrook Winery has it now, though the numbers may be divided between that winery and Congress Springs Vineyards. This has been going on for so long that no one has to worry about a flood of it. In all California only 2,550 acres of it are in bearing, and that total is spread around among fifteen counties in which it is grown for a blend grape as often as it is for itself.

Semillon, like Gewürztraminer, has a tendency to grow bolder in the bottle over its first few years. When the flavors stay fine, that is its strength. Sometimes, for reasons I have not learned to predict, Semillons that start out all polished and understated grow stronger and stronger in ways that are not easy to love.

At its finest the variety reminds one of fresh figs. Sometimes, according to the system of flavor associations devised at the University of California at Davis, it carries a scent of newly ironed sun-dried sheets. Now and again it will have the faintest whiff of a first-quality cigar. Odd as the descriptions may sound, those are the good moments. Occasionally Semillon will get to smelling and tasting like potatoes that have grown too close to the top of the mound and stayed green. Those are the not-so-good moments.

Semillon can be just as intractable as a blend grape as it can alone. Any number of wineries have tried blending small proportions of it with Sauvignon Blanc to fatten the latter and give it some extra dimensions of flavor. One after another, they have dropped the percentage from 15 down to 10, then 5, then none. The secret of success seems to lie in the other direction, blending the two at equal or nearly equal proportions. Varietal regulations being what they are, the equal blends labor under a welter of proprietary names—Chevrignon, Sauvrier, Chevriot all plainly intended to reveal their bases. Varietal and blended bottlings are intermixed in the descriptions here.

A few wineries sell Semillon under its alternative name, Chevrier.

CLOS DU VAL SEMILLON

Of all the producers of Semillon as a varietal, Bernard Portet tames its flavors most fully, makes in fact something delicate of it. A welcome, smooth feel on the palate goes hand in glove with the subtlety of flavor. For all of the taming, few wines smack more specifically of the variety.

We have tucked a couple of bottles away, as usual, to see what comes of age, but most of the annual supply we drink early in company with mildly fatty whitefish—monkfish, sablefish, red snapper, that sort.

Even more than Warren Winiarski's Stag's Leap Wine Cellars Johannisberg Riesling, Bernard Portet's Clos du Val Semillon shows that the winemaker is at least as important as the vineyard in the frontier that is California. Portet's first Semillon, 1983, was all Napa Valley, the second all Santa Ynez Valley, the third from Yolo County, and the fourth a blend of Napa and Yolo. Except for the thinner, less aromatic all-Yolo vintage, they have been peas in a pod. The slight advantages of the 1983 and 1985 belong to those vintages, not the vineyards. As Clos du Val's own plantings at the winery come into play from 1987 on, Napa will be the sole source.

VICHON CHEVRIGNON

The proprietary fusion of Chevrier and Sauvignon advertises a fifty-fifty blend of the two grapes in a wine with a longer history than readers of even Vichon labels might suspect. The proprietary wine started out in 1981 as Chevrier Blanc, but lost its maiden name when ATF ruled Chevrier to be a synonym for Semillon and thus varietal, which the wine was not. Legalities and former names aside, Chevrignon has made pleasant company to a lot of fish and chicken. It is a couple of shades bolder in Semillon flavors than the Clos du Val, and a good deal bigger-bodied or rougher in texture.

Two bottles of the debut 1981 linger in our cellar in 1987, still in perfect health and fuller of flavor than ever, as the opening of a third bottle demonstrated.

The Vichon is an assembled wine, a majority of the grapes from Chiles Valley, the rest from the heart of the main Napa

Valley. The two varieties are barrel-fermented separately, then blended and oak-aged.

MONTICELLO CHEVRIER BLANC

A new entry in 1985, it is compounded from close to 80 percent Semillon, the rest from Sauvignon Blanc, and is astounding because of that. In the normal run of things, winemakers add a touch of Semillon to fatten up extra-lean or harsh Sauvignons. Here, the bit of Sauvignon is there to put flesh on a tart, tart Semillon. The answer is in the vineyard. In general, Semillon takes more heat than Sauvignon to ripen fully. In this vineyard the sun shines just hot enough to get Sauvignon up to the lower limits of ripeness. Thus all goes in reverse, and to excellent effect. In its early days the debut Chevrier Blanc tasted as much of its minority partner as of Semillon, which caused it to fit exactly a dinner of Tuscan dishes, two of them with sweet red peppers.

It is too soon to speak in absolutes, but, given the track record of a Sauvignon that goes back in memorable fashion to 1981, betting on the Chevrier Blanc seems safe enough. All of the grapes for both come from Monticello proprietor Jay Corley's vineyard at the north edge of Napa city, where Oak Knoll Avenue and Big Ranch Road intersect. Corley and winemaker Alan Phillips planned to work longer wood aging into the program for the 1986 and later vintages. Not too much, one prays. It is a delicate soup to season.

This is where Vichon's old name has ended up. Though Monticello treats the wine as a proprietary, the federal government has no objection because this blend qualifies as a varietal too.

ALDERBROOK WINERY

All of the other Semillons I know about share a flavor that is not pure fruit. One great inventor of flavor associations pegged the overtone as potato. The whimsical-sounding but spot-on contribution of UC-Davis is newly ironed sun-dried sheets (which in turn smell like the first few drops of a warm rain). It is something like that. Whatever it is, Alderbrook does not have it. Alderbrook's flavors are all fruit, but elusive at the same time. The hint of fig (UC's other association) is there, but not all alone. Sometimes melon comes to mind, sometimes not. I give up; John Grace's wine is likably fruity.

Different as the flavors are, the wine suggests itself most often where other Semillons do, but also with a whole range of salads dressed with other than vinegar. Grace manages to match the affable taste of fruit with nicely polished textures. A hint of oak adds depth, but is hard to identify for itself. Because the fruit flavors charm as much as they do, waiting for bottle bouquet has never seemed as good an idea as drinking the wine young, but somebody ought to test the limits.

John Grace started making Semillon in his first vintage at Alderbrook in 1981. Through 1986 all of the grapes came from a single vineyard on the east slope of Dry Creek Valley, about midway up its length. Grace's own plantings began to bear in 1987; his plan then was to add them to the blend if they measured up, peddle them if they did not.

CHAMPAGNES AND OTHER SPARKLING WINES

AH, CHAMPAGNE. ITS FLAVORS CANNOT BE EX-
plained but its powers can. A few years back I was one of a
band of thirty condemned to each other's company for a week
of winery touring in Napa, Sonoma, and Monterey. For the
first day and a half it was a convention of shy persons. People
spoke only when spoken to, mostly to their mates, and to them
in near whispers. One got the feeling that if anyone laughed,
someone else would cry. Then came the visit to a sparkling-
wine house, followed by lunch with enough of the bubbly to
suit Jay Gatsby. Lunch turned into a class reunion. For the rest
of the week nobody shut up for a minute.

It is this sort of thing that has made sparkling wines a neces-
sity at weddings, farewells, and other gatherings of emotion-
filled friends and strangers. It may be this sort of thing that
causes people to limit their exposure to sparkling wines to one

or two festive moments a year, on grounds they cannot afford to be so happy any too often. One can, I admit, slip too deep into bliss. A chap I know starts each morning with a glass or two of a fine champagne, and wonderfully amiable he is, but his workday is too short to be a model for society. However, a glass a year is not enough, especially if it is the run of stuff one sees at weddings, and is being taken half for therapeutic purposes into the bargain.

Well-designed, well-made sparkling wines bring incomparable gifts to the table. Few beverages refresh as well. None sets the appetite to stirring half so well. The paragons have dozens, maybe scores of flavors lurking among the bubbles, but even the major themes are subtle, leaving the bibber free to pay fascinated attention or just let the wine slip down. Could anything else be asked of a bottle?

Well designed and well made almost limit the discussion to wines made by the traditional champagne method, but not quite, because one bulk-process sparkling Muscat does not brook exclusion. It tags along behind the traditionalists, not to diminish it but rather out of respect for its dessert-sweet qualities.

Some of you may have noticed that I have been tap-dancing around the words *champagne* or *Champagne*. The semantics have become a burden heavier than the wine itself ever is. According to the French, Champagne is wine made by the champagne method in the district of the same name. Anything made anywhere else is sparkling wine. Other-than-French observers think Champagne, or champagne, is all sparkling wine made by the champagne method and, where needed, labeled with a qualifier (California Champagne, Australian Champagne, etc.). California has supporters of both views, both camps more polarized than they were before because several Champagne houses have established California subsidiaries. The philosophical and philological debate rages. Can only a Cuban cobbler fashion a Cuban heel? Etc. Why continue to lay the California breast bare to French arrows when the wines can stand on their own? Etc. I do not know the answers. I am not sure I care, never having bought a Californian when I meant to buy a French or vice versa.

Champagne versus sparkling wine aside, the Anglo-French nomenclature of style holds. *Nature* or Natural means a wine with no extra sweetness added (dosage), and thus no sweetness at all. Brut means dry to the taste, which in turn means a technical sweetness level of 0.7 to 1.5 percent sugar (in the loftier circles of California sparkling wines it does, anyway). Extra Dry and Demi Sec are patently sweet (and ignored in this chapter because none of the sparkling-wine houses mentioned in it makes any).

For all their frothy reputation as the wine of weddings and bon voyage parties, champagne-method Champagnes do not come easy. The most "made" of all the wines, they depend on one extra step after another, not just for the bubbles but for their curious balances. One of the balances is the familiar push-pull between sweet and tart, sugar and acid. A similar one plays bubbles against sweetness. (Any doubter can make the test handily; let one glass go flat and taste it against one still alive with bubbles from a freshly opened bottle of the same wine.) But the most delicate and mysterious one sets evanescent aromas of fruit against the now-earthy, now-toasty bouquets from autolyzed yeasts and whatever makes up the dosage.

Champagne masters have hundreds of tricks in their bags for shifting flavors a tiny bit this way or a tinier bit that. Dosage alone can take a lifetime of study. It can be brandy, or new wine, or old wine. If it is wine, it can be barrel-fermented, oak-aged, or innocent of any time in wood. Or it can be a blend of all of the above. Little boosts or declines in the amount of sugar in the dosage may have almost as much effect as a change in any other aspect of it. The exact strain of yeast can have as pronounced an effect on flavor as the dosage. We have not even gotten to the main questions of which grape varieties and from where.

If each of these balances is precarious, the sum is more so. Blenders of still table wines can, sometimes, shift a set of proportions by 10 or 15 percent without changing the end flavors enough for a skilled taster to notice. Champagne masters can watch a blend soar to unexpected heights or go altogether haywire with the addition or subtraction of less than 5 percent. Sometimes only one percent, plus or minus, is enough to make or break a broth. I know; I have done it.

Every now and again a winemaker will sacrifice a couple of gallons of wine in an effort to make outsiders understand what goes on between the fermentors and the bottling line. It has been given to me, as one of those outsiders, to try a hand at blends of various sorts over the years. One result after another has been properly humbling, but never so soon and never so thoroughly as with some bits and pieces from the 1985 stocks Edmond Maudière and Dawnine Sample Dyer had at hand to fashion Chandon Brut and Blanc de Noirs during 1986.

Maudière and Dyer handed over to six of us dilettantes samples from three lots of Chardonnay, three of Pinot Noir, and one of Pinot Blanc, plus, finally, one lot of reserve from 1984. As kindly advice, they suggested blending each of the individual varieties to satisfaction, then blending those blends into one master lot. The other participants can speak for themselves, but I found a dozen different ways to drive straight into the swamp. Things would go along fine for a while. A trial blend of Chardonnay would seem passable, and so would one of Pinot Noir. A couple of times the two would come together well enough. But the merest hint of Pinot Blanc or reserve—less of it than the whiff of vermouth in a martini—would topple my house of cards every time. These tragedies call for hours of explanation, but it is a busy world. Suffice it to say my last, best blend went to hell in a hand basket, and that was that. Maudière, ever gentlemanly, said not to worry, it happened to him all the time, and gave us all dinner to ease the ache.

The lesson is that a champagne master has to have a monomaniacal idea starting out, or be self-condemned to wandering forever through the maze. Without a definite house style to work toward, there is no knowing where one is at any point along the long road from grapes to finished wine. Domaine Chandon,

Iron Horse, and Schramsberg lead my list of California sparkling wines, not only because they please my taste, but because they have such consistent personalities.

I do not expect the crowd to be so small for long, for a score of new players has come with the 1980s. Almost half of them arrived from Reims and Epernay with the required, highly refined monomanias, new to California but old to the world of Champagne. Their combined presence will govern what California sparkling wine is to be in the near future because their sheer numbers will dominate the sense of style.

It is worth stepping back for a moment to get perspective. In the early 1960s California's specialist champagne-method-sparkling-wine houses had declined in number to two, each following its own trail. F. Korbel and Bros. had developed a grapy style by using Chenin Blanc, French Colombard, and other varieties not common in Champagne. Hanns Kornell had taken a similar tack, with Chenin Blanc the mainstay of his off-dry styles and Riesling the backbone of his dry ones. Kornell's most distinctive wine, Sehr Trocken, is well-aged Riesling. It has merit but no flavors a Frenchman would call champagne.

In 1965 Jack and Jamie Davies launched Schramsberg on the premise that champagne-method winemaking called for the grapes of Champagne—Chardonnay and Pinot Noir. Beyond the choice of grapes, they were working mostly on their own, with the avowed purpose of developing a wine with as much character as fine Champagnes, but a different one.

In 1972 Moët-Hennessy brought not only the idea of traditional grapes but also traditional styles of Champagne to the game, and established Domaine Chandon on the first knolls west of Yountville, not quite fifteen miles down the Napa Valley from the Davieses. In the process, they avoided all use of the word *champagne* and so sparked up the long-standing debate a good deal.

Then came the deluge that virtually assures a French dominance of style, partly out of numbers, partly because they all seem to hit the track running. The roster:

· In 1980 Piper-Heidsieck and Sonoma Vineyards joined forces to establish Piper-Sonoma at Windsor in the Russian River Valley. (Piper-Heidsieck has since become sole owner.)

· In 1981 Louis Roederer began the explorations that resulted in Roederer USA in Mendocino's Anderson Valley.

· In 1983 G. H. Mumm and Seagram combined to form Domaine Mumm, temporarily housed at Sterling Vineyards, but scheduled to move to a site of its own east of Rutherford during 1988.

· Also in 1983 Deutz & Geldermann established Maison Deutz on ocean-facing hills south of the town of San Luis Obispo.

· And finally, Taittinger launched Domaine Carneros in 1987, with plans to work in leased space while the winery goes up.

It is not that the French are alone. Recently established native players in the champagne-method game include S. Anderson in the Napa Valley, Chateau St. Jean, Robert Hunter, Iron Horse, and Sebastiani in Sonoma County, Parsons Creek and Scharffenberger in Mendocino County; Wente Bros., Mirassou, and The Monterey Vineyard with Monterey County grapes. Spain's Freixenet has an entry called Gloria Ferrer, in Sonoma's half of Carneros. But even among these, the nod to France is ever evident. Iron Horse hired a young *champenois* to get and keep its program in fine trim. The owners of Gloria Ferrer originally had it in mind to plant and experiment with some of the native varieties of Spain's Penedes region, but backed away from everything but Chardonnay and Pinot Noir after looking over the competition. Korbel and Kornell have both added cuvées based in Chardonnay. And so it goes. Still, it is impossible to know just now who is going to do what.

Roederer plans to release its first cuvée late in 1988. At Maison Deutz, owner André Lallier thinks he did not begin to get into stride until his third cuvée, due on the market during 1988–1989, and then he still will be some years away from using his own vines. (The first several vintages are from bought-in grapes from nearby Santa Barbara County.) One of the native entries, Shadow Creek, has just put itself back on square one after winning an early reputation for wines made in Sonoma from Sonoma grapes. In 1985 the owners pulled up stakes altogether, moving the winemaking to Corbett Canyon (which they also own), shifting the grape sources to the Central Coast, and installing a new champagne master.

Generally speaking, there is not much point in thinking about European wines as models for Californians. The conditions differ so much, from vineyard right through to store shelf, that anything that looks like a parallel is most likely an illusion, while everything that looks divergent can be taken for a true picture. But, to repeat a point, France is hard to forget when it comes to sparklers because so much of France has taken itself to California.

To talk about a French as opposed to a California style is to talk about how little or how much the wine smells and tastes of ripe fruit. In the comparison, the French style dwells very little on fruit and very heavily on the toasty bouquets of autolyzed yeasts and the caramellike ones of oxidation in the dosage—the sweetened syrup that goes into the bottle just ahead of its final cork. California, especially traditional California, leaned a bit the other way when Korbel and Kornell were the only specialists in the game, and leaning on fruit flavors from Chenin Blanc, Riesling, and other grapes other than Chardonnay and Pinot Noir. Now the pendulum has gone to the other, French end of its arc.

Up to a point, any effort to imitate France is doomed. The coolest parts of California ripen fruit sooner and more fully than does the district of Champagne. The Californian habit of picking before the grapes develop their full flavors goes in the desired direction, but still gives a different set of flavors demanding a different set of balances among all the other factors. How different depends on how like or unlike the French a producer wants to be, and how warm the district from which his or her grapes come.

NORTH COAST

The sources for Chardonnay and Pinot Noir for sparkling wines are still all in a jumble in the North Coast, with all but Schramsberg and Domaine Chandon running their first few laps in a long race. But the bent is toward the coolest sources—high hills in some cases, a nearness to tidewater in most. By name, the AVAs that begin to dominate are Carneros, Russian River Valley (including the Sonoma–Green Valley subappellation), and Anderson Valley. However, domination and exclusivity are not synonyms. Other parts of these counties contribute now and will continue to do so for more years than I have left to see how the screw turns.

Napa Valley

Conventional wisdom now says the grapes ought to come from Carneros, perhaps from the Big Ranch Road area on Napa's north city limits at the northernmost. These are the valley's coolest areas, where grapes are slowest to get to the desired 17 to 19 percent of sugar (degrees Brix in the trade). In fact, both Schramsberg and Domaine Chandon draw from a broader horizon. As with most aspects of coastal California winemaking, desirable sources turn out to be a property-by-property proposition.

SCHRAMSBERG

In an era when winemakers have tended to become cult figures, it has been easy to forget how important proprietors can be to the quality and character of a wine. Schramsberg is a particular antidote to excessive worship of the employee.

Jack and Jamie Davies launched Schramsberg in 1965 with a clear idea not only of making a first-quality California Champagne, but a firm notion of what that meant in every detail of taste. In the ensuing years they have taught several winemakers what they meant—and mean—by that, all the while driving toward a sharper picture of their ideal. Vertical tastings of their wines are always impressive for the balance between continuity and refinement, the slight but continuous curve that has kept theirs the most distinctive voice in the state.

The Davieses decided early to use a bit of cognac in the dosage, an idea so old in Champagne that it is seldom used there these days. Cognac lends a small but piercing note at the finish, a specific flavor of alcohol, a particular feel on the tongue. In sum, it provides a pointed quality that marks the wine whether one tastes it side by side with its peers from California or its rivals from France, but one that is very hard to find or describe when the glass comes alone, on the way from introductions to dinner.

However subtle, it is this pointed quality that makes Schramsberg the wine for winter, when the fireplace is lighted and a hearty meal is coming, and the weather invites sober reflection on what might be in the glass to warm one's soul.

Schramsberg produces four cuvées finished as Bruts—Blanc de Blancs, Blanc de Noirs, Reserve, and Cuvée de Pinot.

The Blanc de Blancs is Chardonnay with a leavening touch of Pinot Blanc, the Blanc de Noirs pure Pinot Noir. The Reserve reversed course between 1978 and 1979. Originally pure Chardonnay, it is now 80 to 90 percent Pinot Noir and the balance Chardonnay. It stays on tirage three years and more, while its running mates wait on the yeast between two and three.

Trying to draw lines between any two of the three is harder than one might think. The Blanc de Noirs and Reserve, in particular, come so close to each other in color, body, and other characteristics that trying to say which is which in a blind tasting is no easy job. The Blanc de Blancs lacks the telltale coppery tone of its mates and feels a mite leaner, less fleshy in the mouth, but even it can fool a skillful taster whose eyes are closed.

The last of the four Bruts is not hard to spot. Cuvée de Pinot follows the style called Rosé in France. Pinot Noir dominates, but a touch of Gamay amplifies the flavors of the named grape. In youth, it has a pronounced floral-fruity aroma, but this subsides within a year or two, leaving a dry, tart wine with the traditional bouquets of yeast and oxidation as complications. The option of drinking it early for its lightness or waiting for it to get serious poses no penalties for indecision.

All four wines have their bases in the Davieses' own substantial plantings high up the ridge from their aging tunnels and build complexities from several independent properties extending southward through the valley into the Big Ranch Road area.

For my taste the Brut styles show best when they are three to five years old, but the Blanc de Noirs and Reserves in particular hold up well until their tenth birthdays in most vintages, sometimes longer than that. Of the vintages from the 1970s, the 1973 Blanc de Blancs and 1975 Blanc de Noirs seem to have held notably well, while their opposite numbers from the same years have faded more than most. The Blanc de Noirs tasting notes can serve for the Cuvée de Pinots.

1980 One of the outstanding vintages of the past ten years for the Blanc de Blancs, Blanc de Noirs, and Reserve alike. All deftly balanced to refresh early, and all aging well in 1987.

1981 A little stronger of fruit and a little softer in texture than the previous vintage. Type for type, the Blanc de Blancs has had an edge over the Blanc de Noirs all along.

1982 The Blanc de Blancs was showing a particular turn of speed as late as 1987, but both it and Blanc de Noirs ranked near the head of the class then.

1983 Both the Blanc de Blancs and Blanc de Noirs show some of the polishing of technique in recent seasons. Though the vintage was not an easy one, the wines are developing as well as their three predecessors.

1984 Further reflects the technical refinements. The vintage is at least the equal of 1983, probably its superior.

Schramsberg has a fifth sparkling wine that opposes its running mates in every way. It is a cremant, which is to say it is less bubbly than a champagne, is sweet (about 6 percent of sugar), and is based in a boldly perfumey variety called Flora (a University of California cross of Gewürztraminer with Semillon).

DOMAINE CHANDON

Looking over old tasting notes brakes the ego more than anything else, but once in a while it reveals something worth noticing. In the case of Chandon Brut and Blanc de Noirs—and more lately the Reserve—notes from one blind tasting after another remark on how well made the wine is. If technical excellence is Chandon's hallmark for me, the pleasure in Chandon's wines comes from flavors that manage to be intriguing in understated ways year after year.

From the very first cuvée, the Bruts have had a dry, almost dusty note right in the forefront and a toasty one lurking behind that. Fruit has stayed well in the background since 1972. Moët-Hennessy's chief winemaker, Edmond Maudière, set the style and still stands guard over it, though Dawnine Sample Dyer has become increasingly responsible for the day-to-day winemaking. A lifelong winemaker in Champagne, Maudière sets particular store by the strains of yeast he has cultivated in the interest of a Moët house style. He is also insistent on using reserve wine from the preceding vintage to hold style at Domaine Chandon, hence no vintages there.

The Brut usually has between 60 and 70 percent of Pinot Noir and between 20 and 30 percent of Chardonnay, with Pinot Blanc filling in the gaps.

The newest member of the family, Chandon Reserve, out-Bruts the Brut. In fact it is a select cuvée from the wines made to be Brut. Domaine Chandon introduced Reserve in 1985 to mark its tenth anniversary in the Napa Valley. (To avoid confusion, the name of the company is Domaine Chandon, but the names of the wines are Chandon Brut, etc.)

The Blanc de Noirs is something else, pure Pinot Noir patterned by Maudière after the full-flavored, coppery-hued wines that were plentiful in his youth but have nearly disappeared from contemporary Champagne, the ones described as partridge eye. The Brut and Reserve have a faint cast from the Pinot Noir in them, but this one makes no bones at all. Early, it has astonishing perfumes somewhere between rose petals and a scent I associate with hard candy but never have been able to pin down. Its fuller proportion of Pinot Noir gives it more flesh to go with its stronger fruit flavors. With a year or two in bottle, its fruity or candied flavors slip into the shadows, and the family traits show more clearly.

Though Chandon has offered no vintages to this point, the winery has kept back bottles from each year since the beginnings in 1972. In autumn 1985 the firm trotted out a vertical of Brut cuvées from every harvest except the first. All nine wines were disgorged on the same day, and all were left as Naturals so that none of time's tricks would be disguised. What they proved as individuals was that variable vintages are a fact of life, even when grapes are safe in the barn long before the first rains of autumn. (The 1975 has shot its bolt; all the others were in varying degrees of good health.) The field also showed that Maudière and Dyer were—are—still honing both substance and style to useful effect.

Chandon has refined its vineyard selection, based now in the firm's own 850 acres—220 at winery, 100 high up on Mount Veeder, and 530 straddling the Napa-Sonoma line in the Carneros—but still including grapes bought from Napa growers south of Yountville to Carneros. Maudière also has narrowed his choice of varieties other than Pinot Noir and Chardonnay. Pinot Blanc has kept its supporting role. Ugni Blanc never passed the first test. Folle Blanche lasted only for two seasons. Pinot Meuniere is a recent and continuing experiment. Yeast, dosage, and all of the other fine points are under constant review as well.

Sonoma County

Sonoma is Napa's twin in the sense that conventional wisdom about sparkling wines calls for grapes from the coolest parts of the county. More than in Napa, the wineries follow that dictate, looking almost entirely to the Russian River Valley—especially the westernmost parts of it—and to bayside Carneros. In the history of Sonoma sparkling wines to date, the most consistent success for my taste is Iron Horse, one of several firms drawing upon vineyards in the western reaches of the Russian River Valley.

IRON HORSE VINEYARDS

If Schramsbergs are the sparkling wines for winter, then Iron Horses are truly the wines of summer. Type for type among the three houses described here, and all the others in California as well, the Sonomans strike the palate most delicately. Sometimes they seem almost airy.

Electing Iron Horse to this company is, in the comparison, a hasty decision. The winery has had only the vintages since 1980 to prove itself. But Barry and Audrey Sterling and their partner-winemaker, Forrest Tancer, have brought an assistant wine-maker from Champagne each year to keep after the details, and so keep their techniques impeccable and their style on track.

Iron Horse is odd man for being the only estate wine among the three, and one of very few in the state. The notion of building a cuvée out of diverse properties is not for Tancer and the Sterlings. Their 120 acres of vines south of Forestville offer, they say, complications enough all by themselves. The vineyard rolls up and down several steep knolls at the westernmost and coolest margin of grape growing in Sonoma County. The better-drained, sunnier tops yield the grapes for Iron Horse still Chardonnay and Pinot Noir. The chillier bottoms, with their heavier soils, ripen grapes more slowly if at all, and it is from these that the proprietors draw most of the fruit for their sparkling wines. They do a bit of mixing both ways to gain the complexities and balances required for still and sparkling wines, but the generality comes close to a pure truth.

From the single property Tancer and his French second make Brut, Blanc de Blancs, and Blanc de Noirs Wedding Cuvée. A Late Disgorged bottling is in the works. The proportions begin to sound familiar. The Brut is 70 to 80 percent Pinot Noir, the rest Chardonnay; the Blanc de Blancs pure Chardonnay; and the Blanc de Noirs all Pinot Noir, except when a dollop of Chardonnay has to fill the tank as a cuvée is being readied for the second fermentation. Type for type, all four live up to the Iron Horse house style of light body and delicate flavors when compared to the other two familiars in our cellar. While the four are less easy to distinguish than the Schramsbergs and Chandons if one comes to them one at a time, the purposes of their being come clear at any head-to-head tasting.

1980 All delicacy of texture, yet firmly marked by the faintly earthy smells of yeast and the faintly butterscotchy ones of dosage. The Blanc de Blancs seemed to have just a bit the best of it among the four.

1981 A shade lighter of texture and definitely subtler in flavor than the 1980s at comparable ages.

1982 Both the Blanc de Noir and Brut seemed more noticeably flavored by Pinot Noir than preceding vintages. The Blanc de Blancs has struck me as unusually tart.

1983 The Blanc de Blancs made its debut with much the same delicacy of flavor and texture as 1981.

A Postscript in Favor of Muscat

Contrary to the opinions of some strayed Calvinists, wine is not always serious. Some of it is meant to give heedless pleasure, to slip down as something with immediately likable flavors. Take

Muscat in any form. People who know the broad perfumes of this extended family of grapes eat the fresh fruit with pleasure throughout the season every year. With the grapes, I have to worry only about dribbling juice down my chin a couple of times a summer. With the wine, I have a little more restraint, but not much. The closer it comes to the taste of grapes straight from the vine, the less restrained I am likely to be. Add bubbles and I have to put myself on strict rations from mid-April into early October.

Throughout those months the sun shows up early where I live and hangs around all day, holding out invitations to lean back on the oars. Gentle thoughts flood the mind without bubbling Muscat to provoke them. Add it into the mix and, for an hour or two, the world becomes too benign to disturb for any of the reasons advanced thus far.

It is the need to cause disturbances that, to this point, has kept this section limited to dry examples of true champagne-method sparklers. The method is both a source of quality and a statement on behalf of that quality, but it also tends to result in intellectual wines that keep a body social and stirring away in various pots. The drier the wine, the truer this is. Sweet wines, meanwhile, are supposed to pacify, to keep the issues simple until the mind is rested enough to do more battle. For sweet sparklers, Charmat processing in tanks may be not merely as good, but better. If the goal is fresh fruit flavors to go with the sugar, then fermenting large quantities in a pressurized tank does a more certain job than fermenting a tiny quantity in a single bottle, when flavors from yeasts are almost sure to have some effect. If the grapes are Muscats, there is no point in trying anything else because Muscats are going to be fruity no matter which technique is used.

SPUMANTE BALLATORE

A few years ago two friends of ours who are formidable connoisseurs of the great wines of the world found out halfway through dinner that Ballatore Spumante was on sale at our local Safeway. Between the main course and dessert they excused themselves from the table to rush out and buy several cases at the favorable price of $3.99 a bottle, as opposed to the regular $4.89.

Ballatore first showed up in a wine competition in 1981 and won a silver medal. On the rare occasions it has missed out on a medal since then it has been because an inept panel judged it. I dare to say so because the standards are so unambiguous. A proper sparkling Muscat mirrors the flavors of the fresh grapes that go into it. An outstanding one epitomizes those same flavors. As best I understand the flavors of Muscat, having eaten several hundred pounds of the fresh fruit, Ballatore is the epitome. Sometimes we have it with butter cookies, sometimes nuts, sometimes fresh fruit. Sometimes we just have the Ballatore. It never fails us.

Its appellation is California, it draws upon more than one of the Muscats, and its technical balance is roughly 8 percent alcohol and 8 percent sugar. In spite of the numbers, it does not cloy in the slightest. The wine's great secret is rumored to be a tiny dollop of Sauvignon Blanc that somehow accentuates the Muscat flavors, but nobody in charge will say yea or nay. E. & J. Gallo makes Ballatore, but the winery is unaccountably shy about admitting authorship of one of its great successes.

INDEX

323